O̲K̲L̲A̲H̲O̲M̲O̲

C.T. Madrigal

PRISSPRESS

Published by PRISSPRESS

Printed in the United States of America

ISBN-13: 978-0-9987694-0-0

hey, picasso (A Disclaimer)

While this story happens to be autobiographical, I am a writer and not a journalist so I enjoy a degree of creative liberty. I'm older than I want to be and my memory is nearly as old as I am, when it fails I am likely to fill in the blank, sometimes consciously and sometimes not. I don't remember childhood conversations verbatim, I don't even recall all of the Pledge of Allegiance (something about *nation under God,* perhaps the reconciliation of Church and State) so I write them the best I can. Occasionally I'll condense a story or a timeline if it makes a more concise read, I may merge two experiences or two characters for similar reasons. Sometimes I suppose an age or a date when the correct one isn't clear to me. Should I choose to recall old unpleasantness with more levity than it deserves, it's because humor helps with the bitter aftertaste. I might change the name or other identifying marker of a person or place since I am the only one who agreed to have his story told.

Similarly, there's much this book won't say. The truth at its truest can't be told—stories are too long, there isn't enough paper, they are all condensed. In this way, my memoir is an anorexic reflection of truth: information and experiences and people are thinned out, or purged altogether. While the truth is the *whole* truth, that was an impossibility here. To affected parties: I realize these edits are omissions, and those omissions are lies (I was a lying kid and I have not changed), my apologies.

This is not the dossier of my early life, it is the story of it. Is it true? Yes. Has the truth been edited and stylized? Of course. If we commission a portrait and the painter adds a bit of color to the cheeks, if the photographer softens the lens, if a still-life painter adds a third lemon where there were only two should we cry: Liar, liar! This is not truth! (*"Hey Picasso, my nose isn't this crooked. I want my money back."*)

As with painting, truth in writing (except the journalistic, the historical account, the educational textbook, and perhaps diabetic cookbooks) should be filtered through the writer's own aesthetic and creative whim. That's what good art and good writing—especially the memoir—is. I'm not an historic figure, there's room for style in the retelling.

In one story I talk about a conversation I had with a boyfriend in a restaurant. The truth is we were in some place with a lot of pay-phones, I think it was indoors but it might have been just enclosed with sky overhead, it was adjacent to the lobby of some establishment I don't quite recall, maybe a hotel. I think all that lack of clarity is confusing and verbose and irrelevant so I simplify it and place us in a restaurant because the anecdote has more important things to get to. *In another story* I describe the drag queen Phyllis Cheesesteak as being "as big as a refrigerator and just as cold." She was big but I don't really think she was as big as a refrigerator, refrigerators are really big. And she was cold, but probably not enough to keep milk from souring. I was just being clever to be entertaining and to make a memorable point. As with all writers worth reading, I do this at will.

If you feel you are represented in my book and my childhood recollections leave you feeling litigious then you might consider how you earned an ignominious mention in a child's eroto-biography, or how you treated my mother. Attorneys should note that names and locations are changed, characters are merged, and recollections are only that—old memories, too fractured, fragmented and fused to be offered as fact.

I invent words, I conjoin them, I have my own opinions about commas before conjunctions, I don't capitalize nations when they're used as modifiers, I even insinuate Patti Labelle had a mohawk while with Labelle when I know she didn't. I am a writer and not a journalist so I enjoy a degree of creative liberty, I wouldn't want to read the writer who didn't.

CONTENTS

merci:

Divine, Quentin Crisp, Sylvester, Leigh Bowery
Power queens of yesteryear

Stevie Nicks
Gave voice to my lip-sync when I could not sing

Grace Jones, Nina Hagen, Dale Bozzio, Alison Moyet,
Laurie Anderson, Kate Bush, Diamanda Galás
Unstuffed me from a box

Ms Robertson (Kindergarten), Ms Collins (4th grade),
Ms Turner (Art)
Memory-worthy kindergarten, elementary, and junior high teachers

Sally Singer (VOGUE Magazine), Dita Von Teese
For the support they generously gave my business, TheFrock.com

My mother and my sister
Endured more than I did, including unidimensional mentions in this book

Derek Adams, Robert Pierce, Brandi Lewis, Candace Biggs,
David Wallingford, Dale Carroll, Andrea Bastien,
Steven Williams, Brian Buford
Friends from Oklahoma

Patricia, Monica, Diana
Nana and aunts

Robert Glassford
My lady

va te faire foutre:

Mike Q. and Barbara J.M.
Fuck you

preface:

I FEEL NAKED when I'm not wearing clothes. I feel like standing behind a curtain. My curtains are seersucker—cotton, it would feel nice. My stomach is as soft and plump as a baby's vagina. My skin is pasty because I avoid the sun like it's the IRS. My hands and knees have scars—some from clumsiness, some from crime. And I singed a bald spot on the side of my leg where my desk chair sits too close to a wall-mounted space heater. Similarly, my ankles lost their hair. Maybe my body is trying to cool them because I sleep under too heavy a blanket, maybe the hairs were sacrificed to age. Either way, I feel naked when I'm not wearing clothes, not ashamed (I know not to measure my worth in the eyes of strangers, unless they like what they see), just naked. I like men who *look* naked when they're unclothed. Some men don't. Their "hit the gym five times a week" bodies look factory refurbished for nudity, like they anticipated it, prepared for it. Perfectly tanned skin, same thing. The bronze plating cloaks the lovely vulnerability of bare skin as opaquely as a wetsuit would. Tribal tattoos on a knotty bicep (or maybe those matching stars oft-found on inflated pectorals) are for the man who anticipated the exhibition enough to bring props. He'd flex his muscles (and his manly interests) by carrying a greasy engine around the beach if he could, if they'd allow it on MUNI. Naked is sexier to me. It makes the lack of clothing seem accidental, rare, absurd. It teases the child in me that was a voyeur and a Peeping Tom.

When I was adolescent, my friendships were naked. I lived with other runaways ten-deep in small, smelly apartments; we were secretless. We talked about music and art, fate and death. My friend Wally was bashed walking home from a club, his swollen face widely unrecognizable. "Were you afraid they'd kill you," I asked. "No," he answered, "I'm not afraid of death. I'm not afraid of anything but heights." Four years later Wally was thrown two hundred feet off a bridge and died; *fate is a dick*, I thought. I had first-date conversations about addictions, bad parents, bitter ex's. I know the topics are shunned by dating advice-givers but I remember the talks so much better than the polite conversations I've had over coffee with milquetoast. I masturbated with room-mates, just for the camaraderie.

Maybe it was youth—we were too young to be guarded. Maybe it was the proximity of poverty—there was no room for mystery. Maybe it was the era—before conversations were truncated by technology. Whatever the reason, it leaves me nostalgic. I have no talent (or rather, tolerance) for smalltalk, the tepid exchanges make me want to pull out my remaining ankle hairs. It's so wasteful of the few puffs of breath mortality has afforded these lungs. "Are those prescription glasses? Are you far-sighted or near-sighted? Have you ever worn contacts?" Yes, I enjoy living in San Francisco; No, I don't see my family often; Please stop talking about your children.

My grandmother—Nana—died in her eighties. She had a long life and I bet some of it was interesting. Unfortunately, we never talked about it. I tried a few times but she dismissed my interest without recognizing its sincerity, I could've tried harder. Nana didn't speak with much depth: we talked about food (spicy food gave her heartburn) and her pets (they understood her when she began with *Now listen to me, I'm serious*), but never about life. She spoke to me with more affection than she would a mere acquaintance, but with no more substance. I imagine the rest of my family never excavated the nut of Nana's identity either, I know they never cracked mine.

It saddens me to consider my nana at eighty, eighty-one, eighty-two . . . hair shedding, skin becoming translucent, memories disappearing like cookies from a jar. Did she feel sad? Angry? Afraid? Was it like a final installment of the *Final Destination* franchise—with rickety walkers, slippery bathtubs, and miscounted medications all revving-up to take her down? Did she want to talk about death but lacked the words, or did *she* say nothing because *we* said nothing—not wanting her to think it loomed.

I'm not going out like that. I'll think things and say things, I'll even write a book if I have to.

OKLAHOMO

CHAPTER 1

Weeds

There were three places to hide, all appalling to a kid with too few corduroy slacks: between a huckleberry hedge and wood fence that partitioned front yard from back (the harsh sun never hit that side of the house and the hedge concealed everything but my feet, but I'd been spotted there once before and there's no good explanation for skulking behind a shrub), along the other side of the house where I found the fallen piece of aluminum drain (no one looked there because tomato worms made it nearly impassable, but the tomato garden was within pistol shot of Mickey's bedroom window), and the weed field.

We lived in the last row of houses before a large weed field that separated two northern California towns. While ours could be considered a distant suburb of San Francisco, the maverick mecca's reputation of liberality and 'free love' could not have been more foreign to us had they been Buddhism and the *Fatawa-e-Alamgiri*. But Gloria Steinem (by way of Phil Donahue) and the succinct slogans of women's liberation had reached my mother and—after a pregnant exit from high school at age fifteen, and then a second child from the botched marriage with my father—she was back in school. She was learning *Shorthand: The Secret Language of Professional Secretaries*, and I was fascinated by the mysterious support-staff symbols she shared with me. On study days we shared a sofa, our over-tanned bodies soiling its avocado cushions, while I rubbed the sensitive underside of her right forearm as she practiced writing long lists of shorthanded abbreviations on tablets of oddly lined stenography paper with her left (Mom was a lefty, in all respects.) When she finished, I'd write them too. "If you practice, you might be a secretary—or even an *executive* secretary one day."

Mom's teacher—Mrs Something I Can't Remember—took my mother and me to lunch at a restaurant that was nicer than any restaurant I had ever seen, though probably not all that nice. The authoritative woman wore her nails long and her graphite-grayed hair short, or maybe it was just pinned to a length that discouraged frivolity (she seemed a woman who'd've insisted I place a period after the "Mrs" in her name.) Mrs Something ordered an iced tea with lemon and then my mother ordered the same, though I don't recall her preferring tea before. I ordered a root beer and promptly spilled it on the table. "Oh Honey, be careful," Mom said in a maternal voice that sounded as unrealistic as the re-ran 1950s sitcoms she parroted. She used her cloth napkin to unpuddle the pop, tilting her head to cloak a threatening glare (the same *'watch it, fucko'* expression she makes if someone discloses her age) when Mrs Something I Can't Remember had returned to her menu. The waiter brought my replacement and Mom nodded thanks with an ireful and entirely penciled brow.

For the occasion I wore an itchy sweater and my only slacks. Mom said the sweater hides my *impudence*—a word we had shorthanded in just four strokes. (I wasn't impudent, in fact I hardly spoke as a child—partly because of a slight stutter and partly because my acquaintances seemed disinterested so I hadn't had much practice—but I didn't think of this then, then I only thought of the itchiness.) Mom wore a thin, waist-tied dress with a high hemline that posed no threat to her permanently tanned knees, their amber skin shiny with cocoa butter. Her flimsy garment was patterned in sepia-toned portraits of southern belles, the belles' conservative necklines made Mom's suggestive décolleté seem blue by comparison.

The food came and I was very excited in the way hungry kids are, and eager to impress Mom's teacher with my best table manners. "Mrs Something I Can't Remember, will you please pass me the catsup?" I implored with a politeness that I was certain would not go unnoticed, it wasn't too late to redeem myself from the sticky brown stain of incorrigibility found only on my side of the table's pretty white cloth. "Certainly, young man," she replied, her gracious tone sauced with a sweetness that seemed indigestible to my mother and me. I reached up for the catsup and knocked over my second glass of root beer on the way down.

The puddle of wet seemed to electrocute my mother from within, her eyes bugged (one more than the other) and her body tensed as she tried her best to not punch me in the mouth. "I don't know what's wrong with him," she confessed, a false eyelash still quavering from the electrocution, "What is *wrong* with you, do you *want* to wait in the car?" She asked the familiar questions in an irascible tone not befitting a sitcom housewife, using my sweater arm to sop the spill. "Smooth move, Chris, *real* smooth move."

"Dusty, it's okay," Mrs Something consoled.

"I apologize," Mom replied, in no mood for consolation, "but this isn't anything new—he plays this jazz *all* the time," she continued, distancing herself from my recidivism as one would a junkie or a prostitute.

"Dusty, it's just a soda. Let's get him another one and enjoy our meal. Chris, would you like a root beer or would you like to try a cream soda, have you ever had cream soda?"

Mom left early most mornings to catch the BART train to secretary school so it was Mickey's responsibility to wake us in time to meet the school bus at the mouth of the street's nine house Cul de Sac. Mickey was my mother's second husband (by California's *Common Law* standard anyway). He was a biker in the worst sense of the word. Not just the weekend getaway type but the type you'd hope not to anger on a long stretch of sparsely travelled highway. (One night Mickey came home late in his heavily detailed black Chevy truck. He often came home late, without explanation—an infuriant for my mother that made her especially intolerant of any shenanigans from Mona and me. The vehicularly vain man considered the vintage car a showpiece so it was surprising to see the headlight broken and a small dent and scratches on the front end. Mom asked what happened and Mickey said he picked up a jogger, and to watch the news. At 10:00 PM, or minutes thereafter, we saw a story about a man jogging on the side of the road who'd been run down and left to die.)

Mickey woke me each morning with a hard pound on my bedroom door. And from the age of eight until the age of twelve he woke my sister with a hard pound as well. Mona often cried while we got ready for school, though I didn't know why. I'd pass by the off-limits bedroom to find her playing the clarinet, badly, stopping only to catch a breath and to sob. I asked what was wrong and she'd explain something about being worried she hadn't learned the song in time for band class. I admired her commitment to the arts (I myself was no stranger to the trials of a musician's life, having recently played a one-man viola recital of "Twinkle, Twinkle Little Star" at a school assembly) so I let her be.

Mona was two years older than me, though the two-year gap could have been twenty—she wanted nothing of a little brother. Years earlier I was wearing only underwear to water the front lawn when I accidentally crapped my pants. I was too old to soil myself, but there it was. I considered flushing the thing out with the garden hose but my sister immediately ran into the house shouting to my mother, "*Christian* pooped his pants! *Christian* pooped his pants!" which provoked me to cry. (Though my mother had chosen the name *Christian*, she immediately circumcised it to *Chris*. My full

4

name was only used to embarrass me for its fussiness when pronounced by someone who aimed to ape the preciseness of my personality.)

There was no time to ditch the dung, and I knew I was cruisin' for a contusion, so I thought quick; when my sister returned with my mother *Mona did it!* was the explanation I had conjured. Mona's mouth dropped, the tattler hadn't anticipated the backfire. Crying, I swore to God that she stood behind me and pulled my waistband back and pooped inside my underwear. Unfortunately my sister is resourceful under pressure, she threw dirt at me and called me a liar. I think that was the incident that set the tone for the remainder of our relationship.

Mona was an asocial (with me anyway) who pelted me with put-downs whenever I dimmed her bedroom doorway. If I stood some ground we'd trade blows, but I always fell to her age and girth. She was a big girl and Mom and Mickey made a fetish of her imperfection, reminding her at every meal. My sister's self-consciousness about weight was evident when she tugged at her blouse in family photos, and how her sad brown eyes seemed to beg for the flash to malfunction. I loved to answer the telephone (which is odd considering how little I like talking to people), when the phone rang I'd run toward the kitchen shouting, "I've got it. Don't answer it! I've got it." I however did not have it—a fact that only Mona knew as she positioned a chubby, outwardly stuck foot to tumble me to the floor. The subsequent thuds and clanks of a scraggy boy's toppled bones were always followed by a polite, "Good afternoon, Mona speaking," as she smugly answered the call. I explained this to my mother when she found me beating my sister's bare legs with a rubber fly-swatter but Mom was unmoved by the explanation and sent me to my room. I probably would have been slower to retaliate if I had known how her mornings began.

I did know Mickey was tough on adult women though, I kept the three-foot length of aluminum drain that had fallen off our roof for those occasions when the brute would grab a handful of

Mom's hair, and Mom would grab a faceful of Mickey's fist. As my mother's blond shag haircut collided with the livingroom's brown shag carpet I would jump from my plate of baked french fries (or whatever childishness had lulled me into complacency) and run to my bedroom to unearth the weapon from a pile of dirty clothes that expertly concealed it on the closet floor. Mostly I'd swing the makeshift club once before Mickey took it from me and tossed it across the room. Then he'd casually push me to the ground, like Kong swatting a tiny effeminate helicopter from the sky. Unlike me, Mom was a brawler. As the large man pummeled her she couldn't cower (nor abide the safety tip I'd shared with her—the one Mountain Martin, a Calaveras Big Trees ranger had explained to my class: to play dead during a bear attack, and also to carry bear spray). With each hit she'd reboot, bouncing from the floor to throw a wild punch before getting sent back to the ground. The couple would repeat this weekly pyrotechnic display of woe until she lay still or until something valuable, like a mirror or a tooth, was broken. Nowadays I usually remember the frenetic steps of the two lover's oft-repeated dance slowed from its 45 rpms, and scored by Barry White or some other sexy sounds of the `70s.

I knew mom's greatest foible—the unwillingness to back down—would get her in deep trouble one day, if not with Mickey then with his ex-wife Carmen. Like my mother, Carmen Satana was a big-titted biker gal who was quick to fight over a man. We'd drive to her house to pick up Mickey's sons for a visit and Carmen would meet us in the driveway wearing a tight dress under a ruffled apron that was embroidered with the word SPICY (the 'I' was a chili pepper.) She wore big hoop earrings on every occasion. Without speaking, the busty broads traded glares, performing their enmity only through the narrow squints of heavily mascara'd eyes. My mom was a badass, a punching kicking scratching badass, but I feared Carmen would pull a switchblade from the back of her frizzy black hair for which mom's nails would have no answer. As the two women circled Carmen would bark, "Hey Gringo, mess wit me and jou'll wake up dead, and dat'll jus be da warning!" or some other threat that I may have borrowed from a scarcely produced poster for *West Side Story*.

Mickey's two sons, Little Mickey and Mack, were twenty and nineteen years old. Both seemed to have modeled themselves after their desperado father. Little Mickey was the handsomer of the two, with dark latin skin and curly black hair to his shoulder blades which he commonly kept in a single braid at the back of his head and wrapped in a bandana headband. Occasionally Little Mickey untied his mane, unleashing the full measure of his dangerous beauty and driving me nearly to applause. Mack was oddly caucasian by comparison, but I knew better than to inquire. He was attractive by any standard, except the one that compared him to his brother.

The brothers usually stayed at our house two nights each month, sleeping on the livingroom's pullout sofa. Some evenings Mom and Mickey would have another couple or two over, they and Mickey's sons would drink tequila and play poker until long after Mona and I went to bed.

"Hey Dusty, why don't you let the kid play with us?"

"Nah man, cards aren't his bag."

On one of these occasions as I prepared for a leisurely evening shower, I thought how nice it would be if Mickey's handsome sons joined me. I twisted into a bath towel and marched to the kitchen where, with a polite "Excuse me," I interrupted the table full of bikers from their poker hand. "Little Mickey and Mack, I'm going to take my shower now, and wondered if you would like to join me?" My invitation was met with a smoke-filled room full of the kind of silence that only eight stoned bikers feeling sexually harassed by a second-grader can produce.

I was gay since the word meant happy, even in kindergarten I hoped to meet some sandbox stud to share an eraser with. Some nights young gay me was unable to sleep knowing Mickey's sons were prone on the pullout couch in the room next to mine. Around 3:00 AM I'd slink out of bed, stepping slowly enough to creak every floorboard from my bed to my bedroom door. When I achieved livingroom I dropped to the floor as if I'd heard the approaching Viet Cong. From there I began a slow crawl to the sofa bed in the middle of the room. I'd approach, hoping their offset snores would muffle the thumps of my pounding heart, before searching the scene for any bit of exposed leg. Little Mickey's ankles were dark reddish brown—the color of baked beans, they lightened to the noncommittal pale of a fingernail the closer you got to his thigh. His brother was pale throughout—not like a fingernail, more like a tooth.

If courage allowed, I'd begin a slow tug on the blanket until a sliver of white cotton underwear glowed supernaturally in infiltrating moonlight. Mickey's sons were tall with big feet that overhung the foot of the sofa bed, some nights I moved in close to admire the sporadic hair and warm smell. I'd get close enough that my chin inevitably touched a sensitive sole, causing one of them to jerk a little or mumble something or even sit up. I instinctively flattened to the floor like a manta ray, closing my eyes and feigning invisibility, praying snoring resumed.

Big Mickey was handsome too, in the wicked way that abusive father figures sometimes are. My bedroom wasn't far from his and my mother's so I often listened to their sex. Mom was a moaner and I was aroused at the thought of what Mickey was doing to deserve such praise. And I was hurt that she could be elevated to those heights by a man who was as awful to this family as he had been.

One summer Mickey had a motorcycle accident that broke his leg. When he and I were alone in the house it was my duty to carry his mason jar of urine from the bed to the bath. He'd call me to his bedroom—now dank from closed drapes and his unwashed hibernation, his voice softened by lethargy. "Leave the light off," he ordered in the Demerol slur, allowing me only the hall light to find his end of the king-sized waterbed. The brawny man's long black hair was matted on one side and his beard and mustache had lost their sharp perimeter. "Here's a fresh batch for you," Mickey'd say, submitting a foamy jar from under the blanket, it fluoresced like sea anemone in the hallway's distant light. "You're not gonna spill it are you?" he warned, after seeing a previous jar's contents shake when my hand trembled from the excitement of holding his warm fragrant urine. "No, it's just heavy," I lied, adding a second hand for support. I carefully walked the infirmed man's pee to the small master bath, my mother's make-up strewn across its countertop. I stood on the little oval rug—still damp from Mom's shower—cautiously climbing my hand to the rim of the jar. From there, my little gay finger stiffened its backbone and dove Esther Williams-style into the pee. Mickey's waste was thermal and restorative; I felt as Christians do when embraced by pure white light, only mine was yellow. I touched his urine and it touched me; Mickey was holding me, for the first time ever. I heard a cough and quickly gave his manly mess to the toilet as if drowning a lover who'd seen too much.

That summer was the only time Mickey and I spent together. At seven he decided I was too old to be indoors so he and Mom kept the doors locked until nightfall—when I was allowed to come inside for dinner and to ready myself for bed. I wasn't supposed to lurk around our yard either, but I didn't have any friends in the neighborhood (or in other neighborhoods for that matter) so I usually spent afternoons hiding in the weed field behind our house. The dense, unmolested weeds had dried to resemble hay and grown several feet tall so I was able to sit there unnoticed, like an unnecessary extra from *Children of the Corn*, until the sun went down.

Raskell was the nearest I had to a neighborhood friend. He was a dirty little kid with a smart mouth. He lived several houses down and was really more of a nemesis. One day he chased me out of his garage with a baseball bat, but I don't run from a fight—I scamper, I scampered home and knocked on the door. Mom wouldn't let me in but she did give me a broom to go back and do battle. We met Raskell and his family in a neutral yard between our two houses and the adults decided we two boys would fight but no weapons would be allowed—we were civilized afterall. So Raskell and I fought with kicks and fists while our moms shouted (mine: "Kick his ass and I'll buy you an ice cream!") from the sideline. Another day Raskell and I were sitting indian-style by the garbage cans when the foul-mouthed kid blurted out, "Bite me." Always amenable, I leaned down and—with my face firmly planted in his crotch—I bit down, hard. Raskell screamed and I ran home. I again knocked loud and fast on the front door, hoping my mother would offer me asylum. She refused me entry until I explained my bloody lip so I described how I'd scraped it on Raskell's zipper when I bit him on the dick; she sent me to my room. In twenty minutes the police arrived with questions about a boy with a bleeding penis. Mom saw them coming and told me to pretend to be asleep, she would handle the pigs.

For two months—maybe three—I'd walk ten blocks to the little shopping strip that boasted a laundromat, a donut hut, and a "No Horseplay Between Players!" arcade, or so the sign read. The arcade wasn't much, but it was familiar (Raskell's parents walked us there once on his birthday, back before I bit his dick.) It offered pinball machines and foosball tables; I wasn't very good at either. I stole change, anything but pennies, from my mom's and grandma's purses to play the *Planet of the Apes* and *Six Million Dollar Man* machines. 'Maury' or 'Murray', maybe 'Mort' (the man who owned the place) offered to teach me to play the competitive looking foosball table. After a few games he could tell I was a natural, "and if you're good at foosball then I can guarantee you'll be good at soccer." The arcade didn't do much business, some days just me, so Mort even closed early a few times to coach me privately. The balding man inherited the arcade when his father died of an arrhythmia or arachnophobia or something. His mom was still alive but she had no interest in kids or games, he said it sounded to him like our moms were a lot alike. Mort's real interest was photography. He was a professional photographer for one of the top modeling schools in Oregon before he moved to California to take over the arcade. Mort missed photography so I agreed to let him practice by taking pictures of me in the arcade's backroom in exchange for the free foosball lessons. Mort was mostly accustomed to photographing girls so he suggested it would be best if I posed how I thought a girl would pose; I thought a girl would blow a kiss and point a finger toward her boobs, Mort agreed. It was nice to have a place to go, especially on hot or cold days. I arrived one afternoon, earlier than usual to get a jump on my drills, but the door was padlocked. I went back a few days later and it was still locked, and the window sign was painted over. It stayed that way until I stopped checking.

Some days when sitting in the weed field became monotonous I'd climb under a splintered wood fence, into our backyard (we had a dog who dug a hole under the fence and ran away, we never found her so we never filled the hole.) Mom called the disused portion of yard that extended along that side of the house her "garden" though it was really just a plot of dirt that got tilled biennially for a heart-healthy vegetable garden that never came to be. At best, she'd plant a few rows of tomato plants that widely withered and died. I usually stayed out of the garden because the tilled dirt looked too much like the cemetery ground in *Carrie*, where she punches through a grave to grab the wrist of an hysterical Amy Irving. And the dirt was thick with rotten tomatoes and tomato worms. The fat bald caterpillar-like worms stuck little hooks into your legs and hair and they hissed as you tried to pull them off. You'd have to pull so hard their fleshy, mush-filled bodies would crush in your hand before they'd let go. But the tomato garden butted against my bedroom window so I'd some-times endure the threat of clingy bugs and Sissy Spacek's undead hand to press a cheek against my bedroom window and pretend I was inside.

Eventually I made a real friend, his name was Benedict. Benny was a schoolmate and asian of some variety, though I had no idea which. He had more teeth than mouth, or maybe they were just bigger than his big head could accommodate, and his dash-mark eyes and bowl-cut hair made him the perfect mascot for a racially insensitive cartoon. He smiled and giggled at the drop of a chopstick, so much so it made people uncomfortable in a town that was already discomforted by any non-latin immigrant. One afterschool afternoon, Benny invited me to his house. It sounded better than a field of weeds so I went.

Turned out we were both sci-fi enthusiasts and so we made a *Star Trek* style set from marker ink and cardboard boxes. After hasty construction and a brief argument Benny and I decided we would both play Wonder Woman. We traded our trousers for the short skirts that Benedict brought from his mother's closet, by their length (and my shameful unappreciation of women's lib) I deduced his mother was kind of a slut. We pretended to push buttons on the *Enterprise's* cardboard dashboard, "boo bee boo boo boop, uh-oh Wonder-Woman, there is a problem up ahead..." I'd warn. "What is it the plobrem, Wondah-Womah?" Benny would inquire.

Benedict's dad was a petite, gray-haired man. His english was barely recognizable as such, it sounded as though he'd been dubbed by another asian in post-production. He had a stillness and an elegance about him—nothing like the raucous, leather-clad men who visited my house, men whose exhaust pipes sent neighbors into houses and dogs into fits. Benny's dad brought us cups of warm tea, he sat with us and told us stories. (Apparently tea was discovered when an ancient emperor's servants boiled water for him to drink, to make it sanitary. They didn't notice a leaf had fallen from the window into the water pot and served the brown water to the emperor who found it to be very refreshing.) Later, Benny's dad returned to tell us it was time for the afternoon nap. Benny and his father and I climbed into his father's bed and went to sleep.

When I woke, Benedict was already gone. His father remained behind me and was gently rubbing persistent little circles on one of my mini-skirted buttocks, as if he might coax a genie or a fart out. I opened an eye—maybe two—while the rest of me feigned sleep, the knead of an adult hand in my borrowed skirt had choked all movement from my body. For several minutes, a month at most, we continued quietly. Then, as the amateur masseur's hand began to tremble, slightly, he added a mutter, softly, in a language I didn't understand. The exotic words were short and choked, while others were comedically stretched as if spoken by cartoon cats. Whatever the meaning they weren't said to me, but rather seemed to be whispers of self-encouragement, as his breath quickened he became increasingly supportive. When the little circles became little squeezes, the little mutterings became something closer to english, "Yes, uh you ah WunnaWoma [squeeze], you ah WunnaWoma." With each round the squeeze grew harder, though never ungentle. And then, with a final "WunnaWoma!" and a final squeeeeeeze, the massage was over.

I didn't go back to Benny's after that. His english was just too hard to understand, I did kind of miss his father though.

Initially the weed field was a stationary affair. I sat near my house, close enough to see into my backyard but far enough to not risk being seen through the livingroom's rear glass doors (Mickey and my mother wanted no reminders of the pieces of their family that were outside, tossing about like tumbleweeds; if they spotted me, there would be consequences.) Sometimes I saw the couple sitting together on the couch, watching television. She'd bend her shiny legs onto a sofa cushion, then lean into the recess of his hairy underarm for warmth; he'd wedge his forearm under her bust, as if her *3 for $5.99* brassiere might fail. If something funny played on the TV—something out of view to the exiled— the couple laughed jointly, heartily. They were like newlyweds.

But most days the room was empty, there was nothing to see. I'd close my eyes to quiet my disquiet, focusing all my impotent energy on willing the blue out of the sky. When that failed and daylight lingered intolerably, I prayed—to God, then to Satan—for nightfall. I repeated the cycle until one of them conceded, though their untimeliness made it hard to be certain whom to thank. I had prayed to the dueling deities before, to close my bedroom curtains when I woke some mornings to harsh sunlight. First I tried telekinesis, then prayer; none worked. I got the idea to attempt the supernatural when watching the ease with which Samantha (from *Bewitched*) completed her daily chores. I'd also prayed that if my parents became incapacitated—say, if my real father's station wagon accidentally hit my mother's VW beetle in a tragically coincidental mountainside collision—I could live with Aunt Dinah.

Aunt Dinah (my father's sister) was a handsome woman with blushed cheeks and black hair, perfumed skin and pressed clothes. Despite her pretty package, when she hugged you—you knew she didn't mind if it bent her bows. I visited their family a few times yearly. In late afternoons my aunt melted cheddar cheese onto a bowl of Doritos and gave it to me with an icy soda so that I could lay under a blanket to watch a 'Creature Feature' marathon in as much comfort as any human deserved; it was nice to be indoors with the sun still out. Yeah, if my dad was killed by Jaws and my mom by Orca…I could get used to this. I had been charmed by the 'this is the church, this is the steeple' hand-game that my aunt taught me years earlier. When I 'opened the door to find all the people' it gave me comfort to know they were all there. Wherever I went, so did they. After a few months in the field I began unhinging the finger-legged churchgoers and taking them for walks through the weeds.

Though young, I was hardly foolhardy and never walked *into* the field—only along it, just behind the backyard fences. Sometimes I crawled on knees and a free hand so that my two fingers could walk the ground beside me, and sometimes I walked upright and my finger friends leapt from weed to weed like little Tarzans—loyal and brave. From the weeds I looked into backyards of the other houses that edged the field. In one: a wealthy older woman in the back of the street's largest house / she wore a swimcap to sit on the steps of her swimming pool / at times, she shielded her eyes to read a book / at times, she pointed her face to the sun, closing her eyes and squinting her entire face so that I briefly thought she was smiling at me. In another: three boys, probably ten, twelve, and fourteen / wearing dirty cutoff shorts and no shirts / working on the engine of a lawnmower and calling each other faggot. Most days though, backyards were empty and drapes were closed.

A few months later I decided to walk—not the cautious walks I had taken along the edge of the field in previous months, but to *really* walk—*into* the field, maybe to the end. I had no idea where or how the weed field ended, it seemed endless. Maybe it stopped at the Pacific Ocean, or maybe it was like the old flat-earth theories— I would take a step too far and tumble into the cosmos.

That day I saved the fried peanut butter and jelly burrito that the school's breakfast program served the poorer kids, I had no idea how long my expedition would take and I might not make it home for dinner. I had never explored before, I had never created a path. I went places with my mother (or back to places I had once been with my mother) or with a surrogate—anyone who would lead the way. But today, I secured my book bag in a hidden spot behind my house and I walked into the brush.

Within twenty steps a grasshopper landed on my sleeve. I don't mind insects but I hate feeling startled, the bug startled me, I jumped a little and flicked it off. *This is a bad idea*, I thought. When I was so far from my house that I knew I could yell for help and no one would hear me, I paused again. *I can go back, I've gone far enough.* After a moment I pressed-on, certain the three shirtless boys would have walked further. The deeper I walked the taller the weeds grew, I reached up and only my hands overtook them. If something happened I could stand up and wave my hands and someone would see, so I pressed on.

After a few hours—or maybe it was thirty minutes—I heard something sinister in the weeds. It sounded like a gopher or a rabbit, or maybe a gimp bird, or it could have been a man whose arms and legs were severed with a sword, using his jaw and chin to

15

drag his enfeebled torso from weed to weed (Mom told me Charles Manson had settled a man's hash this way, de-limbing him in the desert.) I was quiet at first, turning slowly to divine the direction of the sound. Then the hobbled torso inched closer and I knew that if I heard it—it heard me, so I turned back and I ran, hard. I meant to cry out as I ran but my frantic feet pounding the hard ground turned a sustained scream into the spasmodic yelps of a kindergarten karateka. After minutes of running I stopped because I'd lost my direction, and because I was winded. I looked left and then right, had I run the wrong way? When I swiveled to divine the direction of the sound, did I turn a half circle, a full circle, two? Did I make a cataclysmic miscalculation, was I now lost—lost in a boundless field of weeds and clambering torsos? I considered surrendering to the hopelessness and dropping to the ground, crumbling with the dirt. I could curl into a ball and wait to see if anyone would miss or come to rescue me. As I scoured the floor for a comfortable spot—one that might not stain my recently laundered pants—I heard a thing. Somewhere, over there, I heard a girl laugh. "Haha, hahaha," she laughed again, somewhere over there. I walked a few dozen steps and saw a break in the weeds; I thought to run to the clearing, *I'm here! I'm here!* boiling up inside me. When I reached the end, where the weeds met the clearance, I poked my head through.

There, sixty—maybe eighty feet away, like a mothership, I saw a great mass of futuristic architecture. Towering, complex mazes of silvery gray cubes. Glass grids reflecting puffy white clouds from a bright blue sky. Pristine white paths landscaped with trees and bushes so tidy and green they seemed fake, plastic, like those you'd find in an architect's model. Farrah Fawcett lived in a place like this—in the 24th century supercity in *Logan's Run,* where everyone dies at thirty; sometimes Kirk and Spock went to a place like this, usually populated by tribbles or some other deadly miscreation. But here, at Los Medanos Community College, everyone looked chipper, content. Energetic men and women were walking to and fro, sometimes stopping to talk—to laugh, but always with somewhere to go, somewhere to be. I stayed at the weeds' edge, watching the colony of junior-college coeds until the sun began to set.

I came home to an unlocked front door as the last puff of daylight vaporized from the horizon. "You missed dinner," my mother advised. "We had lasagna," her taunt continued as I passed the kitchen's aromatic doorway, "with italian sausage, real primo stuff." I didn't mind, there was a peanut butter and jelly burrito in my bag, I could eat that.

Mrs Collins (or Sue, as I thought of her) was my favorite teacher and a woman who really liked children and, in particular, me. Always soft-spoken and even-tempered, Sue wore her hair in a tidy black bob that was as shiny as her disposition. Her vest almost always matched her skirt (a feat that seemed impressive to me). The lenses of her big glasses were rounded squares, like a television screen. Once I saw her without them and considered telling her she looked like a model, but when my Mom's heavy-on-the-eyeline/high-on-the-hemline style received unwanted compliments from a boss she sued him for sexual harassment, I didn't want to risk a similar grievance.

Our school had an evening talent show and I told my teacher I couldn't come so she offered to give me a ride. I was mesmerized when three of the fifth-grade girls—bathed in plum and kiwi colored lights—did a baton-twirling routine to "Night Fever." Sue leaned in and asked if I was enjoying the show. She'd given me a plump baggie of home-baked macadamia nut cookies, I swallowed the treat in my mouth and confided: it was the best night of my life. My teacher seemed pleased by my answer, raising the corners of her mouth. Then, as she reconsidered, her bottom lip tightened and raised a bit—giving her smile a doleful center. She patted me on the knee, as if to apologize for identifying the pitiful part of my answer.

Several months later Mrs Collins and my mother said Mona and I would be spending the night with my favorite teacher. I thought that was strange because Sue didn't even know my sister, but I was too excited to mind her intrusion. Mrs Collins and her handsome husband took us to the movies that night. We saw *Star Wars* or maybe it was *The Empire Strikes Back*, it was the first time I had been to a movie theater (unless we count the time my real dad and his new wife took me and a stationwagon full of her young children to the drive-in to watch Al Pacino's *Cruising*, about a series of murders in the city's underground gay sex bath-house community).

Afterward, Mr and Mrs Collins (or Sue and Grant, as I thought of them) took us to dinner and then back to their duplex to spend the night. Mona and I slept on makeshift beds, and in the middle of the night I sneaked a pair of Grant's underwear from the bathroom hamper as a memento. After a nice breakfast Sue drove us home. She gave me a hug that was the best hug I'd ever had, I hoped she wasn't just frisking me for the stolen underwear.

No one ever told me why we spent the night with my teacher, but four days later I came home from school to find my mother on the front porch next to a pair of mismatched suitcases. She stood—mascara-smudged and teary-eyed—in the cement alcove, perched between two large aloe plants like a flaxen-haired damsel being sacrificed by the natives of some fog-shrouded island.

"I've got something to tell you, and I swear to fuckin god it doesn't mean I don't love you…"

It had been decided that my sister and I were moving out of our home and into the house of my every-fourth-weekend father, his wife Berniece, and her four children. I listened to my mother without looking at her, her tears were contagious and I was too angry to cry. I focused instead on a rusty mailbox secured near our front door, wondering how the x-ray specs I'd ordered would ever find me.

"Hey, I know it sounds bunk, but this is still your house," she lied, "you can come visit any time you want."

For twenty minutes my mother foisted the benefits of the new arrangement onto us until we were too weighted-down to stand in defiance. My father's above-ground pool was her final selling point. I enjoyed swimming, but I was clever and knew the news was not good.

Dad's stepchildren were many—we would be heavily out-numbered, and his wife was known to be an enemy of my mother. Though outwardly cordial, she could barely hide her resentment for my sister and me for an entire weekend. I instinctively knew my youth and her girth meant I'd never win a livingroom brawl, but I knew one day I'd be forced to try.

CHAPTER 2

Rich Girl

The screen door closed with the jarring clack of aging hydraulics. I turned away, unwilling to show desperation. I felt confident, hydrated, fit; conditions were favorable for redemption (it would take more than this to break me.) A car drove by, I looked to the ground. An unseen conversation grew louder, dangerously so. The next car honked and I considered pulling the underwear down to hide my face. *Would I get enough air*, I wondered, *would I suffocate?* I sensed a cry coming, at least it would hide that. From the cars, and from Berniece.

My stepmother, Berniece Jean Moritz—she kept her last name as a declaration of separatism with her own children, wanted her stepchildren to have everything her own kids never had, like scurvy and neglect. In the adult homes of Madrigal children 'Berniece' is a four-letter word (starts with c, rhymes with cunt.) Even today my eyes roll and my cholesterol rises as I type the name, if you say it slowly it sounds like young children developing eating disorders. Berniece Jean was a fat woman. Not the affable, huggable young Rikki Lake kind of fat. Hers was a menacing fat, the kind John

Wayne Gacy used to overpower young boys. My father, though similar in scale (I know this because Berniece wore the dingy white underwear he discarded after their elastic waistbands failed), was not threatening in his size. Rather, he was a quiet man made quieter by his abrasive second wife—a woman with a voice like snow chains on asphalt. In fact, between dad's long work hours and diminutive personality, I scarcely remember the man. I do however remember Berniece.

The first few weeks in my stepfamily's eight-person/two-bedroom home were surprisingly smooth, possibly promising. We swam six children deep in a plastic pool that was nearly as large as the dirty house's rusty backyard. It was curious though, that when we—Mona and I—got into the pool, Berniece got out. "I better go inside before I freckle," she'd explain, "I should probably start dinner anyway." My sister and I watched our big stepmother climb the little ladder, her bottom shedding the gallons of water that Dad's old underwear were unable to smuggle up the plastic steps.

Some weekends all eight of us squeezed into a station wagon to sing discordant harmonies with The Beatles' "Paperback Writer" (there were other songs, but that's the one lodged in the memory) during a forty-minute drive to San Francisco. We visited the bustling city a few times, though never leaving the car. At a red light Dad told us to lock the doors as his micro-minded wife recoiled from an approaching black man asking for change. A green light saved us, and Berniece returned to pointing out the city's handholding gay pedestrians as though we were on safari in the biblical city of Gomorrah. "Look, there's two more over there!" she'd announce, excitedly bouncing in her seat as if her unlucky safari camel had just quickened to a slow jog. With each point, six obedient heads whirled in unison, hoping not to miss the aberration. Then we all laughed at the sight of men in love, though I was probably laughing for different reasons.

At six years old my youngest stepsister Candianne was the apple that fell nearest her mother's tree, already echoing Berniece's boorish biases (her favorite insult was "Tar Baby," and I guarantee she wasn't referring to the character from *Mr. Rabbit and Mr. Fox.*) The girl entertained with nightly song and dance, followed by fits of rage if audiences were insufficiently smitten with the less screamy routines. 'Audiences' were the neighborhood's older boys and younger men—the attention addict had no interest in gyrating for women. A watchful neighbor could have prophesied that little Candianne might ripen into a bigoted stripper, "When she's good…she's *very* good, but when she's bad…she's a racist! Welcome to the stage, CANDI."

In the privacy of a bedroom, Candi and I sometimes sang (she would sing, I'd lip-sync) to her 45 of "You Light Up My Life." Her voice was oddly deep for her young age, and mine was oddly tuned. Candi may have been the better singer but at choreography and general stage presence there seemed to be no end to my talent, and no beginning to hers. Despite her mother's influence Candianne and I were fast friends, though she was occasionally underfoot.

Afternoons—after school and before dinner—I sometimes sat on the sofa, watching TV. Lazy Vanne—my older, classically carefree stepbrother—sometimes lay beside me, resting naked feet on my appreciative thigh. I feigned indifference to Vanne's handsome hooves but they could not have been more of a gift had he wrapped them in organza sacks and tied them with two smart bows. It was always then, at that moment, that Candianne plopped her uninvited ass on the couch, exactly between the teen and me.

For the rest of the afternoon my selfish stepsister wangled her biological brother's soft feet for herself. The pair hooted and hollered at the television, no matter the program, each oblivious to me seething at the far end of the sofa. I had a crushing crush on the sun-bleached boy since we first shared the upper level of a twin bunk bed. In the dark, under a blanket, Vanne would tell me to pull his finger. I would, even though I knew it wasn't his finger. The coal-brained boy would laugh and I'd act surprised; nights weren't so bad. Still I cried privately (as sensitive gay boys do) for the absence of my mother and the uncertainty of change.

The first real blemish surfaced during a pizza dinner. I was eating my third slice with a kind of giggly, pizza-fueled elation that still floods me as I eat pizza today, when raspy-voiced Candianne—a girl who ate like a bear at the dump—gestured to the half-eaten pizzas strewn between us. "How come you're still eating? Don't you know you're eating too much of *our* pizza!"

I listened to the harbinger-of-dumb's tomato sauce-stained advice (puddles of it caked in the corners of her unfriendly smile), and then returned to my slice. When it became clear that I had dismissed her *Tiger Beat* wisdom, Candianne tapped the forearm of dunce-faced middle sister Leanne.

Leanne slowly focused her big cow eyes ("She has her father's eyes," Berniece often boasted, as if to explain how an unlucky inheritance caused the dead man's man-sized orbs to rest in the semi-orphan's preteen head), shook off her stupor and demanded, "Yeah, why are you eating so much of *our* pizzas?"

"Whose pizzas?" I asked.

"I don't know," she finished, in the drone of a room temperature IQ.

Then, as if rehearsed, secret-smoker TammiAnn (the eldest and sluttiest of the three stepsisters) tugged up her tube-top and coughed her agreement. "You shouldn't be eating that much of *our* pizzas. Mom [cough], tell Chris [cough] to stop eating so much of *our* pizza! [more cough]"

With surprising quickness and troubling agility Berniece Jean peeled herself from the synthetic floral of a deeply dented sofa cushion, stood, and brushed crust and crumbs and other debris around her wastebasket-like chest. "In case you didn't know, my kids get a monthly 'pension' check from their 'deceased' father," she used pepperoni-greased fingers to air-quote the words *pension* and *deceased* (something she did if a word sounded legal or pretentious, like when she air-quoted the word 'chandelier'), "and we use that money to buy the groceries. So really all the food in the house, including this pizza and that soda [pointing her air-quote exhausted finger to the Mr Pibb in my hand] belongs to them." She made the announcement with great pride, as if she'd solved the mysteries of history and presented them to me in an embroidered pillowfront, then she picked a bit of crust from her t-shirted bosom and chewed it to oblivion.

I don't know if I replied or reacted outwardly at all. But in my metaphorical gut (by way of my biological throat), as it became difficult to swallow the once delicious wad of pizza now trapped in my mouth, I realized something poisonous had been delivered with the pie. The realization climbed through me like the slow triumph of infection.

My journey to a new home had reached its end. The smooth trip had been deceptive—across a benign bridge to a malignant mountain. Now, in one panoramic stare I knew: *this* family was not *my* family and this house was not my home. I sat silently, as interlopers do, at the knotty-pine-patterned formica table of an artless and hostile clan. They were silent too, staring unitedly and unsympathetically as I struggled to disappear the last stolen bite of their long-dead father's sausage and mushroom pizza. I looked only at my plate as I choked the heavy ball of dead-man's dough into the pit of an unsettled stomach.

The next day assignments were made regarding who was allowed to eat which foods from the well-stocked kitchen: Berniece and her children ate from one supply, my sister and I ate from another. Our cereals were generically packaged, our milk was powdered and our cheese institutional, our meats came from cans. Their packages were colorful, their dairy came from a cow, and their meat—thickly sliced ham and flavorful salamis—were tamperproof, alarmed with the telltale crackle of protective butcher paper. Secretly, when opportunity allowed, we gorged the better foods in the cold bath of an open refrigerator; we were often excluded from family outings—like dental cleanings and check-ups, or shopping for new school clothes—so opportunities were many. Berniece took the telephones from the house anytime Mona and I were left there alone so, instead of calling our mother, we ate. At night, as everyone slept, I would creep to the kitchen and feast on bread and butter or a fistful of salami or anything I could smuggle to the bathroom. After the impromptu bathroom meals I'd stop back at the kitchen for the largest gulps of Pepsi that my throat could tolerate, Mona and I were only supposed to drink the discount soda so Pepsi was my silent protest. Sometimes I'd float a booger in the remaining two-liter when I was done.

I realize now it was probably the 2:00 AM Pepsi binges that started a bedwetting habit that would traumatize me and my lower bunkmates for the next eighteen months. Vanne stopped sharing a bed with me which was much worse than the punishments Dad and Berniece threatened, mostly because I didn't believe their outrageous threats; the first time I came home from school to find my yellow pee-stained sheet hanging outside from an open bedroom window and down the front of the house I realized I had been too quick to dismiss their resolve. Taped to the windowpane was a large and proudly written sign in bold black letters that read CHRIS'S PISS SHEET, just in case my school bus and passing motorists might have missed the subtleties of the installation. Years later I worked as a telephone operator for the deaf, a morbidly obese woman named Libby sat in the cubicle next to mine. Libby was so large that she had trouble keeping herself clean. She doused herself in heavy perfume in a failed attempt to camouflage a human odor that was at times hard to take. I liked Libby—she was smart and funny and easy to talk to, aside from the odor I mean. While she was out of the office everyone complained about the smell, and the other operators refused to sit in her odorous chair. Ossie—the owner of the company—confessed to me that she didn't know what to do about the 'situation'. The next day I arrived at work to find her solution: the smelly chair was sitting out in front of the building with the sign *Libby's Chair* taped to the front. I removed the sign and wheeled the chair back to its cubicle before Libby reported for work. And I wondered why no one had ever done the same for me.

After two weeks of the house's new window treatment it became apparent that Dad and Berniece's punishment was not the deterrent my bladder required. My father took me aside, advising that: if I wet my bed again, for two hours after school each day I'd have to wear my pee-stained underwear on my head like a shower cap, while standing on the front porch with a BED WETTER sign affixed to my chest.

Dad had a large, low, credenza-style stereo system. The wood cabinet's plastic side panels lit with an array of colored disco lights to the beat of music, Hall & Oats was his favorite band. I liked the duo too, they were perfect opposites of hair and height (the CHiPs of soft rock). And I liked how closely they stood on the covers of albums, mashing their manes in a melting pot of black and blond. Some days as I stood on my tiny porch perch (wearing the marker-emblazoned sign and urine-stained underwear hat), I'd wipe my eyes to watch the bouncing colored lights through the front porch's dusty screen door, listening to "Rich Girl" and dancing a sad little jig. Sometimes "Hot Child In The City" played on the radio, I closed my eyes to contemplate the ode to sexy prostitute runaways, forgetting about the underwear on my hair and sign on my chest. I decided that one day I'd leave, I'd probably go to San Francisco. I knew a kid in elementary school would have a hard time supporting himself, but I'd seen something on TV about unsavory men who wait for runaways at big city bus stations so at the very least I'd have that.

Once a month, for ten minutes, Mona and I were permitted to talk to our mother on the telephone. The calls were timed and Berniece's kids monitored the conversations from an extension in the master bedroom, sometimes laughing or burping to be sure we knew they were there. On a few occasions we were allowed to go to lunch with our mother. She'd pick us up in her Volkswagen Beetle, we'd drive to the McDonald's drive-thru and sit in the parking lot to eat our burgers and fries. Mom would tell us how much she missed us and I'd ask to come home.

"I swear, I'm gonna come get you—both of you—and we're gonna live in a big house," she'd promise, "a lot bigger than your dad's house."

"Just us?" I'd ask.

"Just the three of us. The Three Musketeers, right Mona?"

"Uh-huh," my sister answered.

I'd ask about my new bedroom, something about choosing my own paint color.

"Oh shit yeah, we can wallpaper it if you want."

"What kind?"

"I don't know...cardinals, you still like cardinals?"

I did (birds, not baseball. I hate baseball.) We talked about my new room, how it would look, while Mona ate quietly from her sack of food. She was too old and too smart for empty promises.

I ate too, as slowly as chewing would allow. Words can't express how much I love a Quarter Pounder with Cheese but my enjoyment of the burger was always tempered with the fear of finishing my meal because I knew we'd be returned to Berniece when lunch was over. I felt like a death row inmate trying to savor his last bites, but it's hard to enjoy an entree when you know the dessert is 20,000 volts of electricity.

After apple pies Mom drove us back, she'd hug and kiss us good-bye. "Take us with you," I'd ask again, grabbing her waist in a bawling beg. She'd cry too, reluctantly pushing me off, then slam the car's little green door and speed away. I always ran behind with bionic speed, "Please Don't Go!, Please Don't Go!" punching its way through a salty waterfall of tears and snot. I ran in the direction of her disappearing car until I couldn't run any more.

Fifteen years ago I dated a guy named Keifer. He was a handsome guy, effeminate in a way that I found to be adorable, and with a butthole so tight it could choke-out a cat. We'd been dating about a

28

year when he told me over a restaurant dinner that he'd slept with someone else. Minutes later Keifer's phone rang and he answered a call from his new lover, telling the illicit voice he'd get a cab and come over. I begged him not to go but he ran out of the restaurant and down the street toward a row of hotel taxis. Even in clogs Keifer ran like a gazelle (this was before I knew it was better to let clog-wearing boys flee), he jumped into one of the waiting cars and drove away. I ran behind them until I couldn't run any more, and then I stood in the street and cried like an eight-year-old who just lost his mother. It had become the worst feeling in the world for me—knowing the person you love is going to run out of your life unless you can catch them. But no matter how hard and how fast you try, your legs and your lungs betray you and you watch them slip away.

One day my six-years-older-than-me stepsister TammiAnne returned home from an afternoon of strolling sidewalks. She often walked the neighborhood in short-shorts (that were tighter than a snare drum) hoping to inspire a "Hey what's cookin, average-lookin?" from passing cars. Apparently catcalls were slow that day because TammiAnne returned in a mood and decided to tell me my mom was a whore. The bitchy brunette was twice my size but in this scenario I played the role of a madman, picking up a branch and chasing her bouncing black bob back around the block. In the two years that we'd been living with my father, TammiAnne had emerged as the worst of Berniece's henchmen—mocking our complaints, listening to our phone calls, reporting our food excesses; she'd have medaled in meddling if the world rewarded despicability the way her mother did. When the screaming teen and I circled back to the house, Berniece waited in the doorway and caught me by the throat. She took my branch, and promised I would be sorry.

"Do you think I have to let you live in this house?" I kind of did.

"Because I don't. You are a guest in my house, one word

29

from me and you and your sister will be on the street," she paused to swallow a mayonaisy sandwich that had been churning around her mouth.

"Do you really think your mother would take you back?" I nodded yes.

"Well she wouldn't. Dusty didn't want you any more, and your grandmother didn't want you, nobody did." Before that comment I disliked Berniece, after it I hated her. "You're here because Dusty and her boyfriend *didn't want you anymore* [she enunciated the four words loudly and slowly, the same way she talked to the mexican immigrant family who lived next door.] If we didn't take you in, Mona and you would be living in a 'foster' home, or worse!" she used her free hand to air-quote the word *foster*, a legal term I suppose. "The only reason you aren't is because my kids felt sorry for you and said you could stay in *their* house. My children and I have been more than generous with you," I assumed she wasn't talking about the Pepsi, and she is a liar and I hate her, "so don't mistake our charity for duty or I promise you—you'll be very sorry."

My dad came home from work and Berniece told him what happened, he decided it was time for *family court*. Whenever there was a punishable disagreement in our house, family court was convened; Berniece's kids were always the jury majority so Mona and I were always found guilty, no matter what the charge. TammiAnne and I sat in the room's two armchairs, Berniece stood in the doorway stirring something in a bowl, and the remaining kids sat on the couch. My dad asked us what happened and we each told our story.

"I told Chris I thought his mother would be prettier if she didn't wear so much eye make-up..." TammiAnne lied, sniveling, raising a tissue to her rapidly growing nose.

"And then he physically 'assaulted' you," Berniece interrupted (air-quoting *assaulted*). Weren't there rules against this sort of thing—against council feeding answers to the witness. "I object..."

I wanted to say, "...Berniece is a pig."

"And she doesn't wear a bra either," middle sister Leanne added, of my mother's ever-present nipples.

"She can't because the straps hurt her shoulders, so there!"

At trial's end the step-jury was asked if I was at fault, they all raised hands to condemn; Mona withheld her vote, knowing it served no purpose. The voting jury decided I should be spanked with a belt, and that I would have to see a psychiatrist. Justice was restored.

The idea of a psychiatrist had floated around the house ever since a phone bill revealed that I'd been waking up early some mornings and dialing random long-distance numbers. I didn't intend to dial long distance, I just pushed buttons until someone answered. I'd curl under the open middle section of a long, double cabinet-style coffee table and listen to the "Hello. Hello?" until they hung up. If the person sounded nice I'd redial a few times (in this season of famine, I was migrating to more nutrient families.) Occasionally they'd tire of my calls and pick up the receiver, set it down without hanging up, and walk away. I'd sit quietly and enjoy the sound of their household until they eventually came back and unplugged the phone. Maybe a psychiatrist wasn't a bad idea.

I had several sessions with Dr. Rick. His airy office was on the top floor of a four-story building, which I explained was the tallest building I had ever been in. "From the roof you can almost see the Bay Bridge," he replied. I wasn't familiar with the reference, but I had no interest in falling off a roof. We sat on swivel stools at a long, book-filled table that ran the full length of a window wall. We talked about everything from cartoons to comic books while watching the tiny traffic below. Dr. Rick was a good listener and a good guy. When I told him about the food situation he began bringing us sack lunches that we ate picnic style in the middle of the room.

After our fifth meeting the doctor asked me to wait outside his office while he spoke with the adults. I thumbed through coloring books while my dad, Berniece, and the doctor talked privately for several minutes. Apparently the conversation heated— voices rose enough that I heard Berniece say in her most unpleasant tone, "Listen *Doctor*, save all the 'rationalizing' [undoubtedly air-quoting the five pretentious syllables] and just tell us what in the hell is wrong with him or we're *not* coming back!" And then, with less volume but reverberating clarity, I heard the doctor retort, "Bad Parenting."

I wanted to run into the room to slap my lunchmate with the highest of fives, but quickly realized I'd just had my last appointment with Dr. Rick. On a Sunday morning later that month, Mona and I were awakened and told we were moving out. Berniece and her eldest children escorted us to the front yard where we found our unpacked clothes piled onto the oily driveway. "Take everything," TammiAnne warned, "or we're throwing it away." My dad had worked the graveyard shift and was still asleep so I tried to go back inside to tell him goodbye (maybe he'd written his valediction on a card that he'd forgotten to hand to me.) I tried the knob but the door was locked. When I was young I got terrible earaches, my dad would sit me on his lap and rub my temples—his adult fingers siphoning the pain away with their little circles; I knew he'd want to say goodbye. I tried the bell three more times then returned to sleepy-eyed Mona, on the curb, waiting for our estranged mother to take us home.

CHAPTER 3

Nigger Lover

There is an unpleasantness to sharing pornography with your mother. But after the accidental discovery of a *Playgirl* magazine in the top of Mom's closet I began periodic snoops of her bedroom. Hers was the first beefcake I had ever seen, and the pages of roughhousing rugby players filled me with the kind of all-consuming bliss that a vampire must feel when his teeth pierce flesh, or that my sister must feel when her fork pierces a banana cream pie. During an otherwise fruitless search of Mom's dresser drawers, I found some thick folders of hundreds of pages of court transcript. I opened one and began to read the story that explained how my mother was able to bring Mona and me home.

Mom's common-law husband had been away for a long weekend "run" (their lingo for a group of bikers riding in force into the California hills to commit petty crimes, drink, and scare locals). When their relationship was new Mom would go with Mickey on the weekend runs, but eventually she was left at home. My mother was a jealous woman and convinced Mickey was screwing around on the weekend getaways—it wasn't uncommon for this circle of men to share their women, and this was a three-day weekend so

Mom was particularly pissed. Mona and I were living with my father so my mother, no longer saddled with children, decided to ignore Mickey's long-standing instruction to stay inside the house. She packed an overnight bag to spend the weekend across town, sunbathing at the apartment swimming pool of my grandma Pearl. Mom knew Mickey would call the empty house to check on her but this time she wanted *him* to worry, *him* to be jealous. At weekend's end, Mom instructed that if Mickey called, my grandma should say she hadn't seen her; Grandma Pearl agreed.

Sunday evening my mother returned to an empty house. Sad and angry that her "husband" was still out carousing with loose women, she stripped off her clothes and went to bed. Near 4:00 AM, the transcript continued, she awoke to the bright bedroom light and a dizzying crack to her head. Mom raised her arms and kicked her feet—trying to untangle long, sun-tanned legs from the mess of blankets that must have seemed in cahoots with Mickey as he rained heavy blows from a wooden board up and down her half-naked body.

When my mother regained consciousness Mickey was standing over her, board in hand. "Where were you when I called?" the attacker asked in a slow monotone that we always knew meant danger. "I was lonely, so I stayed with my mother," Mom explained through a locked jaw and rapidly swelling face. Mickey told her not to move, then he walked her explanation to the kitchen and picked up the phone. "Hello Pearl, I'm sorry to call so late but I wonder if you've seen Dusty?" Mom's heart sank—she knew her mother's answer, she readied herself for his return.

Though Mickey had gifted my mother with many beatings over the years, something about this one didn't sit well with her—she was bored with the board, she'd had enough. Mom quietly gathered her self-esteem and the bits of grocery money that might go unnoticed and, a year later, pulled into the driveway of my father's house to reclaim her two children and their pile of oily clothes.

We lived with relatives, on their couches and carpets, migrating often so that we might not outstay their waning welcomes. Mickey eventually moved out of the house (taking all our possessions with him) so Mom thought it safe for us to return to our empty home. A hollowed house confesses the grief of the family that lived there, our comfortable furniture had been a lie. My waterbed, the one I assumed had been waiting for me these past two years, it wasn't. The twin-sized bed seemed a sanctum, its headboard's dual cubbyholes were the perfect resting place for rabbit's feet, my calculator, a pair of red ceramic bulls. (The bulls were a gift from my great-grandmother, we met her once in Oklahoma. The feeble woman told me to pick any one thing from her house, to remember her by.) I couldn't take any of these things when I moved in with my father, we only took clothes; I thought they'd be here when I returned, they were not. Mickey didn't just take my things, he took my sister's things, my mother's things, everything.

Our rug was gone, it hid bullet holes in the corner of floor where drunk Mickey once made my barefooted mother dance. The livingroom furniture was gone too, like a long couch that never moved from beneath a gold and black painting of a bridge over an overly reflective lake. The paint was glossy, like wet tar carefully dripped onto a board. It had an artist's signature, as if he had created something important. The heavy wood and wrought iron coffee table was gone, and so was the cabinet television and a pair of his-and-her chairs that I imagine my parents once sat in when they were married. Everything was gone from the room except a shapely red glass ceiling lamp with dozens of clear drop crystals, it swagged on gold link chain to the corner of the room. The lamp was only illuminated on special occasions when it bathed everything in thick red light, giving a bawdy bordello feel to birthdays and Christmases.

The lamp seemed to have a mate—a twin reflected in the room's mirror wall. The long sidewall was covered entirely in twelve-inch mirror squares, each heavily marbled with gold-stenciled veins. If one watched the room's goings-on through the mirrors, as I-for-one sometimes did, then one's family appeared to exist through the censor-protected filter of a 1960s television program. But now, with everything gone, it appeared as though the program had been cancelled—only the unlucky ghosts of a few cast members lingered, waiting to crossover to another program, another station.

That night we closed drapes and locked doors and windows, Mickey was gone but his menace still occupied the house's creaks and shadows. I wasn't worried though, I was nearly two years older and what I hadn't grown in muscle I had gained in speed—I could gently toss a punch and then run for help. On *Charlie's Angels*, Farrah escaped diamond smugglers by kicking over a trash barrel and jumping onto a skateboard—I might try something like that. In discreet light we ate a variety of gas station sandwiches then went to sleep under a shared blanket on Mom's bedroom floor. I didn't have a waterbed, but I had my mother so I knew I'd sleep happier and dryer than I had in years.

Mona screamed near 3:00 AM. My startled mother dove for the borrowed gun in her patchworked purse with the feline speed of a young Shelly Hack or any of Charlie's other lesser-known Angels. She held the little mother-of-pearl handled pistol she'd gotten from her pawn-broker brother in one hand, and gestured us into the bedroom closet with the other. She closed the sliding door, telling us to wait inside in a semi-hushed voice that was almost drowned-out by the incessant fist that had woken us and was still pounding hard and loud on the bedroom window. Mona and I huddled in the closet, she cried and I attempted to comfort her by crying as well. After a minute or two we sneaked down the hall and were met at the front door by a small crowd of neighbors telling my mother how they'd chased away the two men who were pouring gasoline and lighting fires at our doors and windows. The neighbors had used our garden hoses and theirs to douse the small flames, they explained. We stood in our underwear and thanked them for their heroism. Then Mom called her brother, then the police. And we left the house and never returned.

Our new apartment was luxurious compared to my grandmother's sewing room floor where we spent several weeks following the fire. Mom sold the lightly charred house that she and my father bought when they first married and—after the county court gave half the profit to arsonist Mickey—we spent our half on furniture for a new three-bedroom apartment in another town altogether. The new couch was L shaped and covered in a pale weave that my mother knew would show stains, but she thought we ought to have something nice. A pair of matching display cases flanked a new television set and all three were decorated with a collection of glass and ceramic bells that I would help my mom grow over most of the birthdays, Mother's Days, and Christmases that followed. A coffee colored coffee table had a wicker and glass top, its center boasted a large asian style brass gong—the crown-jewel of Mom's bell collection. And we bought a better car. I was deliriously happy—I had an unbattered mother, showroom furniture, and unrestricted access to a refrigerator. Mom debated changing our names, believing her ex-lover would be looking for us, but our new home was a few towns away and the handsome new apartment gave us a confidence we had never known.

Mona and I started a new school and Mom started a new job, which kept her away from home until 7:00 PM most evenings. My new school was only a few blocks from the new apartment, after a challenging day of fifth-grade social politics I'd walk home and let myself in for a renegade afternoon in a latchkey life. Mom's new schedule and blossoming independence made her a taskmaster with the household chores so, after a free-for-all snack, I'd empty and scrub and dust a variety of things. When tasks were complete I watched two episodes of *Eight Is Enough*.

I'd often fantasized about living with the octadic television family, perhaps as a distant cousin whose parents had died (say, in a hot air ballooning mishap) and I thought we could change the title to *Nine is Even Better*. I'd also begun a new hobby of watching a neighbor in the apartment complex next to ours. My bedroom window faced his window from across a parking lot, giving me a decent view of the often-shirtless man sitting at a desk that he'd positioned to take full advantage of the apartment's parking lot view.

Some days I noticed the man standing away from his desk, still facing the window and possibly nude. In this position he sometimes seemed to make curious movements, but—through all the window glare—it was hard to be certain. And I was uncertain if the bare-chested man ever saw me. As weeks passed I grew bolder in my stalking—standing on top of my bed, wearing no pants. I held a modesty pillow over my privates and watched my neighbor stand in the rear of his room making the mysterious movements. One day as I squinted for a clearer view of the elusive man, the heavens momentarily disappeared the ever-present sun behind a sympathetic cloud—miraculously erasing all window glare and granting me my first undiminished view.

I watched dumbfounded as the man's busy hand swung back and forth across his erect penis. The hypnotic site untethered me from the middle of my room and propelled me toward the window glass, my pillow dropped to the carpet—introducing the world to my unpillowed crotch. My eyes travelled from the hairy man's bouncing penis, up to his heaving chest, and finally to his handsomely mustached face. When my eyes reached his I flustered to find them looking directly at me, and then I noticed his free hand stretched toward the window and motioning slowly and unmistakably for me to "Come Over."

The lesser part of me was delighted by the one-handed invitation, the greater part was aghast that I hadn't been somehow been shielded by a cloak of invisibility. I hopped away from the window and began a frantic half-naked back-and-forth across my bedroom, just out of window view. As I bent down to pull up my pants a bullet of fear shot through me; like a younger, hornier Christopher Walken I froze with a nearly psychic prediction: Tomorrow...on my way to school...the sexy pervert will be waiting in the bushes...he'll grab me...carry me up to his apartment...shut the door...and no one will ever see me again. My hands quaked as I dialed my mother's work number and warned her of my impending doom.

I closed certain curtains and locked all doors as my mom had instructed, then I grabbed a kitchen knife and waited. Mom came home and the cops arrived a few minutes later. I told the policemen what I had seen, though I may have omitted my pantsless peek-a-boo pillow dance from the story. The police made notes on a tiny notepad then left to speak with the man who, they later reported, denied wagging his penis or inviting me over. From my room I heard the officers assure my mother that they'd left him with a stern warning.

"That's it," Mom asked, "a warning?"

"I think he got the message," an officer assured.

"I got a message for him: Tell him he fucks with my kid again I'll cut his dick off."

"I know how you must feel..."

"Yeah? Cuz I feel like cuttin' his dick off. I keep a blade in my purse, tell him that."

Mom eventually settled down, she thanked the officers for their heroism and promised to keep a safe distance from our neighbor; I wondered if he would be angry with me, and if I could take a raincheck on his invitation.

Later that evening I asked my mother why the man had been handling himself so furiously. "Okay, first off he was a sacka shit for doin' that in front of you—you're just a kid so I'm sure it was scary. But when you're a little older and some Sweaty Betty's doin' it...trust me, you'll be jazzed." Then, with no bit of embarrassment, she explained he was masturbating, "That's when you touch your penis or when I touch my vagina to make it feel good."

"It feels good?"

"Oh yeah, really dynamite."

"Why does it feel good?" I pressed.

"Well, when a man's penis or a woman's vagina is stimulated it can get an itchy feeling inside, and if you keep touching it—it gets itchier until it feels like a sneeze, but better!"

"Really?"

"Bigtime. I'm talkin' top shelf, really blue-ribbon stuff."

Before this conversation, the only schooling my mother had given me about sex had something to do with the Nazis (that they strapped naked men to tables, inserted glass tubes into their flaccid penises, then had sexy women dance for them until the glass snapped inside their erections) so her new enthusiasm for masturbation made me wonder why she'd withheld this information until now. I went to bed that night and shook my penis in a variety of directions (back and forth, forward and back, and like a windmill in an easterly wind, and then a windmill in a westerly wind) trying to produce the mysterious sneeze. Handling myself felt good but it was no blue-ribbon sneeze. Still, I had a hunch this was a puzzle worth solving. Cautiously, I wrestled myself in the dark corners of dark rooms, semi-certain I'd be snatched by demons and yanked to hell; still, I was persistent. Just like the box in *Hellraiser*, if I rubbed it just right it might open, and all the world's wicked pleasures might spit forth.

Eventually the box opened, Mom had a copy of Grand Funk Railroad's 1973 LP *Flint*, the album's interior photo of the four naked band members had been the key. I opened the album and it opened the box every day after school and every night before bed. Within a few short weeks I had completely mastered bating, and would eventually become as inveterate a box opener as Pinhead was a pincushion.

Eventually I tried new methods (the other hand, our apartment pool's water jet) and more exotic lubricants (maple syrup, grandma's hand cream, an imprudent vapor rub). When I lived with my father, Huck—a delinquent, and some sort of relative to my stepmother Berniece—sometimes shared our bedroom, Vanne's and mine. Huck was the oldest kid in the house, flirting with adulthood. He had long blondish-brown hair that was thick with boyish barrelcurls, bright white skin and a fake tooth. He looked like a badass but he smiled at everything, a big slow glassy-eyed smile that made marijuana seem like a good idea. Huck had a troubled past, the details of which were secreted from me, but it was the reason he stayed with us and the cause of his artificial tooth. One night, long after bedtime, Huck came home later and clumsier than house-law allowed. From my bunkbed I heard the shouting of explicit words and then the tumbling of inexpensive furniture. We all ran to the ruckus and found Huck in my father's headlock like a wild buck with antlers caught in an iron gate. Before I could say 'Stop it, you're messing his beautiful hair' Berniece screamed us back to bed. From my bunk, through a wall, I listened as a war prisoner might listen to the torture of a beloved comrade, praying that one day we'd rise up and defeat the commie, Charlie. Huck eventually came to bed, unvictorious and still handsome, though angry and bruised. We were alone in our room that night, Vanne was away, and Huck wanted to talk. He told me things, worldly wisdoms largely learned in juvenile hall. Adults think they know everything, he explained, but they don't. And people will fuck with you just to keep you from having a good time. And he said to listen to Foghat, especially *Foghat Live*. Huck didn't mind going back to juvie, "There's no pussy in jail," he complained, but if you take a towel and soak it in warm water, and then roll it around a plastic breadbag, then grease the tube's interior and tuck it between two couch cushions…it feels just like the inside of a girl. I took mental note of these things, especially the last. Turns out he was right, about all of it: people, Foghat, the breadbag—which felt just like the inside of a boy too. I used the breadbag technique often, thinking of Foghat, thinking of Grandfunk Railroad, thinking of Huck. I still think of him sometimes, I know from a bit of internet research that his happy-go-lucky personality was ravaged by an unhappy-went-unlucky life. A prison sentence left him covered in racist prison tattoos and probably piqued with a hatred of homos. Still, he'll always be an heroic pothead to me.

Masturbation was my new best friend and life was good. Life was good for my mother too. She was home less but her mood had improved. My sister told me that Mom was dating a man from work, the news knotted my stomach a bit. Mom introduced her new lover to us over a ski-weekend. I didn't know how to ski, I hated the cold, and my mother's romances had given me a lifetime of bad experiences so the ski-weekend sounded like a wonderful idea. Mom sported a snow bunny style fur hat with pom-pom ties—a new look for her and an old look for Joan Collins. I wore a new pair of snow boots and an old pair of my mother's Isotoner gloves, but wasn't afforded anything that Joan might have worn to such a weekend.

Aside from artlessly tumbling down a number of snow-packed hills, and learning to perfect the curt answer to unwanted conversation, I remember very little of the trip—possibly a result of all the tumbling. I do remember eagerly holding the car door handle as we entered the apartment complex's parking lot on our return home late that Sunday afternoon. When the car stopped I jumped out. My mother—embarrassed by the lack of graciousness I had shown her new lover over the two previous days—yelled-out, "Chris, don't you have something you want to say to Norm?" I know now that she expected me to say 'thank you' but at the time all I could conceive was "Bye."

Apparently my speech infuriated my mother because—after what I am certain was a long, tongue-drenched goodbye—she bounced her furry pom-poms up the stairs and into my bedroom, swinging her belt as if it were a winter olympic event. I instinctively fell backwards onto my bed as Mom indulged herself with a dozen whacks. This wasn't the first time my mother and I had played 'uppity slave' but this time felt more unjust. She wasn't disciplining me to teach me some important life-lesson, or to otherwise protect me from myself. She was hitting me out of anger—because I had posed a threat to her new relationship. She was beating me up the way she would some bar floozie who had tried to buy her man a drink. When Mom and Mickey were together he would sometimes walk her into the house like a boxing coach escorting his prizefighter back from the ring. She'd nurse a bloody lip with a bar napkin, and he'd pull bits of bar floor debris from her hair in the manner of a back-alley cock fighter tending a triumphant rooster.

I don't know if I or my mother was more shocked when my indignation for the undeserved beating (and my distaste for her self-righteous expression) lifted my snow-booted foot and planted it directly in her snow bunny gut. Mom folded forward and dropped her belt, looking at me as if I had just telekinetically slammed-shut all the doors and windows and proclaimed, "Momma, things are gonna change around here."

She left my room and we never spoke of it again.

In the days that followed, Mom returned to work and my sister and I returned to school and the mood in the house returned to tepid. One morning as Mona and I feathered our hair (clanking our raised elbows like elks' antlers, vying for space in the shared bathroom mirror), Mom yelled from down the hall, "Chris! Get me the keys from my purse!" My mother's careful application of the many shades of eyeshadow that sculpted her lid and brow-bone caused her to run late most mornings, I was accustomed to assisting her in catching-up.

I abandoned my comb and reported to her bathroom with the ring of keys, then waited quietly while she rolled a straight bit of peroxide-lightened hair to a round brush before searing it into submission with a blowdryer. She did this with the proficiency of a Cuban rolling a cigar; I'd even said I believed she could do it professionally. The dryer quieted and Mom requested in a semi-polite tone, "Bring me the carton of cigarettes from the back of my car," before returning the dryer to full speed. I loved to watch my mother apply make-up and fluff her hair, but I obliged.

I ambled outside and down the building's cement stairs, toward Mom's single-owner silver Honda Civic. I stopped short to read a message in **big bold black strokes** sprayed across the driver's door.

NIGGER LOVER

I read it again, NIGGER LOVER. And finally a third time, it said the same thing. The four tires were slashed, and SLUT redecorated the windshield. I stood in a stupefied stare, forgetting all about the cigarettes in the trunk, uncertain why I had come downstairs. I wasn't confused by the SLUT accusation—I'd heard my stepsisters describe my mother as a slut before, but NIGGER LOVER only perplexed. I knew from watching a night or two of the miniseries *Roots* that "niggers" were old-fashioned black people—from around the time of *Little House on the Prairie*, but I didn't understand how or why my mother would have loved them, I didn't think she even saw the program. Whatever the reason, I knew this was bad.

I told mom, she and Mona and I ran back to the car (Mona with curling iron in hand, bangs in curling iron). Mom inspected her pretty silver Civic, she seemed fine—pissed but fine—until she called my Grandma. "He fuckin found us," the words barely escaped her lips before a sheet of tears washed across them and down her trembling jaw. My grandmother's car had been re-detailed as well, with MY DAUGHTER IS A NIGGER LOVER scribed across the hood (wordy, but effective). Mom called her brother, who had some social connections to Mickey Satana's inner circle—connections I never really understood. Mom's brother made some calls and learned that Mickey knew the apartment complex we lived in, but he didn't know which building or which unit was ours. My uncle's connection said the word on the street was that Mickey found out my mom was dating a black man (she wasn't, not yet anyway) from her work, and that Mickey was using the money he made from the sale of our house to pay for hits on my mom, her new boyfriend, and my grandparents. I don't know if I was more shocked to learn of the mob-style hits, or to realize that this sort of information was available in "word on the street" format. Within a few days my sister and I, my grandparents, my mom and her new boyfriend were handing our hastily packed belongings to Mayflower Movers, and driving our [1]nigger-loving cars to Oklahoma—the panhandle state.

---

[1] In the spirit of an apology and the format of a footnote, I'd like to explain that I didn't use the N (as in *noxious*) word lightly. It wasn't an attempt to be shocking or comedic or entertaining, rather it hoped to relay the character of a man who considered "nigger lover" to be an insult. I considered not using his words at all, but with some endoscopy I discovered a belief that I'd be doing no one any favors by rewriting the childhood racism that was literally spelled-out before me, and before the black family who shared our parking lot.

CHAPTER 4

Lady Drinks the Booze

In June 1929 Great Britain darkened to its first solar eclipse in nearly two centuries; the body of a Canadian serial killer's last victim was discovered in a Winnipeg rooming house; and in the hardscrabble area near Slaughterburg, Oklahoma, a black-haired infant with a great sensitivity to alcohol was loosed upon the world. Fanny was one of many born to an alcoholic chicken farmer and his fertile wife. The Sissom family patriarch was an abusive man—most of the Sissom family sons had committed suicide or died of liver failure by the age of forty, many of the daughters joined the war effort abroad to escape more immediate dangers at home. In total there were eighteen children in the Sissom family, a clan residing near the agricultural region that would later incorporate as the town of Slaughterburg, Oklahoma (a community briefly made famous when an animal rights group asked the town to change its name—which suggested the murder of innocent animals—to Veggieburg, a name that encouraged animal compassion. The organization offered free veggie burgers to those at the town council meeting, though the residents of Slaughterburg opted for meals from a meat cart brandishing the sign, SLAUGHTERBURGERS, IT'S WHAT'S FOR DINNER.)

Fanny was my grandmother's sister and—when I was very young—my low-wage babysitter on those weekends when my mother left town, clung to the leathered back of her biker boyfriend. At an age long hovering around forty-nine, Aunt Fanny was sharp as a tic-tac (she kept a box of them in her purse to add minty nuance to smoky breath.) She had the kind of body that only a lifetime of cigarettes and barstools could sculpt (not to say my aunt had a drinking problem—she was more like a workaholic, but with alcohol.) A mostly thin woman, Fanny seemed too frail to sustain the number of bar brawls she had undoubtedly started, her limbs too wobbly to gracefully support her booze-logged hub. Her breasts were small, but brassiereless decades rendered them lower than most. And her rear end had widened and flattened to the dimensions of the wooden seats of the three-legged stools at the bar of the Palomino Wine & Whisky Room, conveniently located just four blocks from Fanny's residential hotel.

Aunt Fanny's gray-rooted, black-dyed hair was sponge rolled, teased and pinned with black wiglets, then sprayed into a bouffant that might have been attractive in an era twenty-five years earlier on a woman twenty-five years younger, but I doubt it. Fanny's babysitting usually involved dousing her polyester pantsuit in drugstore perfume—a pungent sweet she hoped might cover the brown tobacco mist that seeped from the pressed-on nail tips of her heavily knuckled fingers—and throwing on a marmot ("How do you like that, it's *real* fur!") or opossum coat before kissing me hard on the mouth and clomping thick heels toward the front door. "I'll only be gone an hour or so [that meant 2:00 AM] help yourself to the leftover TV dinner in the fridge, it's Salisbury Steak! And if your mother calls tell her I just stepped-out for a pack of ciggies. And don't answer the door unless it's for me, tell them I'm at the Palomino, they'll know where to find me."

Still talking, Fanny slammed the door behind her—rattling the wooden *Give A Hoot, Don't Toot* sign decorating its backside. Alone, I'd climb into one of Fanny's kimono robes for a leisurely evening of picking through tin-foiled leftovers, smoking lengthier cigarette butts, and watching *Eight Is Enough* on the room's only luxury: a wood-paneled, rabbit-eared television set that doubled as a stand for styrofoam wig heads and a toaster-oven. While I was indifferent to actor Dick Van Patten as a father figure, I believed actress Betty Buckley might be the world's most perfect mother. She was an effortlessly beautiful woman with the sensitivity of a poet, and she had the ability to love all the Bradford children as though they were her own. In fact, it was Betty Buckley who once rescued Sissy Spacek when she was tormented by bullies and telekinesis, crouched in a locker-room corner and covered in lady blood. That's the kind of woman you want in your corner, the kind you want making your lunch. I knew the Bradford kids would welcome me into their primetime home, just as they had welcomed stepmother Betty Buckley. Little Adam Rich and I could ride the school bus together, with matching bowl-cut hairdos we would easily be mistaken for brothers. Older brother—actor Grant Goodeve—could teach me to identify the different types of wrenches needed to fix a car, and Susan's new fiancée Merle "The Pearl" could teach me to catch a baseball (he was in the minor leagues after-all.) Middle brother Willie Aames and I might lay in the sun together, a little lemon juice in my hair would likely give it the same golden highlights Willie enjoyed. We could surf a bit if the waves permitted. If not, we'd have a picnic of fried chicken and exotic cheeses in the back of his van (I learned Willie drove an oceanwave-themed van in the *Tiger Beat* article "Will You Take A Ride In Willie's Van?") And if there weren't enough beds in the Bradford house, Willie and I could share.

My aunt Fanny eventually came home, she'd announce the arrival by dropping keys several times before successfully inserting one into the front door. Her stupor afforded me the time to abandon my shorty kimono and hide any other embarrassing paraphernalia I'd collected throughout the evening.

"How ya doin', kid?"

"Fine."

"Yeah? Your aunt Fanny's doin' pretty good too." *Pretty Good* meant unsober—a definition she illustrated by stumbling through the removal of each shoe.

"Hey Chris, how's this?" she'd ask—of her girdled figure, "Not bad for a grandma, eh?" (Fanny was grandmother to two kids—a boy and a girl that were roughly the same age as Mona and me. We were friends with the cousin siblings until a maternal rift forbid us from further contact.)

I wasn't sure how to distinguish a well-girdled figure from a poorly girdled one, but the truss looked like an armless straightjacket, as though Fanny's midsection had been found to be a danger to itself or to others. "Not bad," I offered, "not bad."

After a final cigarette and some wine-stained mutterings, Fanny would fall asleep beside me on an unfolded folding couch, beneath a nicotine cloud that lingered like unresolved pain throughout the hundred fifty square feet of her studio apartment.

The small room was always dimly lit, with green curtains that never opened. It was drably furnished with mostly office-style furniture from the 1950s and 60s that I suspect came with the unit. Other than a few Tom Jones records, a disused litter box left behind by a runaway cat, and a small collection of stretch pants, cocktail dresses, and open-toed shoes—Fanny had not assembled any personal possessions in the first five decades of her life. She had however assembled a long list of men who had briefly entered and then dramatically exited her rented room. There were many "uncles" who might follow Fanny home from the Palomino on a Friday or Saturday night—an Uncle Hank or Uncle Vic, or perhaps Uncle Chet. On those nights, I slept on the floor (Fanny's discarded rat fur coat made for a nice second blanket) so that she and Uncle Hank might enjoy some private time on the springy platform above.

Fanny's lovemaking sounded a lot like crying. Crying was something Fanny did often (she didn't suffer her tragedies, she performed them), which is what I usually assumed was happening on the bed above. Fanny would lie under the man and cry for several minutes in her hoarse, whisky-soured voice until she seemed to hyperventilate and then pass-out. Hank would often leave as Fanny began to snore long and aggressive snores; I'd try to watch as he clumsily searched the room for underwear in the early morning light. Sometimes Fanny and one of the Hanks would argue as he left. Aunt Fanny would scream profanities punctuated by fits of coughing (a comma) or a thrown shoe (an exclamation point). As the man retreated, the slam of the front door would cause Fanny's tears to amplify to the biblical, as if her husband or an armful of her children had been thrown to the lions. Her widow's wails would permeate the thin walls and echo through the slumbering community until an upstairs neighbor might bang a heel on the floor, reducing Fanny's fit to a watery whimper. And finally—with her black bouffant's finely teased wiglets jostled askew—she'd call me up to the sofa bed, hug me tightly from behind, and softly cry herself back to sleep.

My mother was mostly more elegant in her consumption of spirits—I rarely saw her drunkenly throw a bowl of salad, or vacuum a pile of vomit—but I never saw her without a Margarita or Bloody Mary (made with spicy Clamato juice) in hand. I was Mom's most regular bartender once I became old enough to pilot the blender, taking great pride in my ability to evenly salt the rim of a fresh lime Margarita glass. In youth I never attributed my mother's peculiarities to alcohol, they just seemed to be the antics of a bored and mischievous woman.

Mom was usually up at the crack of lunch, but some winter mornings—when boredom had crept in with the cold—she'd wake me for her early morning entertainment. "Chris, get up," she'd say in excited whispers, "I'll give you a dollar to jump in the pool." My disbelief of the ridiculousness of her suggestion was eclipsed by my greed for money; at seven years old Mom's dares were my only source of income so I crankily accustomed to the rigors of the working class. Half asleep I'd stumble to the backyard and up the pool ladder then hurl myself into the frigid water. Other mornings my mother woke me with an urgent shake, insisting I come to her room to watch Jim and Tammy Faye Bakker's *PTL Club*. Mom wasn't a religious woman, in fact she was an atheist, but she was tickled by the Bakkers and wanted to be sure the irony of her 5:00 AM program selection wasn't lost on an empty bedroom. Mom proudly sang-along with the famously teary-eyed Tammy Faye while I tried not to fall asleep.

My mother could tickle and terrorize her children in a single gesture, one of her favorite gestures required only nudity and a fresh book of matches. She'd pluck a match from its book—the tip of her index finger pressing the match head against the rough strip—then thrust her finger toward an unlucky target (Mona and me); the lit match propelled across the room like a fiery little cardboard missile. Mom's unique talent for repeating this attack in rapid succession had alarming precision, even while running naked after screaming children. Mona and I scattered and hid from Mom's firestorm, and from her nudity. Once Mom settled down my sister and I would get ready for school.

When Mona and I were very young, Mom fed us stories to relay to our unsuspecting grandmother. "Nana, can you tell us how to heat up a can of soup? Mom and Mickey went away for the week and we haven't eaten for a few days and we're really hungry." We heard a thud as my grandma dropped the phone. My aunt June-Ida—my grandmother's sister and roommate—picked up the receiver, "Oh My God, she fainted! Pearl, wake up!" My mom would laugh and we'd giggle and confess the prank as my grandmother stirred into consciousness. I imagine Mom would have booby-trapped our jungle gym if she thought it would get her on *Funniest Home Videos*.

On Halloween my mother expressed her drunken creativity by putting a thick coating of black shoe-polish on our hands and faces. She braided our hair in a few dozen sprigs that were rubberband sheafed and LiquiNet sprayed to stand perpendicular to our scalps. Oversized bras were padded with nylons full of uncooked pinto beans, and pillows over our fronts and butts were held in place by tightly cinched leather waist belts. The fat lady padding was hidden under big comfy long-sleeved cotton nightgowns, the kind Laura Ingalls might have worn had she shopped at JCPenny. Mom gave us each a wastebasket and a kiss on the cheek before sending her two black-faced Aunt Jemima children into the street to beg for candy.

My mother's favorite way to spend an afternoon was sunbathing, a bottle of baby oil in one hand and mixed drink in the other. I'd grease her like she was swimming the English Channel then lay on a deck chair beside her. She read pages from a book, usually Helter Skelter, and I kept away the yellow-jacket wasps that lived in the ivy privacy wall that edged our small patio. If I needed a break from the heat I'd pick out the bits of dead goldfish that circled the drain of our poorly maintained rock fountain pond (I didn't know if my parents built the little pond or if it came with the house, but either way the exposed PVC pipe and dead fish tumbling above the filter suggested it was not up to code.) Mom bought a tanning lamp to maintain her color while she lay on the couch in winter months. I watched soaps on a nearby slab of carpet while she passed-out under the bright UV light. By early evening my eyes had swelled shut. They crusted over and I wasn't able to open them or leave my bed for a week. If my mom hadn't been badly burned herself I'm sure she would have been available to comfort me or to take me to a hospital, but she mostly slept through the ordeal on a strict diet of pain pills and mixed drinks. A week later—when she finally emerged from her bedroom—she was thrilled with the weight she'd lost, but disappointed that her tan had peeled away.

When I was in junior high Mom met some local highschool dropouts. They were the scofflaws in the town we lived in, in their early twenties, living off marijuana sales and a bogus workman's comp claim. Buddha was a giant of a man—nearly four hundred pounds—with a massive unkempt afro. He planted a hair pick over each ear and would retrieve them in unison like a Samurai pulling two swords. Clem was tall too—at least six foot five, but probably weighed less than my fourteen-year-old sister. Clem's scraggly hair was the color of cream corn, and his teeth were the color of his hair. His skin was pockmarked and one of his eyes was noticeably bigger than the other which gave the somewhat lewd impression that he was always contemplating a wink. Both men had long fingernails and smelled of pot and unwashed clothes. Despite the duo's scary exteriors they were soft-spoken and always nice to me, though I suspect it had something to do with their infatuation with my curvaceous mother. (Mom was a sexy woman, she could have been Loni Anderson's stand-in when the *WKRP in Cincinnati* lights needed readjusting; we never went to a gas station or a grocery store without some man staring at her like he wanted to tolerate her kids.) I knew my mother had large plastic bottles of something hidden under her bed that I suspected had something to do with Buddha and Clem. I was embarrassed by my mother's association with these men, we were already pariahed by poverty and I was afraid the stench of her new friendships wouldn't be one I could perfume.

We lived across the street from the town's popular Baptist church, some Sunday afternoons my mom and her new friends would lay on our couch, looking out the window and making fun of churchgoers returning to their cars. I woke late one Sunday, had an overdue pee then lumbered to the kitchen (Mom worked every other Sunday so those days were the best of my month.) I brought a bowl, a box of Captain Crunch, and a gallon of milk to the livingroom and turned on the TV—it was going to be a good day. A few thirsty bites into my mid-morning meal I noticed the Sunday Baptists, a small group of them assembled at the edge of the church's well-manicured lawn (the lawn was just across the street from our little house, its fresh-cut smell our only incense). I choked down my chew and bore below the window line, the Christians were watching me eat.

Cowered and confused, I made certain I was wearing bottoms and then crawled the length of our four-section sofa, when I reached the wall and its large open window I peeked from beneath the curtain. One...two...three dozen well-dressed men, women, and children were all looking across our narrow street, looking directly at our house. Many seemed to salute our home—an army of onlookers holding hands as visors over sun-glared eyes. My concerned gaze followed their concerned gazes to our front yard, where I noticed a strewn beer can and then another, then a shoe and then a foot.

Underwear clad, I ran out the front door to my unconscious mother where she and her unconscious boy-toys were displayed on our liquor-littered lawn like a white-trash nativity scene, or like something you'd see outlined in chalk just before the coroner carted it away. ("Looks like she got ahold of some bad booze," he'd say, "what a shame, she could have been a stand-in for Loni Anderson.") I reached down and shook my mother's shoulders, "Mom. Mom Get Up," I pleaded, I shook her again. On a third shake my mother opened an unfocused eye and mumbled something about being late for work, then Buddha and Clem sat up like hibernating zombies catching spring's first whiff of delicious brain. Mom noticed the Baptist audience—four dozen now, she regained her legs and clumsily achieved vertical, pushed her boobs forward and slur-shouted across the street, "Stare hard, lasts longer!" then "Take a picture, Retard!" then more things less eloquent.

I don't know how or when my childhood sitter, Aunt Fanny, died. I never saw her after we moved away. I do know that any glints of promise she'd had as a little black-haired baby born in that June of 1929, any chance of a happy marriage or meaningful friend-

ships or an interesting career, were suffocated in the smoke of a hundred thousand cigarettes and drowned in the flood of as many glasses of wine. However Fanny died I can be certain her coffin was cheap, her black hair was a wig, and her funeral was poorly attended.

I'm an anomaly in my bloodline—I never fancied booze. I rarely tasted a beer, a wine, a mixed drink, or a shot that I didn't want to spit out. I've been drunk but never without dryheaving into somebody's bathtub the next day. By the time I was old enough to drink legally, I'd given up trying to drink altogether. Maybe it was the flavor, maybe it was the fear of ending up like Fanny. I had my own afflictions to overcome, but none that came in a can or bottle.

"HOW MANY TIMES DO I HAVE TO TELL YOU THAT YOU SOUND LIKE A BROKEN RECORD?"

We drove and drove and drove and drove. I spent most of those hot days unsticking myself from backseat vinyl. Mom and Norm kept Bob Seger turned up and their windows rolled down so that Mona and I could enjoy the arid air at interstate speeds while being flogged by our own overgrown hair. The unrecognizably barren landscapes of Arizona, New Mexico, then Texas, looked like wastelands to the under-travelled, and every desert cactus looked like a mutant murderer might be hidden behind it, waiting for the plant's sluffed needles to pop our west coast tires.

"Isn't it pretty," Mom asked no one in particular. She raised a warm beer to toast the terrain, "Shit!" the wind knocked the bottle from her hand. Without instruction, Mona opened the iceless cooler and handed her another.

"How about there?" Norm unstuck his hairy pointing finger from the steering wheel and aimed it at a sign; it was his first conversation in a hundred miles.

"I have to pee," Mona added, closing the cooler to return to untangling permed hair from the metal closure of her denim overalls.

"We all do."

We sat in the hot parking lot for many minutes while Mom corrected her hair and make-up, each of us unwilling to ask that she move it along. "Okay", she said, "let's see what they eat in Oklahoma."

"Welcome to Bread Lobster, table for four?"

"Yes," my mother confirmed, watching Norm to see if he noticed the hostess's beefy bosom.

"How's this?"

"It's fine, thank you."

"Someone'll be right along to take your drink order."

"I'll have a bloody Mary."

"Oh I'm sorry Ma'am [Mom hated being called Ma'am], we don't have any hard liquor."

"Or bras?"

"I'm sorry?"

"Nevermind, please send the waitress."

We silently studied our menus, flipping page to page, looking at the seafoods, baked potatoes, and steaks that Oklahomans ate.

"This looks just like the Bread Lobster menu at the mall," Mom complained.

"It's a chain," Norm explained.

"No shit."

"Don't you like seafood?"

"*Yes* I like seafood, but would it kill them to put cornbread on the menu?"

"Maybe they could make…"

"Nevermind, forget it."

"Wail, Hello Thayre!"

"Hello."

"Om Sissy, n'I'll Be Yur Waytress! D'yall Want Sumthin Nice n'Cold Ta Draink?"

Mona and I laughed, "What did she say?"

"Ow, Yew Tew Gaught The Giggles, Don't Ya?"

"Ignore them, they've never heard an accent like yours before."

"Aixccent? Em I Talkin Fuhnny?"

"Ah, hah ha. Say it again."

"Say What?"

"Say my name."

"Owkay Sugar, What's Yur Nayme?"

"Chris!"

"Chreeus."

"Ah, hah ha."

"Whur Yew Fokes Frum?"

"California," someone answered.

"Ow Gawd, Yall're a Lowng Way Frum Home, Aint Yuh?"

"She said: Y'all!"

"Ah, hah ha."

Mona and I ordered Oklahoma shrimps, Norm ordered an Oklahoma steak, Mom ordered an Oklahoma beer, then another.

"Did you see the boobs on the hostess?"

"What?" Norm looked up from his steak for the first time since it arrived.

"Her boobs, didn't you see her boobs?"

"I don't know."

"We'll did you or didn't you?"

"I guess so."

"Of course you did. They're nice, right?"

"What?"

"Are you deaf? Her boobs—they're nice, right?"

"Should we get dessert?"

"I guess he *is* deaf. Kids, better learn sign language, your new daddy's deaf."

"Haow Yew Fokes Dewin Over Heer? Cain I Geit Yew Anuther Beeir?"

"We're fine. And yes, I'll have..."

"Maybe you should slow down, babe."

"Slow *what* down?"

"Nothing."

"*Nothing?*"

"Nothing."

"You know...every time I ask what you said, you say *nothing.*"

"Do I?"

"Yeah. It's like you're afraid to say it, like you don't have a spine or something; he's like one of these shrimps, you know, no backbone."

"They're exoskeletal."

"What?"

"Nothing."

"Nothing! See, he said it again, nothing. *Nothing nothing nothing,* he sounds like a broken record; honestly, how many times do I have to tell you that you sound like a broken record?"

"Seeeew... Shud I Geit Ya Thayt Beeir?"

"I'm sorry...Sissy, you'll have to excuse us. You can probably tell it's been a crap week."

"Oh Gosh Hun, Yew Muhst Be..."

"I am. Honestly, it's been a shit month, all of it. Six days to pack three houses, if you can imagine that."

"Thray Howses, Thayt's Alottuh Howses. Hey, Yew Keeids Wanta Nuther Soder Pop?"

"Ah, hah ha. Say *soda pop* again."

"Soder Pop?"

"Ah, hah ha."

"Their grandparents came with us..."

"Thayt's Sweet."

"But *somebody* lost 'em, somewhere near Santa Fe."

"Albuquerque."

"Shut up Norm, watch some titties."

"Ow Dear."

"We came to Oklahoma for a fresh start, you know, a new life..."

"Sure, Hun. Whay Don't I Geit Ya Thayt Beeir."

"You're sweet. Listen, Sissy, we're gonna leave you a nice tip. And please tell that hostess I'm sorry he was staring at her breasts all night, apparently he's deaf but his eyes work fine, and they've never seen nipples before."

"Ma'am?"

"Maybe you can split the tip with her, so she can buy a brassiere."

"Ow, Okay…"

"And I'll take that beer to go. Come on kids, get your shit, let's go start our new lives!"

CHAPTER 5

Balls

I hear today's gays like sports, they like watching them and they like playing them. They like them so much they type, "Must Love Football" in the "Must Be Straight, Must Love Football" titles of their Craigslist personal ads. (And if you're the type of self-loathing gay who writes those ads please know that I hate you. I hate that you believe what theists think of you, I hate that you pollute the dating pool with your bigotry, I hate that you bought my book, and please buy my other books. I don't really hate you, I've just spent more time contemplating the offerings on Craigslist than the offerings of museums or libraries so I've over-observed your hetero-fetish. But please consider respecting yourself enough to want to date someone like yourself, someone gay. Love yourself. Love your fat, stupid, ugly self. You are perfect, you smell bad, and you're perfect.)

I don't buy it—all the sports-loving gays of today, when I wouldn't know the Boston Red Sox from the Cleveland Steamers. The gays of my youth feared sports, we fumbled balls, we struck out. Failure at sports was our first indication that we were misfits, outcasts. We were the Carrie Whites in a world full of Chris

Hargensens. It's why all gays loved Sissy Spacek, we related when she swung at a ball and missed—both athletically and socially—and we shared her bloodlust for revenge.

Don't misunderstand: I took pride in my tweenage gayness… it's part of what made me feel like a rebel (rebellion doesn't just come from sticking it *to* the man, but also from sticking it *in* the man.) Still, I wouldn't have minded being a little more athletic. I've stood somewhere in the deep left of a baseball field—hope high, breath held, glove outstretched—as balls struck the earth like hail all around me. It may have been this percolating gayness that prevented me from finding the balls that loomed high in the sky above me, or it may have been a not-yet-diagnosed nearsightedness (much like childhood birthday parties and era-appropriate clothing, eye doctors and dentists were not the priorities to my mother that they were to the mothers of my teammates.)

Mom married Norm. I had second thoughts about her third marriage, which I mostly kept to myself. We all moved to a rental house in a lower middle-class section of the oil-rich city of Giddyuptown, Oklahoma. I thought Oklahoma would be a lot more like *Little House on the Prairie*, I thought we'd ride a horse to school, and come home covered in dust. Instead our school bus drove us past some of the largest homes I had ever seen—homes that made me realize how poor I was. I hoped their children attended private schools and would not be my seventh-grade peers.

In every school I'd ever attended I was always late to every class. I am inexplicably easily disoriented in both unfamiliar and familiar surroundings, but never so much as when I am at school. I rarely used a locker because the detour usually ended with me asking an impatient janitor for the same directions he had given me the week before.

The door of my new gymnasium closed behind me with a lengthy hydraulic clank that reverberated through the otherwise silent gymnasium.

"Terribly glad you could join us, son," I hoped that wasn't

sarcasm, "I presume by your late arrival and those satin shorts that you like to make an entrance?"

"Yes. I mean no."

"Well in case no one told you, the bell means that gym class has started. Are you familiar with the bell system?"

I was.

"Oh wonderful, then tomorrow I'm sure you won't be late, am I incorrect in assuming that or am I not?"

"Yes. I mean no."

"Terrific, terrific. Well then how about you do me a favor and sit those pretty little shorts down so I can start my speech all over again now that we're all here."

The newly formed team of sports-loving boys watched as I scurried to an open spot of polished wood floor at the tail end of the pimple-faced horde. I wedged between two boys. The asian kid to my right scooched over an inch or two, the italian kid to my left glanced up as I sat down; I'm certain I looked dumbstruck as I glanced back. The boy—Richie—was a twelve-year-old, moppy-haired, Gregory Harrison type ("Gonzo Gates" from television's *Trapper John, M.D.*), and the single most attractive human I had ever seen; he made the rest of us look like primates. He sat with the kind of confidence that only beautiful people have, as if they know a lifetime of german chocolate cake and Cadillac cars awaits them. I sat beside him, stunned by the proximity of his lap and the symmetry of his face.

The coach began his speech, it started with the importance of being on time, and then there was something about punctuality. Occasionally one of the boys would turn and look at me as if to say, "This is because of you." Normally this sort of thing would have troubled me, I might have scribbled notes in a notebook as an excuse to lower my head. But right now, I was broadly oblivious to the coach's condemnation and the resentment of my teammates. I was concerned with nothing but the tenuous touch that had sprouted between myself and Richie Marcasetti's finely hair-dusted, indian-style outwardly bent knee. For a kid who was rarely happy, sitting with the closest thing to a boyfriend I'd ever had—I was.

I don't know if tardiness and the dangers it presents to one's character were still being explained to the class because the room and the world had become perfectly silent, perfectly still to me. Richie and I sat joined at the knee in an impenetrable bubble that would surely carry us through junior high, high school, and into a state-denied marriage with matching his and his Cadillacs. We'd buy a big house, I decided, one of those seen through my school bus window, we'd adopt a baby and name her Morgan Fairchild. I thought to turn to Richie, to tell him the news, but the beautiful boy turned to me first. The asian kid at my right also twisted tersely at the neck so to stare in my direction, as if each had suddenly succumbed to "Captain Howdy" or some other Ouija Board ghoul.

Their four wide eyes startled me, clearing my head of the opiate of young lust, and opening my ears to a profound cinematic fart. It squeaked (or screeched really) out of my ill-fitting satin gym shorts, wailing like an angry Chewbacca across the hard lacquered floor. The nylon satin-muffled saxophone sounds seemed to play a half dozen ill-considered notes. Each echoed through the middle school gymnasium with all the intensity of a determined young broadway diva, as if Sarah Brightman were crying a warning from deep within my anus, "PRETEEN BOYS BEWARE! A SATIN SICKO SITS AMONG YOU! HEAR HIM...THE PHAGGOT OF THE GYMNASIUM!"

Seconds passed before I corseted my shock and shut down the faulty sphincter, bending the diva's final note from a brassy F-sharp to an abrupt B-flat. I instinctively turned my head to the right and looked accusingly at the asian boy, as to deflect ownership. But his little asian eyes stared back at me, hard, as if he were made of wood, teak. When his splinterless scowl made clear he wasn't having any of that, I looked around the room and all eyes were only on me.

"Son, was there something else you wanted to share with the class or can I get back to my speech now?"

"Yes. I mean no."

Mom's new husband Norm was tall and strong, though lanky and slightly awkward. He was handsome in a twelve-year-old-boys-are-attracted-to-anything kind of way. His thick brown hair was carefully combed, with the occasional wiry gray separating from the pack. He wore it parted on a distant side, each hair about four inches long, his hairline receded about half that length. His tall shiny forehead looked as if it had been factory lacquered, and corduroy was the only fabric his legs had ever felt. Norm seemed to be much better to my mother than Mickey had been, but I now lacked the ability to trust her romantic choices or to accept any man other than Dick Van Patten as a father figure.

Since our move to Oklahoma my married mother had grown tired of city life. With secretarial schools and bar brawls behind her, Mom decided she was a country girl at heart. She and Norm bought a recently constructed house on the outskirts of civilization, in a barely populated area a few miles outside of Puddin Foot, a small Crow Hop County town forty miles from the comparatively civilized Giddyuptown. The house sat on several wooded and weeded acres, and was in fact the nicest house we had ever lived in, though probably not all that nice. Mona and I were offered dogs and horses when we objected to moving for the second time that year, "We might even get you some chickens," they promised, the possibilities were beginningless.

There were two kinds of kids in my new seventh-grade classes: preppys and hicks. Jocks might successfully fit into either category, an interloping artistic homosexual fit into neither. I did have one friend in my new junior high, art teacher Mrs Turner. Carol Turner was the coolest woman I had ever met. She was smart and talented and had no bullshit to her personality—she was an artist and she was above it. She talked to students like they were fellow artists (even though my "art" was an acrylic portrait of a horse with a Santa Clause hat in his mouth, which I gave my mother for Christmas). And Mrs Turner never acted like I spent too much time at her desk, though I did. During the winter break I found my teacher's number in the phone book and called to ask how she was doing. She was fine, but thought it was best that I not call her at home anymore.

When Mona and I got our yearbooks I opened mine and immediately saw a picture of a boy named Decker Abbott. Because of his last name, Decker's photo was the first to appear in the book. He was a senior at the high school so I'd never seen him in person, but Puddin Foot was small enough that all grades shared a single annual. His photo burned through my chest like one of Aunt Fanny's fallen cigarette embers. I spent hours contemplating Decker's curly black hair, confident grin, and left-of-center gaze. About a week later I found Decker's number in the telephone book.

"Is Decker there?" I asked.

"Decker, it's for you! He'll be right here." I nodded a thank-you.

"Hello, this is Decker." I grinned my excitement.

"Hello, this is Decker." I grinned wider.

"Hello?"

I wondered how long the handsome highschool senior would wait for me to reply; when he hung up, I had my answer. I called the Abbott's house and asked for Decker several more times over the next few months. I never did speak, but I felt our connection was undeniable.

Mona was a highschool freshman and had blossomed into an older tomboy. She'd learned to play bass guitar and was obsessed with the band KISS. My heavy metal, tomboy sister wasn't the type of girl to wear a dress so we were shocked when Mona announced that she was going to the school's first formal dance of the year.

Mom bought her a ruffled robins-egg blue chiffon dress that would have looked wonderful on the lido deck of the *Love Boat*. My sister curled her hair and wore a shade of eyeshadow that matched her blue dress. Her escort was to arrive at seven o'clock, we all waited excitedly to meet the young man who would be Mona's very first date.

My mother and sister wanted to appear casually aloof so I was given the responsibility of answering the front door. The ding donged and everyone took their positions, and I prepared my "You must be Mona's date, please come right this way" speech. When I opened the door I first noticed the corsage, and then the outstretched hand waiting to shake mine.

"Hi, I'm Decker...Decker Abbott. I'm here for Mona."

I said nothing.

"Is she here?"

I said nothing.

"Chris, aren't you going to invite him in?" my mother breezed past me when my silence had reached the livingroom. "Don't mind him, he's just shy," she explained. I watched in disbelief as my yearbook boyfriend introduced himself to the family, and gave my sister a beautiful corsage that should have been mine. I stared at my feet and cursed myself for having worn a dirty t-shirt, shorts, and no shoes.

Mona and Decker had nothing in common. *She* was a pot smoker, a scofflaw, and a bruiser. *He* was refined, gentlemanly, preppy—with ironed jeans and crisp upturned collars. And he came from one of the town's richer and most popular families. The Abbott boys—Decker, Deke, Dewey—were Puddin Foot's answer to the Baldwin Brothers; my sister had no business dating any of them.

Nonetheless, Mona and Decker dated for the worse part of a year, both blind to the emotional entanglements of our invisible love triangle. He'd come to our house to pick her up and was always more friendly to me than my social awkwardity deserved. The sparks of excitement for his brief visits were perpetually doused by the flagrant fact that he wasn't there to see me. Still, I'd rather he came to pick up my sister than not at all.

I never got the horse they promised but I did get a dog. Really my mom got a dog and that dog accidentally had puppies—one for me. Edwina was a mutt, we didn't know who her father was but she happened to look just like a Weimaraner. She was only the second dog I'd ever befriended. The first dog, I met when my grandmother and Mona and I spent a few days at the idyllic farmhouse of my grandmother's best friend, Pippa. Pippa and her husband were wonderful people, they retired several years earlier and had been my Grandmother's friends since they were all very young. Pippa's big teeth and playful personality would have made her an excellent addition to Carol Burnett's show—her big expressions perfectly designed for the back of a room. Their farmhouse could have been pulled from the pages of *Town & Country, Oklahoma Edition*. Everything was painted a warm country white, with fruits and baskets and cottons and laces on barnwood surfaces. Their land was a handsome collection of bucolic green hills, populated by roaming chickens and friendly cows. Their only unfriendly pet was a dog named Ernest. Ernie was a peculiar breed—a perfect mix between dachshund and poodle. His low body was long enough for a dog several times his height, and covered entirely in tight black poodle pincurls. His adult legs were only a couple of inches long, but he put them in overdrive whenever I approached. I spent two full days following little, indefatigable Ernie through the house and up and down the farm's rolling hills before he finally allowed me to rub his belly. I presented our relationship to my grandmother and her friend. Pippa bent to me and touched my shoulder, "Oh, Chris" (her hushed voice suggesting the importance of a Bay of Pigs briefing) "he likes you—he never lets *anyone* do *that*." Ernie and I spent the final day of my visit like young lovers, afraid to spend even a minute apart.

Edwina and I were very close. I never asked her to retrieve a ball or tried to teach her tricks because I knew she would find it demeaning, but I was certain she was very smart. Norm gave me a polaroid camera for Christmas (I gave him socks and a coupon for a day of father and son fishing, at my mother's insistence), I used the camera only to take pictures of my dog. I tried photographing people: my mother, my grandparents—but they insisted on smiling and I couldn't tolerate the hypocrisy. I'd pose Edwina for a photo, like sitting with head bowed and paws crossed in front of her on the stump of a chopped tree—as though she were in prayer. Edwina would hold the pose with the equanimity of an olympic archer. She was composed, and as patient as she was photogenic.

We had tarantulas around our new country home. Edwina and I had to shoot the spiders off the walls of the front porch with my BB gun before Mom would agree to leave the house. If I took a shot and missed, the tarantula attacked. The hairy spider would leap—taking surprisingly big hops at me as I retreated. Edwina trounced the approaching spiders, killing them before they reached me. Sometimes while I'd lay on the floor watching TV, a scorpion would sting me. Edwina was afraid of scorpions and not much help there. It's hard to enjoy *Ryan's Hope* when a prehistoric super-insect might climb into your shorts and shoot you full of venom.

In the summer our house was bombarded with June bugs. We closed the windows and doors but some came in through the laundry room's dryer vent, and a hundred more breeched the garage. Edwina lapped up the two-inch flying beetles from the garage's cement floor, swallowing them whole. June bugs are strong, hard to pull from your hair and clothing and hard to smash. Fearless Edwina ate them all. Then she lay down from fullness and exhaustion, her stomach grinding from the bugs crawling around inside.

Norm had the curious habit of humming as he ate—a long droning sound. It seemed like he might be saying "mmmmmm" because the food was good, only it never stopped. We didn't notice the hum until we moved to our country house, perhaps the city sounds had drown it out. But now, pondering our reflections in a smoked glass dinette, without traffic or neighbors, his hum was deafening. It was funny at first—Mom and Mona and I giggled into our napkins; a few months later it started sounding like the lower frequencies of insanity. When Mom and Norm's marriage tensed (as my mother's relationships usually did) I knew his nightly reverberation filled her with loathing. She'd stare at her plate and roll her eyes, quietly contemplating the sharp prongs of a dinner fork.

Mom liked that the June bugs came. They must have been attracted to our dining room light, thousands would stick to the screen of the room's uncurtained picture window. By the time our salads were eaten we could no longer see outside through the clamoring beetles that had entirely blanketed the large plate glass. For the month of June we didn't speak when we ate, we only watched the teeming bugs and listened to their hiss—a hideous sound my mother preferred over her husband's incessant hum. I was not a fan of the besieging insects, they made our dining room feel like the epicenter of some brewing biblical apocalypse, *After a window of June bugs comes a swarm of locusts, then a herd of midgets, then a coven of Jews* (or however the story goes).

For my mother's birthday she and Norm took Mona and me camping at Puddin Foot's untamed lake. On the second day Edwina and I sat in shallow water between the sedges, looking deeply into each other's eyes. We had the habit of sitting nose-to-nose for several minutes without looking away; it was how we bonded. Sitting face-to-face in the brim of the overgrown lake, under the low canopy of an aging tree branch, we listened to the sounds of unseen frogs and the faint encore of a distant Bob Seger song that played and replayed on Mom's birthday present tape-deck. Edwina's eyes stayed on mine, except when our sagging tree canopy dropped a brown leaf into the green water—she'd glance to make certain it presented no danger (yesterday the dog and I had a brief scare when a dead water snake floated nearby, so today we were on high alert.) Edwina maintained our gaze as I slowly lowered my nose into the marshy water. Without breaking eye contact, I blew air out my nostrils causing a rash of bubbles between us. Then I slowly raised my head, reconnecting our noses and waiting for her reaction. Sans hesitation, Edwina tipped her head forward, gently immersing her long nose into the murky lake and—her eyes still locked on mine—blew a little jacuzzi of bubbles of her own. Once her point was made, Edwina raised her moistened nose back to mine. I planted a kiss on her soaky snout and jumped from the lake to tell my mother that my dog was a genius.

I found Mom and my sister back at our campsite, Norm had gone to town to buy more Clamato juice. She and Mona were huddled in a peculiar crouch, staring intently at the ground between them. As I approached, my mother picked up a little package and—teary-eyed—showed me a tiny animal that she'd wrapped in a paper napkin.

"Rosie brought it to me," she sniffled. Mom's dog, Rose (named after the Bette Midler character), often brought my mother little gifts from our yard—anything from dead mice to dead birds. "It's still alive," she finished, "it must've just been born."

"What is it?" I asked.

"I don't know, maybe a squirrel or a chipmunk." It really could have been anything; I'd have believed any mammal other than giraffe.

"It's so small, it must be only a few hours old, it's gonna die if we can't return it to its mother," Mona predicted.

"Maybe its mom is dead," I offered, ever delicate in sensitive matters.

"We looked but we cant find the litter," Mom continued. "I tried to feed it some potato salad but it won't eat. It can't even open its little eyes, there's no way it'll survive."

"Oh."

"So me and Mona think that it should be put out of its misery, it's the only humane thing to do." It was a question.

"Hmm," I answered.

"We can't do it, Chris. I need you to be a man for me and take it some place and smash it with a rock."

"Why me!"

"Because I love you and you're macho and I know you can do it. Here's a rock we found for you. I don't wanna watch so go back to the lake and do it there."

I looked at my mother as if she'd just asked me to murder a tiny animal, but she is immune to argument so I reluctantly received the critter in one hand, the rock in the other, and slowly walked away. I found a little clearing and laid the napkined animal on the wet ground. The thing was wet too, sleepy, eyes closed and waiting for his mother. After a respectful hesitation I raised my rock and took a little swipe, but withdrew the blow before it reached its furry little target. I tried twice more—stopping myself each time, and then my fourth swipe connected. The rock split the two-inch infant roughly in half; I was shocked to see the contents of his interior. It wasn't the bloody mess I would have expected, rather it looked like a three bean salad that I might ignore on the side of a dinner plate; I wouldn't ignore them any more. The image haunted me for years—partly because I felt bad for the little creature, partly because I was too young and too obsessive to be confronted with the warm contents of a mammal, and partly because I suspected that other moms protected their children from the ugliness of death, while my mom gave me a rock and told me to cause it.

Bed Wetter ; Mother Issues ; Kills Animals. I now had one more box checked on the FBI list of how to make a serial killer.

My mom was prone to headaches, leg cramps too. Possibly the result of a diet involving the not-as-directed use of an over-the-counter something-or-other. One late afternoon, lying on the livingroom sofa—a cold cloth on her head, she asked for the aspirin from her medicine cabinet. "Be quiet," she instructed, "Norm's sleeping." I accepted the task, walked down a short hall, cautiously opened the door to Norm's and Mom's bedroom, and stepped inside.

Norm was asleep, flat on his back atop paprika-colored satin-finished nylon sheets, and naked. He lay near the edge of the bed with arms crossed over his chest as if the waterbed were his final resting place. The room itself had the feel of a funeral parlor—overfilled with satins and dark wood. The bedposts, the stenciled mirror headboard, the nightstands and the large hutch dresser were all mahogany stained solid oak (a fact that gave my mother much pride). A mirrored wall clock hung over the bed, the kind of clock you might win at a county fair. It had a photo of a 1920s Duesenberg car as the clock face, Mom called it her "antique clock," possibly believing the photo of the antique automobile signified the contemporary 1970s clock was an antique as well.

I'd had sexual thoughts about my stepfather before, he was a decent looking man. In truth, I'd had sexual thoughts about most men so I felt nothing shameful nor incesty on laundry day when his big-n-tall underwear gave me a long-n-hard erection. But I hadn't seen Norm naked before, in fact I'd never seen any man completely nude except from across a parking lot, the site was almost more than I could handle. I approached the sleeping man, cautiously kneeling beside his endless torso at the side-edge of the waterbed; he was magnificent. Norm's work shirts and corduroy pants had kept the secret of his many muscles, patches of hair were everywhere. The skin on his powerful thighs was a delicate pale, his dark forearms seemed dirty in comparison. With almost no debate I leaned in, easing my face toward my stepfather's hairy scrotum. Then I drank him in, sniffing so hard I thought his heavy balls might levitate.

(There is a smell to a man's balls, the good ones anyway. Like something milky and buttery with Christmas spices that your grandma placed near an open window—to cool, and to tease hungry children with its pungent goodness. You can't help but lean in for big whiff, stopping only when adolescent lungs insist they flow in two directions. *Balls*, if they made an air-freshener in the scent, I'd buy it.)

After a minute I wondered if my mother wondered what I was doing still lingering in her bedroom, but she was busy with her headache so I didn't step away. Another minute passes and my wonder ticks to worry, the looming threat now threatens to overtake the lecherous thrill; another sniff. I look at the Duesenberg—ticking quickly, my eyes pendulum from wallclock to doorknob, sniff. On the next tick, Mom and her cold compress will burst in, demanding to know why her husband's testicles are vacuum-sealed to my nostrils. More ticks still, more sniffs, the antique car races now—burns rubber; what will I say, it's hard to think with a face full of nuts.

"What took so long?"

"They were really hard to find."

Mom took a handful of tablets from the bottle and swallowed them in one gulp of Margarita, never peeking from behind her towelette.

"Do you want me to put the aspirin back?"

"No."

"But I can…"

"Leave them here."

By summer's end the hissing June bugs had nearly died off. And—thanks to an if-it's-not-working-don't-fix-it attitude toward relationships, and the belief that the way to a man's heart was through his sternum—so had Mom's marriage. We all sat down to a June bug free dinner when Norm began to hum. Mom closed her eyes and put down her fork.

"Why do you make that sound?"

"What sound?" Norm asked. Mona and I looked at each other because we were afraid to look elsewhere.

"Why are you humming, do you not know that you're humming?" Mom pressed.

"I don't know, I guess so."

"Well why are you doing it?"

"I don't know," Norm grinned, "it makes the food taste better."

"It makes you sound like an idiot."

"An idiot, huh?"

"A fucking idiot."

Mona and I recognized that Mom was on a mission (when our mother was determined to escalate a fight she always tossed a "fucking" into the conversation, like a grenade into a foxhole), we buried our faces in our plates, hoping to clear them before she exploded.

"Sorry, I didn't know it bothered you," Norm sounded calm but his glassy eyes looked like he might snap.

"No shit, it fucking bothers me. You sound like a retard."

Norm put his napkin onto his plate and stood up to carry the half-eaten dinner to the kitchen sink. Mom stood too, and knocked the plate from his hand. Mona and I used both hands to stuff food into our mouths, knowing we'd never be allowed to leave with dinner on our plates.

"Don't fucking walk away when I'm talking to you," Mom warned, grabbing her husband's arm.

"I'm going to bed," Norm explained in a tone that made clear: he'd had enough.

"Mom, we finished our dinner, can we leave the table?"

Norm jerked his arm out of my mother's clinch, she reached up and slapped him hard in the face.

"Hey Mom, we're done eating, can we leave the table now?"

The large man grabbed my mother by both arms as if to shake her into sobriety.

"Let go of me, you COCKING FUCKSUCKER," Mom lifted a knee and aimed it at his crotch.

Before the night was over a wrist would be sprained, a testicle would be bruised, a window would be broken. Police would be called, bags would be packed, and someone would move out.

CHAPTER 6

Window Pains

If I had been this young and this adept at playing piano or field hockey I would have been considered a prodigy, but no kid's ever been christened a 'whiz' for dressing a chilidog or battering Pickle-Dough's (fried pickle slices). Still, juggling thirty-hour workweeks with a fledgling junior highschool career was more than my twelve-year-old peers were doing. Luckily I had no friends and could usually do homework uninterrupted during school lunch hours so, while more popular classmates might squander their free time playing 'cowboys-and-indians' or 'kick-the-gypsy' or whatever games smalltown boys play, all my nights and weekends were free to work the fast-paced kitchen at the town's most popular late-night eatery.

There was a strip in Puddin Foot where teenagers drove a slow cruise. It began at Wal-Mart on Broadway and ended at our Saddle Burger Drive-In where they ordered cheese tater-tots, looped their cars, and began the short trip back again. Sure, it was embarrassing wearing a puffy, striped hat and milkshake stained pants, carrying trays of food to their sporty cars. Especially Friday nights when the lot would fill with noisy honking hordes going to or from some football party or baseball dance or wherever it was that I wasn't invited. But my mother was the "restaurant" manager so working there was this semi-poor kid's only chance of earning enough money to buy the clothes that might convince classmates that we lived on more than fast food income. In youth I blamed most of my unpopularity on my family's lack of money; looking back, I suspect my ungainly personality was the likelier culprit.

We lived well-outside Puddin Foot's city lines, after nightshifts I'd walk across the hillsided town to sleep at my grandparents' house instead. Their little wooden house was charming in the way rural grandparents' houses are—with artichoke plants in the window and chicken coops in the backyard, but it was too small to be a comfortable place to spend the night. I slept in a guestroom at the center of the house, it shared a doorway with the kitchen, not a door, just a doorway. Once everyone took their teeth out and went to bed I'd smuggle a yellowpages-sized department store catalogue from the creaky-floored livingroom to the creaky-floored bedroom to quietly masturbate to the underwear photos in the back of the book: fathers and sons, standing in log cabins, wearing only underthings. The dads had hunting caps or cups of coffee, the sons had grins that said, "betcha wish you were me."

By junior high I knew I was different than other kids my age (and not just because I could out-cook them). It was apparent to me, if not to my grandparents, I didn't belong in the belly of their little house or the bowels of this hidden Oklahoma town. Those 2:00 AM cross-town walks from Saddle Burger had changed me, and probably not for the better. Sensitive twelve-year-old boys shouldn't walk on unlit streets—streets travelled only by those who scuttle through nights on nefarious errands. "Hey kid, wanna party?" or "Hey kid, need a place to stay?" Yes, my path was dark and its shadows were deep, but no lecherous men ever made the lewd offers I'd hoped they would.

I clocked-out after long shifts, usually working side by side with Donald Simpson (I've changed his real name—Delmer

Simpson—to protect his anonymity), a dirt-poor highschool junior with sun-bleached shaggy blond hair, no deodorant, and an irrepressible grin. Donald was known simply as "Pickle," I wasn't sure if that had anything to do with making the Saddle Burger Pickle-Dough's (something he happened to be very good at). Some nights Pickle would drive me to my grandparents' house in his AMC Gremlin. New, the car was worth exactly $1,879; covered in dirt, smelling of b/o, and filled with garbage…priceless. The garbage was mostly Saddle Burger wrappers, and the smell was really a combination of spilled beer, overflowing ashtrays, and Pickle's unwashedness. I sat in the passenger seat, grooving to Pickle's cassettes and pretending we were a couple en route to a Loverboy or Eddie Money concert or some other fancy, out-of-town event. Maybe we'd make a brief stop at an all-night shopping mall, I mooned, where we'd buy new, fresh-smelling and possibly matching outfits to wear to the show (I knew I looked good in Hawaiian print shirts with upturned collars and could practically guarantee Pickle would as well.)

Sometimes before starting the engine, Pickle—his blond hair and tan skin shiny with airborne cooking grease—would sit in the driver's seat and change in to his street clothes. He wore a well-worn jockstrap between outfits and seemed oblivious to my twisting and contorting, trying to find head and hand positions that might allow me to watch without appearing to be interested (or maybe he just dismissed them as bouts of palsy). Usually though, Pickle forgot to ask if I needed a ride. And so, smelling of double-knit polyester that spent most of its professional life just inches away from a deep-fat-fryer, and horny from sharing a tight kitchen with Pickle and his b/o, I'd hit the streets.

You see things at night, things you could never see during the day. You see young women sitting on stoops, smoking and quietly crying, their feathered hair lit only by cigarette embers and passing headlights. They look at you through spotty mascara, like you might have the answers they need. You see collarless and downtrodden dogs and cats sniffing alleys for edible garbage, briefly made curious by the smell of your uniform. And you see windows—glowing with TV light like flickering blue beacons, pleading for unwanted attention. Big cities don't have windows like that. City windows are too high for twelve-year-old, or even thirty-eight-year-old eyes. And prosperous neighborhoods don't have windows like that—nice houses have lit yards and closed drapes. Only poor neighborhoods in small towns have the kind of early AM windows that could seduce my particular version of perversion.

Trailer park windows were the most seductive. Easily eye-level, rarely curtained, and usually dimly lit from within—no matter what the hour. Most nights I'd look in a few windows, rarely with reward but only hoping to briefly see a man in briefs as he watched Channel 34's Late Late Movie. Or I'd watch a bit as he slept on a couch while the movie played on. One night I saw a couple in a trailer—a man and a woman lying on the couch, both in underwear, talking lazily about something that I could almost hear. They were an attractive couple, probably mid-twenties. She was pretty, but forgettable. With panties and long auburn hair she looked like the sort of girl Michael Myers would have killed in the early part of a movie. But *he* was special. He had the kind of long and lightly curing thick black hair and pale/lanky/hairy body that looked like he might have been a roadie for Grand Funk Railroad. I was determined to stay at this window even until sunrise, I could sleep some other night. And so I watched, with dim soul and glassy eyes, feeling all the sweet pain that is a part—or maybe the entirety—of every unrequited crush. I knew I would never be draped across a man the way she was, but in the cold 3:00 AM air—with only a pane of glass between us—I was almost there.

I don't recall who made the first move but, before I could decide what to do with my twelve-year-old erection, the couple retired their dingy underthings and began a slow, purposeful missionary fuck. I had never seen fucking before, but I immediately knew it was the greatest thing I would ever see. It must have been how Neil Armstrong felt as he pushed open the *Apollo 11* hatch, or how Moses felt at the burning bush. I was so moved by its greatness—as their pace harmonized and muffled moans began to penetrate the window glass—that I swelled with blind courage, reached up, and opened the trailer's front door. I didn't open it much, just a sliver really, only enough to lay my head below the door and press an eager eye against the trailer's musky interior. And I marveled.

The carpet level view ushered my eyes directly between the couch-couples' legs. My orbs locked on his, keeping perfect pace with the man's buoyant balls. With every pump we rose and fell in an ocular/testicular tether of sexual synchronicity. I studied each up and down intently (Oklahoma schools hadn't offered me a sexual education, this was mine.) As their bounce quickened, so quickened the bounce of their pupil's pupils. I calculated that the man's enjoyment was measured by these increases in speed; hers was measured by increases in volume. And mine was measured by a brief belief that I was an integral part of the threeway.

When the lanky man finished he fell off the woman and both lay flatward and perfectly still, like evidence in a double suicide (or homicide, to anyone who saw me lurking outside). Then the girl popped up, all her parts jiggling victoriously as she walked toward me and into the bathroom. In the little well-lit room—just across the hall from the door I'd narrowly opened—she rubbed an unfresh bath towel over her vagina. As she wiped all evidence of the man from herself (something I never would have done) her lazy gaze wandered to the barely open front door and travelled along its narrow opening until it reached the very bottom and rested on my wide, unblinking eye. There was a great stillness as our eyes locked, no sound anywhere, only the slow build of dread as her expression crawled from satisfaction, to confusion, and finally to terror.

And then she screamed.

Hers was a long and soulful scream, starting at the center of the earth and rising up through her bare feet and finally out her gaping mouth. I remember only a rushing blur of spiraling fences and snapping tree branches—jumping over them and being struck by them—as I flailed my awkward twelve-year-old self through an endless maze of night-blackened front and back yards in an attempt to escape the echoing reverberations of her primal shriek. Slamming into garbage cans and igniting choruses of barking dogs, I hurled my body in the direction of my grandparents' house, never really sure if I was close or even on the correct path but desperately hoping to arrive before the mob of angry villagers that were surely just steps behind. Prior to this I had seldom crashed into anything, I had no experience with disorientation, no talent for terror. But with each fall I picked myself up again, I kept running until, miraculously, I found myself on my grandparents' front porch. Hands fighting to gain control of the front door key, I overcame the lock and scurried inside the little unlit house, crouched, and waited for an angry knock that mercifully never came. In the few hours until sunrise, as my heartbeat slowed to normal, I listened to the snores of the elderly and reflected on the monster I had become.

The next morning my grandmother ("*Nana*," she insisted, "*Grandma* is an old biddy's name") welcomed me into the kitchen and into the day as she always did, with a bowl of cereal and slices of banana. They were covered with milk and then a quick pour of Half & Half, the creamer was her way of saying 'I love you'. Nana was not just a loving grandmother but also a vain woman, never succumbing to her return to Oklahoma nor life in this little kitchen. I suspect she'd anticipated another life when she left Oklahoma as a young woman, she probably envisioned an early retirement in a southern California bungalow, the glamorous wife of a retired TV executive, throwing splashy dinner parties (overlooking a rice paper lantern-lit swimming pool) for her husband's industry friends.

"Pearl," (my nana changed her name from 'Gertie Lorene' to the more exotic 'Pearline' a long time ago, a fact I wasn't supposed to know), "Pearl, these Cheddar Apple Puffs are divine," they'd probably say, "I could make a whole meal out of them!"

"Aren't they delicious," Nana would have replied, "I got the recipe from Connie Sellecca, do you know Connie?"

But instead my grandmother had boomeranged back to her home state where, aside from getting her thinning hair teased and set once a week at the Holy-Rollers Hair Salon, she had very little social life. Instead she had settled for a second marriage to a stodgy factory supervisor retiree, a modest house in an unfindable Oklahoma town, and the weekend visits of her young Peeping Tom grandson.

Arlis—my Nana's husband—spent his days golfing, or fidgeting when no sports programs were available on their basic cable plan. Once, smelling of Vick's Vapo-Rub and sick with the flu, he took an afternoon nap; I spent several minutes watching him sleep flat on his back, naked, on top of their patchwork duvet. He was a tall, broad-shouldered man with an arctic wolf's thicket of silver hair and a door-to-door salesman's pushy personality. He gave the impression that he had travelled the states and believed he knew a great deal about life. Golfing with Arlis was like watching a marathon of *Matlock*, and as grueling an afternoon as any twelve-year-old kid could endure. Still, none of this deterred me from watching the naked man sleep.

My mother spent some afternoons at my grandparents' house, to baste herself in baby-oil and lay in a lawn chair in their chickenwire-fenced backyard. She drank a margarita and spritzed herself with water, each every twenty minutes or so. After she baked her front to a crispy reddish-brown she'd flip and roast her back. Her bikini top was usually untied in the second position so I typically timed my backyard visits as to avoid any bit of breast that might squeeze its way out from under her. Despite these efforts I often found myself with the unlucky responsibility of baby-oil applications to mother's rear self. A dutiful son, I greased her thoroughly and hoped the neighbors were travelling abroad.

My grandmother and my mother were close, trading stories of marital misfortunes and courtship catastrophes, like recipes from across a kitchen table. Despite this sisterhood, I had the anecdote-fueled impression that Nana had been a bully not only with men, but was also a harsh disciplinarian to her children, and that my mother had been a difficult teen.

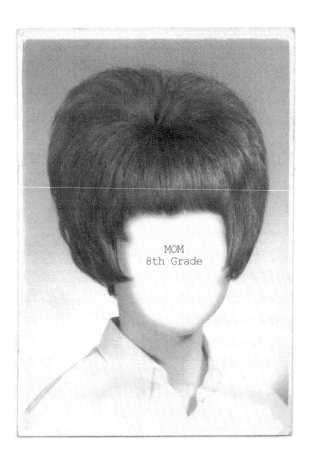

MOM
8th Grade

Mom backcombed her hair in the junior high bathroom before school each day, she smoked cigarettes, and she was pregnant by fourteen. My nana sometimes joked about Mom smuggling her bad-girl bouffant into the classroom, "I can't tell you how many times I had to take away Dusty's hairspray. I whooped her so hard it pulled the power cord completely outta my iron! I swear to god I had to buy a new one!"

Mom would listen to the story and pretend to laugh.

Over the years my grandmother softened into the doughy little woman I knew. She rarely drank—maybe a Coffee and Kaluah on holidays, and cursed only when scared (like when Mom or Uncle Mick crept-up behind her as she handwashed the dinner dishes, grabbing her by the soft skin under her chin and scaring a little fart out of her. She'd curse them for the scare, though really it was for exposing her toot.)

Like many—I imagine—I was too self-absorbed to consider that my grandmother'd had a life before me, but she did. I don't know the details but I do know that after a dustbowl youth she Lemon Pledged herself off and emerged as quite a beauty. I learned this sepia-toned truth by way of small picture frames tucked high on her bedroom bookshelf. The images of my dewy-skinned Nana with willowy limbs and red lips astonished me, as though I'd found her starring as 'Henrietta Hump' in an old stag film. Nana's youthful splendor faded gracefully as time and diabetes took their share, but she never abandoned her elegance or her vanity. I often wondered if my vain nana's ego could recover from the hot summer day when my mother told her that my stepgrandpa Arlis had visited her in the backyard and, after a brief conversation, leaned down and kissed her hard in the mouth. After what I'm sure was a spectacular evening of broken hearts and broken dishes, Arlis moved out of their sixty-year-old house and fifteen-year-old marriage, and was never seen by me again. Nana kept the house and my mother eventually moved in. As Nana's health began to decline and walking became difficult after a series of unsuccessful back operations, the two women eventually sold the house and moved into a two-bedroom apartment in a pastel peach and mauve lacquered retirement community in an uncelebrated California town; my Nana had finally made it back to the golden state.

Nana lost her hair and began wearing a wig—Mom called it "Nana's hat." My mother quit her recent job as a mail courier and received a small government salary for acting as my elderly nana's full-time caregiver. I visited Nana after I had started a business selling vintage and antique clothing. I knew she had some sparkly cocktail dresses from the 1950s and early 60s—an era when she had been a hot-ticket in the Martini lounges of northern California. In those days it wasn't uncommon for a woman to measure her worth by how easily her dancing might inspire a man to buy her a drink, and my Nana could drink for free with the best of 'em. I asked if I could sell the dresses for her (living mostly on Social Security I knew she could use the money). Bent-over a walker, her gray wig leaning leftly, Nana decided, "I better not...Doctor Rajabhusinhji says they're working on some new type a surgery, so, who knows, I may need my dresses if I take-up dancing again." I was happy my nana could pronounce Rajabhusinhji, but sad she'd someday realize her days of disco had turned to dusk. "Dusty," she called to my mom, "do they still do the jitterbug?"

On a glance Mom and Nana's marriage was indefectible. Holiday visits began with Nana praising the delicious meals her duteous daughter cooked for her, and from the nearby kitchen Mom would emerge with a tray of celeries—half of them dressed in peanut butter, the other half buried in one of the zestier cousins of Cheeze Whiz—insisting that Nana tell us stories about the time she did this or the time she said that.

"Oh gosh, that was forty years ago," my grandma would say. "Let's see, I was living in Pleasant Hill and working for Mister Wesselmann, taking care of him after his wife died. He used to say,

'Pearly, if I were twenty years younger I'd take you on a date,' how would you like that Chris, if you had a *millionaire* for a grandfather!"

"That'd be cool, Nan," I'd say.

"Anyway, I would bring Walter his lunch, that was his name, *Walter*. I would bring Walter his lunch and set it down on his bed...on a tray, you know what I mean?"

"Yeah, like a tray," I'd say.

"Right, a tray. And when I bent over with the food Walt would look at my bosom and say, 'Well I see we're having melons again,' can you believe that! Oh, he was such a card."

Halfway through the story my mom would charge the room again, insisting Nana should get her facts straight. "He didn't say *melons*, he said *muffins*."

"Chris, tell your mother I think I know what the man said," Nana would insist.

"And his wife wasn't dead, she was in a coma," Mom continued.

My grandmother would lean toward me, as best she could, "Chris, tell your mother to leave me alone and let me tell my story."

"Then tell it right," Mom would snipe in a pissy tone as she retreated to her kitchen fortress. (In hindsight, I wonder if the storytime tyranny wasn't bitchiness so much as my mom's fear that she would lose Nana, as her essence slowly dimmed with the twilit memories.)

"Your mother walks all over me," my Nana would continue. "I should have driven all over you," Mom would clarify from the next room. And then the two women would, as cloistered couples do, bicker for the next few hours until old hostilities over lost husbands and unrealized dreams boiled over as dependably as the brown gravy did on their unvented kitchen stove.

The 5:00 PM meal was served at the dining room end of the apartment's narrow livingroom, in a dense atmosphere of mutual contempt that had replaced the room's sweet smell of marshmallow-candied yams. But still, Mom was a good cook and the turkey and stuffing were the perfect compliments to the two ladies' annual dinner-theater production of *Grey Gardens*. While they may have lacked the pedigree of the film's fallen Bouvier socialites, this local troupe knew their roles as well as any veteran actors. By the time dessert was served Mom's face was sweaty and her hair disheveled, with a light dusting of flour that made it look as though she had stumbled in from an old western where she had been dragged behind a horse (a metamorphosis designed to relay the hard work that went in to preparing a family meal). Uncle Mick would suggest a few hands of poker—he was a gambling buff and loved to excuse himself to the bathroom by proclaiming, "Time for me to play my deuce, if you know what I mean." But Nana, disgusted by the lot of us, would feign sleepiness and retire to her bedroom. Mom would begin cleaning the kitchen clankily and without conversation to be certain we holiday guests understood the time for departures had arrived.

When Mom's marriage failed we moved to a little house that was closer to the Saddle Burger Drive-In where we worked. The new house was close enough that I no longer had to spend nights with my grandparents and no longer had the opportunities for late night walks through Puddin Foot's sexiest trailer park communities. I missed the young couple I met that night—in fact I still do. But within a few months at our new house I spotted Colton Fisher (real name Clayton Tisher), the handsome rednecked older brother of a junior high classmate. I was thirteen and he was twenty-four so we weren't friends, in fact we never met, but I had seen his photo in an old yearbook and knew there was a connection. Weeks later I found myself in his backyard, crouched outside his bedroom window as he ate Taco Bell and watched TV. Eventually, I'd let myself into the little unlocked, unkempt house, usually on Saturday afternoons while Colton was at work (a factory of some sort I imagined, or maybe a rodeo). I'd lie on the disheveled bed's unfresh sheets, eating taco and burrito leftovers, pretending we shared the messy little home where we were mostly very happy. I knew if I lived there it would be tidier so sometimes I straightened up a bit, once I vacuumed, often I'd nap. When I heard a car I'd regain my pants, steal a piece of laundry from the hallway hamper and leave hastily, reluctantly, through the rear.

Sometimes I wonder where Colton is now, how he's doing. I'd call but it would be a lot to explain.

CHAPTER 7

Balls II

The back porch of our newly rented house shared a wall with my bedroom and the kitchen. The wide, featureless porch was walled by our landlord to create additional living space, but the cement floor and subsequent washer/dryer made it unconvincing as a fourth bedroom. Still, my mother rented the room to Rodney—the assistant manager at the Saddle Burger Drive-In where she, Mona, and I still worked. At twenty-three, Rodney was a decade older than me. He grew up in Puddin Foot and his family lived there for generations. I knew he had been in the military, and gossip around Saddle Burger said he was dishonorably discharged after psychologically snapping—by way of pulling a gun on a superior officer. Having pulled a pistol or two herself, Mom and Rodney were fast friends so when we needed money she invited him to move in. My bedroom window, which once opened to a backyard, now opened to Rodney's makeshift room. He seemed stable but I kept the blinds closed just to be safe.

Mona stopped dating Decker. I was sad that he didn't come around anymore but happy to be untaunted by her unfair affair with my illusory boyfriend. I don't know what caused their break-up (if it had been a dramatic ending with a torn blouse and a police escort, or if they just got bored and moved on) but I suspected it had something to do with Varla—my sister's new gal-pal. We met Varla when the tough-talking blonde worked briefly as a Saddle Burger carhop. The two girls vowed inseparability after Varla was fired for slapping a dissatisfied customer while she sat in her car.

Our new house was in town so I no longer rode a school bus. I walked to school on a path that crossed Decker's house but I never saw him, after graduation he probably moved away. Letter jackets were the uniform of the happiest and most popular kids of my junior high (oddly, the elephant-eared bell-bottom corduroy pants and velour shirts my mother bought me were not), and I was determined to wear one. I was inspired to athleticism by the 1980 olympics, and would be again in 1984, and customarily every four years thereafter. It was lanky men in bulging speedos that caught my eye, back then men wore only the tiniest bathing suits to swim competitively (I hear they switched to today's knee length suits because they make men swim faster, but I suspect governments knew the skimpier suits were turning young boys gay). So every four years I'd tune-in for the swimmers and divers, but as days turned into more days, I stayed-tuned for the Mary Lou Rettons, the Carl Lewises, and the Scott Hamiltons.

Mary Lou was the greatest athlete I'd ever seen, a lady Olympian (and not like those from my grandma's generation when downhill ironing—ironing her husband's slacks while tumbling down a hill—was the leading lady sport) with thighs thick enough to crack a stepfather in two. The whole world cheered its approval each time Mary Lou landed a vault, or chalked a hand, or grinned a toothy grin. She was all smiles, her perfect teeth were racist-white and her ass was solid muscle. This tiny dwarf of a woman was America's sweetheart and probably the happiest person alive. The athletes at my school were happy too, they were the only kids in our little farm town who didn't look like their blue-ribbon cows were just slaughtered. If sport was the key to happiness then I would be an athlete. I signed my name on the tennis roster and was unceremoniously added to the team.

Our coach—Mr del Rio—also happened to head the marching band, the spanish man's three hundred extra pounds made it surprising he could do either. But despite a belly that looked like he might be pregnant with fat twins, Coach was surprisingly agile—even graceful on the court. He sort of taught me to serve a ball and that was pretty much it before our first match against Saint Reba, a private Catholic school and the top ranked in the county. I'd like to say I returned one ball during my match against the eight-foot tall opponent, but—though my memory is fuzzy as a tennis ball—I know it's unlikely. I do remember his professional looking tennis outfit, an expensive looking haircut, and glimpses of pity on the boy's handsome face. I don't know if he pitied my tennis skills as he pelted aces all around me, or maybe it was the cut-off brown corduroy pants with stapled hems that I wore as tennis shorts; either way, I like to think I got into his head.

Our out-of-town meet had produced no wins, but Coach packed ice cream sandwiches in his cooler and was in a generous spirit. When the bus returned to school he offered to drive several of us home; exhausted from fatigue and shame, I accepted. I hadn't known the kids who piled into Coach's car long enough to consider them friends. Some were popular and most seemed rich, and all of them devoured fashion trends like they were going out of style (as our knees touched and the staples holding my shorts began to pop off, I wondered if I didn't belong.) Apparently my address was the closest, and as we neared my street I flushed with the fear that this car full of rich kids would see my dumpy little house. In a moment of panic I pointed to a big, stylish home I had admired a few blocks from mine, "There, that's it," I lied, "that's my house." The coach pulled into the driveway of the gated residence and I opened my door. "Wow, your house is really nice," one of the kids said. "Yeah, it's okay," I agreed.

I walked to the front gate, slowly, hoping coach would pull

away before I had to try to open it; he didn't. I tugged a handle and the gate opened, I turned and waved a suggestive 'good-bye' to my teammates and went inside. *Drive, damn it, drive*, I thought, but the car only sat so I continued my mosey to the front door of the impressive, rock-walled house. Inevitably I reached the porch; someone was inside and walked to meet me at the screen door.

"Hi," a cheery-faced boy a few years older than me offered.

"Hi, um, is this your house?" was all I could think to say.

"Yeah, who are you?" he asked, still smiling.

"Oh, um, my name's Chris and well I live on Broadway in a house with my mom…"

"Okay," his smile starting to flatten out.

"…and I locked myself out and wonder if I can use your phone to call my mom?" God, I was brilliant.

The screen door opened and the teenager welcomed me in. His name was Billiam—not quite Bill, not quite William. I wasn't sure if it was a clever meld of the two or perhaps an ethnic name, his skin was dark and he seemed Hawaiian or Samoan or something equally unfamiliar to me.

"Do you play tennis?" he asked.

I trusted it was my racket and not my corduroy shorts that gave me away. "Yeah, I'm on the tennis team," I hadn't said that sentence before; it gave me a flash of pride.

"I used to play tennis, but I sprained my wrist. The doctor said I have weak wrists so my parents decided it was too dangerous so I quit. They're so lame."

Billiam went to a private school in Sawbuck, the next town over. His father was away on business and his mother shopping for wedding dresses or wedding cakes or something weddingy with his older sister, he wasn't sure. Their house was very modern by Puddin Foot's standard. It was one level, but much larger than mine. The walls were all rock, inside and out. Its front room surrounded an enclosed courtyard. The glass-boxed patio housed a fat-baby-riding-a-dolphin fountain and had a pebble floor—these people really liked rocks. The encasement served as the large livingroom's main source of daylight, the windows of the outer walls were all blanketed with heavy drapes as if his parents were hiding something indecent inside. This seemed to contradict the house's appearance of being designed to impress guests. Some of the structure's dividing walls were a lattice of white woodwork—the kind ivy might climb. I watched Billiam through the openwork when he excused himself to the kitchen to bring us some mango juice, which he served in wine glasses. There was a large lit aquarium in the livingroom, partially recessed into a rock wall, it was full of confused-looking exotic fish. There was another tank in Billiam's bedroom, which he was eager to show me. "The phone's in there too, so you can call your mom…"

"It's ringing."

"Cool."

"Hi Mom, it's me Chris," I pretended.

"At the tone the time will be…"

"Guess what, I locked myself out of the house," I continued.

"6:10 PM…"

"Ok then, I'll see you when I get home."

"exactly."

I sat the phone down and Billiam sat down too, on the bed beside me. "So everything's okay then?" he asked, sitting closer to me than seemed necessary.

"Yeah, she's gonna let me in when I get home."

"Cool." Billiam laid flatward on his bed, "So whatcha wanna do now?"

I leaned back against the headboard, wanting to seem relaxed with my new friend. "I don't care, whatever you wanna do." Billiam seemed to like my answer, twisting toward me and looking intently at my shorts. "I like these shorts, are they Lee-Vigh's?" he asked. "I don't know, I think so." Billiam leaned in closer, "Well what does this button say?" leaning further in to read the text on the small top button of my cut-off shorts. "It says Lee-Vigh's," he informed me, looking up from my lap and grinning at his discovery. *Wow this guy really likes Lee-Vigh's,* I thought, and *I think he might be near-sighted.*

"What does the next button say?" my Lee-Vigh's-loving friend persisted, unfastening the first button so that he might better read the second. "It says Lee-Vigh's too," he marveled. "Oh," I muttered. "This one says it too," he said again about the four or five remaining buttons.

Ten minutes in, we heard footsteps stepping down the hall. With an interruption of suction sound, Billiam spit my saliva-shellacked penis out of his slobbery mouth, and I quickly fumbled over my many 'Lee-Vigh's' embossed buttons. The bedroom door popped open and Billiam's mother entered the room with only her head—saying something about not knowing he had company, and that the front door had been left ajar, and then suggesting it was time for me to go home (I got the impression it wasn't the first time she had stumbled into such a scene.) Billiam stuffed a piece of paper with his phone number into my pants pocket as he escorted me to the front gate, "I had a *really* good time," he giggled in the demeanor of a mini-skirted girl. "Thanks for letting me use your phone," I replied, trying hard to understand the gate handle. "Anytime, Sexy!" he squeeled, the gate slammed behind me before he'd finished the sentence. I speed-walked home, uncertain if I was happy to have had my first blowjob, or sad that I was still wet with the spit of someone so keenly unappealing to me. Either way, I might be 'sexy'.

I had no intention of calling Billiam, something about him made me want to take a shower (probably all the saliva). Still, a few days later I called. I wasn't hoping for another slobbery BJ, I just had never known a gay person, and in this small town it seemed unlikely that I would meet another. Then, when I realized Billiam could talk only about sex, I stopped returning his calls.

Our boarder Rodney and I became friendly, mostly making fun of each other. We often worked the same shifts at Saddle Burger so it was nice to have rides to and from work. Because my bedroom window looked directly into his room, I'd sometimes see him watch TV late at night. There was enough of a gap alongside the blinds that I could watch undetected from the window's edge when my bedroom lights were out. On hot nights—lit only by his small television and a digital alarm clock—skinny Rodney would lay in ill-fitting underwear atop mismatched sheets, giving me sustained views of his lengthy legs. He was a tall man, at least six foot four, but his broad shoulders and goofy stride made him seem a few inches taller. His pale skin was covered in freckles and light brown hair, with the occasional boyish scab on a scraped knee. And like me and the other Saddle Burger cooks, he always smelled of fast food. Some nights Rodney suspected I was watching. He'd leap from his thinly mattressed bed, springing toward our shared window. It was a fifteen-foot trek and I had the reflexes of a mongoose so I always dove into bed before he could be certain.

My sister was hardly home these days, staying instead with new best friend Varla; the unusual closeness of their friendship made Mom and Nana nervous. With Mona away I was free to listen to her stereo after school, she had Stevie Nicks' *Bella Donna* album and the witchy anthem "Edge of Seventeen" sent me into a frenzy. I'd wear Mona's headphones to screech out the choruses, draped in imagined layers of billowy chiffon. One day as I neared a big elusive note, I was rammed by what must have been a bull or buffalo, and sent flying face-first onto my sister's waterbed. "Get out of my room, Fag," Mona demanded. "You and Varla are fags," I mutter-shouted as I ran past her.

Other days I came from school, immediately dropping books to coffee table and pants to ankles. I usually had two hours of post-school privacy and often used the first fifteen minutes to masturbate on the livingroom couch. In my last phone call with Billiam—in the deeper reaches of our conversation—he mentioned, "Oh my gawd, orgasms feel *way* better if you make some noize!" (emphasizing an imagined second syllable on the word *noize-uh*, like Little Richard or a charismatic preacher might); halfway through the weekday ritual I thought to test his theory. Nearing climax, I tried a loudish 'Ohhhhhhh, ohhhhhh' but other than a twinge of embarrassment I detected no difference. Still, I decided to play it through to the end, and with additional gusto. For the next minute I 'Ohhhhh'd and 'Ahhhhh'd, and then with a final booming 'Yeaaahhhhhh!' I consummated the experiment.

Satisfied my method was thorough and confident Billiam was an idiot, I reached for my towel and, with unnerving clarity, heard the refrigerator door close.

Our kitchen was only twenty feet from the couch I'd just sullied (with a volume that would have driven Angus Young to earplugs) so certainly my sex bellow had reached the refrigerator. I yanked up my pants and searched for an explanation, and also decided I should start checking the house before assuming I was alone.

Rodney emerged from around the corner, not letting-on that he'd heard (and probably seen) my matinee performance, but we both knew he had. We said a few things about work and then Rodney threw a couch cushion at me and excused himself to his back porch with what looked to be a smug grin.

I thought the indiscretion might jeopardize my budding friendship with assistant manager Rodney, but instead we grew chummier. Ever since I'd shared a bunkbed with my estranged stepbrother Vanne, I pined for an older brother; with Rodney's new interest in roughhouse, it seemed I had my wish. On the Saturdays when my mom worked a morning shift, Rodney would wait for her to leave—then charge my bedroom, waking me with a pillow to the face or an elbow to the ribs. Some mornings I anticipated the attack, feigning sleep after positioning my erect penis to raise my comforter like an x-rated teepee. Rodney would jump onto my bed with an "I'm gonna kick your ass," and we'd wrestle. Rodney was strong for a skinny guy, and he loved to wrestle. His favorite hold was the one where he uses an arm and a knee to pin my arms down, then uses his free hand to gently massage my penis (I've never really followed wrestling so I'm not sure if that move has a name.)

Mid schoolyear, Mom came home with an announcement: *Pack your shit*, it began, we're moving to Twisterton. The Saddle Burger Drive-In there, 40 miles away, needed a manager. Mona and Rodney and I were all transferring as well, and we were leaving in less than a week. I was excited by the news, other than Billiam and Rodney I had no friends in Puddin Foot and maybe the kids in a larger town would be more like me. I called Billiam because I needed to tell someone my news, and his was the only phone number I had.

"You're gonna write me aren't you, Sexy?" maybe I shouldn't have called.

"If you don't write me I'm gonna come find you," he threatened. "I tried to call you a buncha times but you never called me back. I have a friend who *really* wants to meet you. Can we come by and pick you up tonight?"

I wanted to say no but a friend had never picked me up before, I didn't know when I might get another invitation like that. "Okay, but who's your friend?"

"It's someone you already know," he teased, wanting me to play a guessing game.

"Tell me who it is or I'm not going," I wasn't very good at games.

"You're no fun. It's Decker Abbott. I told him we fooled around and he said he knew you."

I thought to throttle Billiam for telling people we fooled

around, but was too stunned from hearing Decker's name to see it through. "Are you lying?" I asked. "Pinky-swear," he promised.

Mom made taco salad for dinner. The bag of Doritos with hamburger meat and cheese and salsa was my favorite but I could barely swallow a bite without feeling like I might throw it up. I excused myself from the table every few minutes to check the clock. 7:15, 7:19, 7:24. Finally, at 7:41 the doorbell rang. I ran to a mirror and then to the door, steadied my hand and turned the knob.

"Yummm, something smells good!" It was Billiam, alone.

"It's taco salad."

"Yummm. Decker's in the car, you guys are gonna drop me at home if that's ok?" It was so much more than okay.

Billiam and I walked to the curb where Decker was waving from behind the wheel of his shiny car, his gold bracelet sparkling in the early evening light. I opened the door and scurried into the back seat, cursing myself for the mole-ish move. Decker's car smelled like Decker, and his expensive department store cologne made him smell like a rainbow that only touched down in gated communities.

"What have you been up to?" Decker asked, looking at me through the rearview mirror.

"Nothing. I'm on the tennis team, [god his eyes were beautiful] do you still live around here much?"

"Oh my gawd," Billiam squealed, plopping into the passenger seat, "Do you remember when you came to my house and you had your tennis racket and you had to use my phone because you locked yourself out..."

I searched the back of the car for a button that might eject the passenger.

"...that was so crazy!"

Button...

"I can't believe my mom walked in on us! She's so lame…"

Where's the damn button…

"…I woulda swallowed too!"

Decker gave Billiam a look.

"What?! A teaspoon of semen has the same nutritional value as eating half a baby."

"Oh look," Decker announced, "here we are, here's your house."

"Well I guess I'll leave you two boys alone then. Don't do anything I wouldn't do. Or should I say don't do anything I *would* do. Oh my gawd, I'm so terrible!" he confessed, waving and walking in unmanly manners.

I stayed in the back seat as though I were Miss Daisy until Decker patted the empty passenger seat, "Why don't you sit up here with me." I shot to the front, careful not to slam the car door. "That's better," he grinned—his handsome face lit by the impressive dashboard light. With both hands still on the steering wheel of the parked car, Decker leaned over and gave me a soft kiss on the lips. "It's good to see you again," he said, with no indication that he'd detected taco salad on my breath. "How's your sister?" (He asked this casually, as though he hadn't just kissed me on the mouth. If this was his plan to get back together with Mona then I would kill us all.) "She's fine."

We drove twice up and down the strip, from Walmart to Saddle Burger and back again. I had always wanted to cruise the strip that the popular kids in my school drove, and I couldn't believe I was doing it with the most perfect guy this school system had ever produced. I wanted to lean out the window and scream, "Hey Puddin Foot, I'm with Decker Abbott," but thought it might seem overzealous.

"So do you wanna come over t'my house?" Decker asked, resting a soft hand on the bony of my knee.

"Okay."

Decker had been at college and was back for a few weeks, his mother was away and we had the unlit house to ourselves. His room was wood paneled—not the wood linoleum that had covered walls of some of the houses I'd lived in, but real wood. Open cardboard boxes lined two walls, like someone was packing or unpacking in no particular hurry (if the boxes were going with him back to college, I could fold myself to their dimensions, to stow away inside.) An ironing board dressed in a freshly creased pair of jeans stood proudly in the middle of the room, a spray bottle of water waited nearby. His highschool diploma and some photos of the Abbott brothers and their friends were pinned to the wall, so was a photo of my sister. "Is that Mona? I asked, sounding too dumb to recognize my own sister.

"Yeah."

"Oh, I thought so."

"Doesn't she look pretty," he asked, admiring her clumpy mascara.

"She farts in my face," I wanted to reply.

Decker told me he kept her photo stuck to his wall because he would always think of her as a friend—their relationship ended as friends, even though they hadn't spoken since. And then he told me something else. Decker said he dated my sister for as long as he did so he could come to our house, because he wanted to see *me*. The information made me want to laugh or cry or possibly choke. I did none of these, I said nothing—too overtaken by the comedy and the tragedy of a year of yearning to speak; my stupid expression said it all. *Why didn't you tell me*, it said, *Why did you move away, Why didn't you take me to prom.*

I called my mom to tell her I was spending the night with Billiam, then Decker and I got undressed for bed. I didn't expect that someone like Decker Abbott would sleep on a twin bed, he didn't seem as rich as I had imagined him to be, and I wondered why I'd thought it mattered. His family was comfortable— definitely more than mine, but their house wasn't fancy and didn't suggest they tried to seem that way, it was just a nice messy house. I was impressed that Decker always looked so well groomed, despite a room that was similar to mine, aside from the wood paneling. Decker was polished—he took care of his clothes, his hands, his presentation. If I thought it was privelege that made him look so refined, I now believed it was just something he did for himself.

His soft skin appeared undulled by the sun—unmarred by any clock-punched hour of manual labor, he wore it like cashmere from head to toe. His black chest hair was as fluffy and manageable as the hair on his head, it cradled a gold-nugget necklace like a bird nest cradles a fragile egg. As our naked bodies mingled it was impossible to pretend mine wasn't shuddered, nearly convulsing with nerves drunk on electrochemicals and sheer disbelief. I was embarrassed by the quaking and said something about it being very cold—an obvious bid to disguise my unworldliness. I thought he would judge my rattling limbs as proof of immaturity, but he brought me a thicker blanket instead. Today I imagine that anyone bedding an adolescent relishes those manifestations of their inexperience (a trepid touch, a nervous shudder, an early release), some may even fetishize it. But I make no accusations, Decker didn't like me for my youth alone. I think he appreciated me in a way no one ever had—I was a crush realized, just as he had been for me. Wanting someone you can't have is torturous, finally getting them…transcendent. It's a rare gift bestowed only on the very patient. Our nights remain some of the best of my life. They made me realize a rich boy could like a poor one, and a sophisticated boy could like an ignorant one, and that an elegant boy could like an awkward one. When Decker sat across my hips and rubbed himself off on me, so rubbed off some of his confidence. When I toweled him from my chest, I left that part, and it soaked in.

By month's end we'd moved to Twisterton. Mom, Mona, and

I lived in a three-bedroom apartment, Rodney moved into a studio in the same complex. I saw Decker once more—he visited me, saying an uncomfortable 'hello' to my sister; "Hey," she replied. After dinner he and I retired to my room where we slept on my small bed with the door closed. In the next room Varla slept with Mona on her small bed, with their door closed. My mother stayed in her room, with her eyes closed.

CHAPTER 8

Hot Child in the City

"Well, aren't you a little angel."

"Hi."

"Honey, I've been in this bar a buncha times, and I have *never* seen *you*. Are ya sure you're old enough ta be here?"

The heavyset man asked the familiar question in salacious tones. I always wondered if there were undercover cops waiting for me to say 'thirteen' so they could throw me into the back of a paddywagon, on top of a glittery pile of drag queens and street prostitutes. Or maybe cops don't have paddywagons anymore.

"Yeah, I'm twenty-one."

"And I'm twenty-one too," he chuckled. I wasn't sure how old this nosey person might be, he was so oversized it obscured his age, and his gender. "If you don't wanna tell me how old ya are, you don't have to. I'm not here ta judge anyone."

The stranger seemed nice enough, but it was getting late and I needed to meet someone before 'last-call' was announced. I was stranded in the city and knew that—once the bar lights lit—I'd be homeless until someone drove me the thirty-five freeway minutes back home.

"I'm gonna get something before they call 'last-call' sweetie, can I get ya a drink?"

"No thanks," pointing to the Coke I'd nursed since midnight, "I have one."

Two weekends ago Rodney (the Saddle Burger assistant manager) and I came to Giddyuptown, to this bar, and I met a tall and particular-looking man (he looked like he would be particular about things.) He wore a buttoned-up shirt over a well-shouldered frame, and his dark curly hair appeared petrified by mousse—like it would leave the impression of a brick of ramen in your cheek if you rested your head to his for too long. He had full, wet lips and a beautiful face and his stuffiness made me want to sit in his lap. I didn't, but sitting there at the bar we kissed and I gave him my phone number before Rodney insisted it was time we leave—we had to be back before mom finished her night shift.

Brentley (the curly-haired man) called the next day and we talked for most of an hour. He was thirty-three and a scientist. He seemed very smart and was impressed that I was good at math— his sister was a math professor and he thought we would probably get along well. Brentley said he could drive to Twisterton to pick me up the following Friday afternoon and I could spend the weekend at his house in the city. "You need to come meet me down the street though, I don't think it'd be smart for me to knock on your door." I told my mom I was spending the weekend on a camping trip with my mostly fictitious friend Billiam, she wasn't aware that I stopped returning Billiam's calls shortly after we met.

Brentley's house was the nicest house I had ever been in that didn't belong to someone's parents. He said it was lucky we met because he didn't go to bars much, but Rick's Playroom was only six blocks from his house so he'd stopped in for a quick drink.

"I'm not a big drinker, but sometimes after work I like to have a glass of wine," he confessed, finishing his second glass, "we should order some dinner later and watch a movie."

A movie and dinner sounded nice, I'm not sure if you have to leave the house for it to legally qualify as a 'date' but if not, dinner and a movie would definitely make this my first date. "What movies do you have?"

He closed his eyes to appreciate a big gulp from his third helping of wine, "I'm not sure, let's take a look."

Brentley jumped from the couch, catching himself from a little stumble, "Let's see what this one is…" he stuffed a cassette into the player. The television was large—probably wider than I was tall, its big screen lit up with engorged genitalia as one man's penis plunged another man's throat, as though the throat had been clogged with a particularly stubborn clump of pubic hair.

"Have you seen this one?" Brentley asked, wondering if I recognized this particular penetration. "It's *Dumper Humpers 2*," he clarified.

The truth was I had never seen any porno video. Shortly after assistant manager Rodney moved into our house—after we started fooling around, he took me to an x-rated bookstore so I could buy myself a *Playgirl*. I bought three magazines, none were *Playgirl*, most were naked bikers in leather hats working on their motorcycles (a task that is impossible to complete without spilling some motor oil on your dick). They were a dramatic jump from baseball player Jim Palmer's Jockey underwear ad that ran in the back of *TV Guide*, a photo that had served my pornographic needs for the last few months. But video—this was new. The closest thing I had seen to pornographic video was a speedo'd Scott Baio climbing a ladder during *Battle of the Network Stars*. "I don't think so," I answered.

"This nexx pard is my favrite," Brentley slurred, landing near me on the couch so we could continue side-by-side like teens at a drive-in.

I don't recall the characters names or their backstories, I do remember the lead actor swapped holes, apparently finding a second clog in his co-star's butt. For several minutes plunging-man routed the troublesome hole, and for several minutes plunged-man howled the lamentations of the damned; Brentley studied the screen as if prepping for the SAT. Near the end of the scene, smelling of wine and hair-mousse, my drunken host whispered into my eye, "Do you like this?"

I wasn't sure if he meant the video or the rub he was now administering to my pants' front, but I didn't answer—assuming the lump in my underwear was an adequate reply to either question. "Well do you?" he persisted.

I actually like when some people talk during sex, but never if it's in the form of a question that is more than rhetorical. "Uh-huh," was the only answer I offered.

Before the scene was over, and after kissing me with enough tongue for ten rows of teeth, Brentley was trying to mirror the film's action—an action I had done only once before. I tried (as much as laying still constitutes effort) but each time he pushed-in, I pushed-out. Each time he poked in again, I twisted aside. I wanted to, I think, but something made me pull away (I suppose Jesus explained it best when he said "Ouch!") Finally, after four or five attempts, when it was obvious I lacked Christ's talent for impalement, he rolled off, faced the other direction and refused to speak.

"Sorry, it just hurt," I explained. He said nothing.

"Do you want to get some dinner now?" I asked, watching the movie credits roll, but still looking forward to the dinner portion of our date. He said nothing.

"Are you mad at me?" I asked. He said nothing, only staring at the wall as if *Dumper Humpers 3* might be projected there at any moment. Confident the answer would be 'no' I asked, "Do you want me to leave?"

"Yeah, you should probably go. It's getting late and I have to be somewhere tonight anyway."

"I know ya said you didn't want a drink but I got you a Coke anyway, yers looks like it's on its last leg," the returning round man said, gesturing to my glass of soda. It had divided evenly into a brown underlayer below a clear overlayer, so that some day geologists might find the glass and be able to determine exactly how long I stood in the bar nursing a single drink. "It looks like a lava lamp," the man joked as he swapped my drink for the fresh one. "Yeah," I agreed, "thanks." He sat my soda and then took a strawed sip of his mixed drink, stepping back and shifting his attention around the room, showing delayed restraint in his trespass of my corner. Still, I wanted to walk away—I had only a few minutes to scan the room for someone cute who might let me stay the night with them, and maybe to date—but walking away from someone who just bought you a drink is hard, I suspect it's why they do it. The music dimmed and a bartender yelled LAST CALL and a couple of the remaining two-dozen people scurried to the bar. "It was nice meetin' ya," the Coke buying man said, giving me a crooked-toothed smile before turning to rejoin his fuller-figured friend who'd been waiting impatiently by the door. I leapt up and began a desperate cruise around the bar, hoping there still might be someone I could risk making eye contact with.

I first came to Rick's Playroom & Dance Hall four months ago, I'd never been to a gay bar but Rodney talked about it like it was Euro Disney and said I needed to see it for myself. I wanted to go on a weekend (he said those nights were the most wild) but Mom was working the Saddle Burger nightshift only during the week so that's when we went, and early at that. We, Rodney and I, sat nervously on wooden stools in the widely empty two-story establishment, wondering if I'd be asked for ID, and then to leave.

Rick's had probably been a small honky-tonk a decade earlier, but now it was Giddyuptown's most notorious gay bar, though most of the men still looked like they belonged in a honkey-tonk. One half of the lower level was a dance floor with an array of spinning disco lights that seemed at odds with the barnwood walls. Stairs stacked along the edge of the dance floor led to a narrow upper level where Rodney said you could get a BJ.

A coke and a half later, the bar got a little busier and the dance floor started to stir. Rodney asked me to dance but I didn't know how so he excused himself with a shrug of the shoulders then sauntered up to a blonde handlebar-mustached guy wearing a toolbelt with a beer bottle in it, and the two synced their pelvic thrusts to a song I would later know to be Chaka Khan. It was funny to see Rodney dance, not that he was a bad dancer—I wouldn't know a bad dancer from a good one, it was just funny in the way it would be funny to see your mom as a lingerie model or your grandma jump out of a cake. The only dancing I had really seen were the high-kicking, leotarded kids of *Fame*—a movie and a tv show I watched faithfully and had in-fact practiced some of their more passionate dance routines around the livingroom whenever no one was home.

It was still fairly early, maybe nine-thirty, and the bar was still more empty than not. There was one man who siphoned my attention, he had layered blond hair to his earlobes and a little bit of a mustache. I'd guess he was twenty-five or thirty years old. He was wearing dark jeans and a tight tee shirt and a thin leather jacket—not a motorcycle jacket, but more like you'd see on a guy loitering at a bus stop. When he saw me looking, the blond guy gave a little smirk and picked up his cigarette and beer and walked to me.

"How old are you?"

"Thirteen."

"You probably shouldn't tell people that, they might kick you out."

I really did know that. "I mean twenty-one," I corrected.

"Cool. Have you seen the back, there's a couch back there, wanna check it out?" He used the top of his head to point to the back door, then walked away—swinging with sureness, content he had plucked the cherry from the branch; my lemon Coke and I followed close behind.

Behind the bar was a small cement patio. There was a cinderblock fire-pit in the middle—no fire but some glowing orange embers, I wondered who tended them since we were the only ones there. The area was enclosed by the bar's brick wall on one side, and by tall chainlink fences on the other three—they were almost entirely obscured with overgrowth and stolen street signs. Clint, that was his name, sat down on a long dirty couch that was littered in dry leaves and a few beer bottles. It smelled mildewy, obviously not made to be outside. I sat too and as soon as I did Clint leaned in and gave me a taste of the beer on his tongue, I hated the taste of beer but this time it tasted good. We kissed for several minutes before someone else came out and walked near our couch. Clint waved the man back inside—like a lion with a carcass, warning an opportunistic hyena away. Alone again, he opened my pants and tugged them to the ground, then dropped his own. I'd never had intercourse, I'd had a slobbery blow job from my neighbor…and wrestling with Saddle Burger Rodney had gotten outta-hand a few dozen times, but this was different—we weren't playing around. When Clint lifted my legs above my resistance (located somewhere around my ears) I knew this would be the moment when a boy became a sluttier boy.

I was so nervous I had butterflies in my butt, but then—with a palm of beer-contaminated spit, and a few selfish thrusts— beautiful blond Clint replaced my nervousness with pain as he stored the most valuable part of himself inside me; I was like a safety deposit box, for penis. It hurt (maybe not from the size of the drop, but for the frequency of the deposits and withdrawals) but I didn't want to stop, in fact there was nothing I wanted more than to *not* stop. This beautiful man was embedded…entombed inside me, and I only hoped someone else would come to the patio, to wrap us in a great length of cordage or gauze, so that we might be conjoined—like Siamese mice in a jar of formaldehyde—for eternity.

Eyes closed, Clint truncated eternity with a final thrust, and the advice: "Alotta the guys here are gonna be after you, you better be careful." I nodded but wasn't worried—if Clint and I were dating then we wouldn't be cruising bars anymore, I lowered my legs and lifted my pants and we went back inside. With my experience (and anus) widened, I found an excited Rodney, "Where have you been, it's late…we gotta get you back," looking for me near the bathroom. I told him about my patio date (or maybe I screamed it in all four directions) and he gave me a hug, like a mother hugging her daughter after the first curse of blood. The bar had transformed while I was gone, the music was louder and the lights were faster and the dance floor was crowded with shirtless men.

"I don't wanna go."

"We *have* to go, your mom will *kill* us," Rodney pleaded, "and the guy I was dancing with wants me to come to his house to show him some wrestling moves."

I thought (as well as one can think in a disco) for a moment and decided, "I'll call my mom and tell her I'm spending the night at Jemma's, then I can stay the night with Clint." (Jemma was a Boy George-loving lesbian who worked at Saddle Burger too, she hadn't confessed her lesbianism but her appearance couldn't keep the secret. I'd sometimes go to Jemma's parents' house so we could record cassette tapes of ourselves introducing the latest new-wave singles; we hoped the cassettes would help us land jobs as MTV veejays. We'd read some tidbit from an album's liner notes and then, "With their smash hit that's topping charts from the UK to the US, it's 'Don't You Want Me' by The Human League!" Culture Club was the only band Jemma ever introduced, I thought she'd have a hard time getting the MTV job if she remained unyielding in that policy.)

I called my mom from the 7-Eleven payphone and she said I couldn't stay at Jemma's, but "Tomorrow's a school day," she cliché'd (like school mattered when I'd just fallen in love). I told her Jemma would bring me home in a couple of hours and she said that was fine, then I told Rodney he could leave without me—my new boyfriend Clint would drive me home. Rodney agreed, assuming I wasn't so fatuous as to not have secured the ride. He wrangled the blonde handlebar-mustached guy and the two men left arm-in-arm, like they had been together for years.

Clint wasn't sitting at the bar (when I left he was talking to a shirtless black man with engorged nipples, though I hadn't realized he was there with a friend—in fact I thought he said he came alone, I told them both I'd be right back.) I checked the bathroom and the patio, upstairs and down, but couldn't find Clint or his nipply black friend. I looked through the crowded dance floor and a sweaty italian-looking guy in running shorts and a leather harness wrapped his arms around my waist, humping me to the disco beat; if this was dancing, it wasn't so bad. I watched for Clint as I nudged out a little spot on the dance floor and auditioned a few cautious moves.

After a dozen songs the floor got roomier, I was glad—other dancers had cramped my boldening limbs. My shirt was sweaty and my eyes burned from cigarette smoke, machined fog, and disco light; I didn't care—I only wanted to dance. Then Irene Cara's "Fame" played and I thought I might lose it. I quickly calculated that enough people had cleared for me to show some of the choreography I had learned watching the show's "You got big dreams, you want fame…" choreographer Debbie Allen. I finished a brief mental run-through of the dance steps and then with a '5-6-7-8' I raised both arms and "started paying—in sweat."

At the midpoint of my routine, as I got to the 'shoulder rolls', they gave me a moment to catch my breath and to gage the crowd.

Lots of the men were watching me, I was certain they had never seen anyone move like this (outside of Harlem and the Bronx, most bar dancers probably don't pay much mind to choreography, they probably don't have the discipline.) When the chorus hit again I decided to finish big with a roundhouse kick and then a pirouette. The kick went fine but the spin ended in a minor stumble. Still, all-in-all, I think it went pretty well. A guy came up to me and asked if he could buy me a beer, I told him I didn't drink (a dancer really shouldn't.) I asked him the time—he said 1:40 AM, and I almost fell again. I told my Mom I would be home three hours ago and I had no idea how I would get there. I ran back to the 7-Eleven and called her collect.

"Where the fuck are you?"

"Jemma's dad had a car wreck so we're at the hospital with him," was all I had thought to say, with no real plan as to how I would get the thirty miles home.

"Oh no, is he okay?" Mom asked, in a reconsidered tone. I assured her he was fine, just a cut on the head. I promised to be home as soon as I could. "Oh, is Rodney home? Jemma wants to talk to him," I asked, hoping he would pick me up and take me home.

"No, he called earlier, he's spending the night with a friend." Mom said to tell Jemma to drive carefully—we both agreed the last thing we needed was another accident. With no way home, I hustled back to the bar. Maybe Rodney finished his no-holes-barred wrestling match early and came back for me. Maybe Clint's back for me too.

It was 5:00 AM when I finally got home (I was sitting outside the closed bar with my knees to my face—a position my adult stomach would discourage today—when a shadowy man in an El Camino pulled up. He wondered if the bar was open. It wasn't. He asked if I needed a ride. I did.) I entered the unlit house quietly, but with the feeling that I was not alone. After a dozen nervous steps I thought to shout, "Show yourself, Spirit!" but chose a more hurried pace instead.

I achieved bedroom and rewarded myself with breath, the first since I came indoors.

"How's Jemma's dad?" a doorward voice asked as Mom materialized like a spectre or some other otherworldly visitant.

"What?"

"How's Jemma's dad?" she asked again, in a tone that suggested she might shed her skin to reveal her true intent.

"It was touch-and-go for a while," I explained, "the doctors thought he might have a concussion but he should be okay."

"That's funny because I called Jemma's dad and he was at home in bed, he didn't realize he'd been in an accident. Maybe it was the concussion?"

I only stared at her, too red-handed to lie.

"You're not going to school today. When I get home from work I'm taking you some place else to live."

I remember when we first moved to Oklahoma, Mom's dog Rosie heard a thunderstorm for the first time. Oklahoma storms are different than California storms, they're scary. Sirens blare tornado warnings and the sideways-blowing rain hits your windows so hard you think they'll break. When the black sky shot white with a big bolt of lightening the dog's ears stood up, and a few seconds later—as the thunder cracked—she pissed herself. Right there in the middle of the room, on Mom's new carpet—she pissed. Rosie was an impressive canine and a loyal protector (Mom swore her dog was half wolf), she hadn't peed in the house since she was a puppy. We were as shocked as if Linda Blair had descended the stairs and relieved herself in the middle of a piano party.

All season long, every time there was a thunderstorm, Rosie peed on the carpet. Mom would push her nose in the wet spot and yell at her and hit her on the ass with a rolled-up Dollar Saver. She hated being disobeyed and the dog knew it but still, she pissed. Mom never sent Rosie somewhere else to live.

I didn't go anywhere else to live either, not yet anyway, though I stayed up all night wondering if I would. I wondered about Clint too, if I'd ever see him again. I'd cry if I didn't, I'd miss him; he held the key to Pandora's Butt, and would always have a special place in my hole. I don't know why Mom didn't follow through, maybe her threat was a bluff or maybe my dad wouldn't return her call (or his wife didn't want me back again) and Mom realized there was no other place to send me, military schools aren't free and you probably need connections to sell a kid on the black market. Instead she didn't speak to me for a month. Except for my silent birthday, I didn't mind—I didn't want to have to tell her where I'd been.

That was four months ago, now I was back at Rick's Playroom—stranded again with no way home. I just started up the barnwood stairs (to see if there was anyone who might let me spend the night or the weekend with them) when the music stopped and the lights switched from PARTY to GET OUT. I turned around and slowly stepped back down, wondering where I would sleep. I considered walking back to Brentley's house, maybe he had sobered up and maybe he wasn't mad at me anymore. I don't know why it hurt so much when he tried to have sex in me, maybe I just didn't like him enough—when Clint popped my chocolate cherry on the patio couch I didn't care if it hurt. With Clint the pain was welcome, in the manner of a much-needed surgery. It was like recovering a missing organ, like living your whole life without a liver or a pancreas, and then having it miraculously implanted by some brilliant back-alley surgeon. Maybe the butt knows what the heart wants.

After a slow, reluctant exit from the closing bar, I entered the outside—passing through the same dozen people who are always lurking around the doorway of every closing bar, all waiting to be invited to an amazing afterparty that only ever existed in some desperate person's imagination: *There might be underwear models handing out free ecstasy, I better stand here just in case.* I bet in the whole history of the world, there has never been an actual afterparty.

"Hey angel-face, are there any good afterparties?" the globular guy who bought me the Coke waved the question to me from his side of a parked car.

"I dunno, I'm just waiting for my friend," I lied.

"It looks like everyone's about gone, do ya need a ride somewhere?"

I considered saying no, but I desperately did. "I think maybe they left me."

"Well were gonna go get some breakfast, pancakes n'stuff, do ya wanna come with?"

I looked around and saw only a balding transvestite warming her hands in an afro wig, lurking by the bar's locked door. "Yeah," I nodded, and squeezed into the car.

Phyllis Cheesesteak and Sloppy Joe-Ann were drag queens, not the 'dress-up for kicks' type but bona-fide female impers-onators. They were in town twice a month performing at Yellow Brick Road—a very large and largely lesbian bar for larger lesbians. They drove to Giddyuptown from Cowboy City, staying in hotels during their twice-monthly gigs. After their show they'd de-wig and un-makeup and drive across town from the lesbian bar to Rick's Playroom to look at all the sweaty men, or so they told me over our pancake breakfast. "Order whatever you want, my treat," Joe-Ann whispered in my ear as I pondered the menu prices. Phyllis liked to look at the ethnic men—blacks and latins, middle-eastern men were his favorite—the other preferred white men, having no use for men with "names you'd need a calculator to pronounce."

I hadn't seen many drag queens (other than those like the wigless one holding her afro like a hand muff, standing outside Rick's Playroom tonight, Joe-Ann explained she was a "transy" [transvestite] prostitute named Lamar; or tonight, 'Lamarjorie'), but they seemed decent—especially Joe-Ann, who patted my knee under the table much like my grandma would. Joe-Ann, the one who bought me the Coke, made a lot of jokes but I mostly didn't get them (or they just weren't funny). He was very large and wore sloppy clothes—a sweater vest and slacks that were rumpled, both several inches too long. He had the kind of haircut that farm moms give their youngest children. His voice: womany with a thickset twang, it had the inflections (and he had the mannerisms) of somebody's great aunt. I got the impression Sloppy Joe-Ann was more of a sidekick to the larger, stouter Phyllis.

Phyllis Cheesesteak was the size of a fridge and equally cold. He had a demeaning demeanor (and a witch's nose) and seemed to be the worldlier of the two, having once been Miss Gay Arkansas or Alabama or somesuch state; I wasn't sure what that was but it sounded impressive. Phyllis wasn't unfriendly with just me, but was also sour with her drag-sister, the two bickered like forgotten film stars: "Honey, I wouldn't eat that bacon if I were you,"—"Honey, I couldn't *spell* bacon if I were you," or something like that. I did notice Phyllis only looked at me after a punchline, rating my reaction; we sat near a window and he otherwise watched the non-happenings on the other side of it. "So why aren't you at home on a school night?" was one of the few questions he asked me, only it sounded more like an accusation. "Leave him alone," Joe-Ann answered.

When the check came Joe-Ann said, "I've got this one," causing Phyllis to roll his eyes—maybe Joe-Ann bought pancakes for a lot of boys, or maybe Phyllis just had lash glue in his eye.

"I guess we better get outta here before they throw us out," Joe-Ann said, "do you need a place ta stay tonight?" (Phyllis rolled his eyes again.)

Their Best-N-West room wasn't fancy—two full-sized beds and a table. Both men rubbed some cream on and off their faces, then Phyllis removed his pants (giving me a moment of silent panic) and got into bed. Joe-Ann and I left our pants on and got into the other bed. "Don't worry, I won't bite," she said (they called each other 'she' so eventually I did too.) She turned off the bedside lamp, resting her head on my shoulder and arm across my chest like she was my baby, my old gargantuan baby.

Phyllis's choppy snores wake me. Dazed, I look through dim light for Joe-Ann but she isn't there; I hope she'll buy me breakfast before she leaves, an omelette or a cinnamon roll. A few seconds pass and I regain as many wits, enough to notice that the Best-N-West comforter is rising and falling—bobbing marionettishly, like a puppet ghost—between my knees. A second more and I am aware of my erection, and then of the discharge that is being methodically suctioned from it like crude from a Texas oil field. The thought of his big dark lips (not the luscious full lips of Brooke Shields or Sophia Loren, but like some bloated uncooked meat that's been frozen and thawed, frozen and thawed, and then frozen and thawed), the thought of them nursing my penis makes me sick. I sit up and give the gluttonous comforter an angry shove. The butterballish body rolls off me, flailing like a turtle that's accidentally flipped onto its back. "I'm sorry," he says—or sputters really, because his mouth is full of semen.

I stand, dripping, and walk into the bathroom. When the door closes and locks I turn on the bright light, raising both palms to cover my sleepy eyes from the harsh wattage and the harsher realization: I am stuck, stuck with these cocksucking drag queens. I can't walk out of a hotel into the middle of a night—I have no one to call, nowhere to go. After a moment of exhausted deliberation I rezip my pants and climb into the bathtub. Under a towel blanket, on a folded towel pillow, I curl up, hunker down, and wait for daylight.

CHAPTER 9

Fourteen and a Thirty-Eight

We'd been to the wig store twice before, but never after dark.
Last time I tried on a dozen of the brunettes and Scooter tried half
the longer blondes—shifting the little chinese lady's voice from
sharp to shrill when we didn't purchase.

"Why try so many you no buy?"

"We're just browsing," we apologized.

"Browse, browse, browse, everybody, all day long."

"Yeah," we agreed, retreating to the front door.

"Next time you buy or you no try!" she shouted over the glass
door's little cowbell.

"Hurry, before she goes for the chinese throwing stars,"
Scooter joked in a volume I hoped the wig lady wouldn't hear,
Scooter joked a lot. Tuesday, the amateur contest at Yellow Brick
Road would kind of be our coming-out party. We felt like
debutantes too. Everyone who had seen us in make-up said we
were beautiful, and we believed it—Phyllis and Joe-Ann knew how
to paint a face. Last weekend I ran into the two rotund drag queens
when I went back to Rick's Playroom, I guess it was inevitable

since I'd been there several nights a week.

"Hey angel-face, I was hoping I'd see ya again."

"Hi," I answered, wishing I had worn a cup.

"How are ya, did you get home okay? You didn't get in more trouble with yer Mom, did ya?"

"No," I answered, intending to stop there, then blurting-out, "I moved out anyway." Despite a BJ that left me with LGBT-PTSD, there was something about Joe-Ann that made his concern sound sincere.

"Whaddaya mean you moved out, where ya livin' sugar?"

"Downtown, I got an apartment with my friend Liz," that was half true. I was staying with Liz, but we didn't really have a place.

"Well that sounds real nice. I remember my first apartment, you probably weren't even born yet. It was the tiniest little studio, I probably wouldn't even fit into it now! Would ya believe I use'ta be small as you?"

I wouldn't.

"I won't bore ya with that though, I gotta have a tinkle…will you be an angel and watch my drink for me?"

"Sure," I agreed, wishing I had said 'maybe you should take it with you'.

Liz and I were squatting in the empty apartment her friend vacated a couple of weeks earlier. I met Liz when my Mom moved us to Twisterton. The kids at my new school didn't like me. Girls expressed their dislike by way of a passed note, or during the conversational frenzy just before a teacher enters a room.

"What's wrong with your hair?"

"It hates dumb questions."

"It looks gay."

"Thank you."

"Um, sorry but that's *not* a compliment. God made Adam and *Eve*, not Adam and *Stan*."

"Steve."

"What?"

"God made Adam and Eve, not Adam and *Steve*. You said *Stan*. It's *Steve*. Steve rhymes with Eve, it's only clever if you say *Steve*."

"Whatever, Fag."

And boys expressed their dislike by knocking books out of my hands or throwing things at my head.

My hair became a talking point during the previous summer after a record store visit introduced me to a blue-black androgyn on the cover of a record that I would later know to be *Nightclubbing* by Grace Jones. I bought the record and played it a dozen times, then asked my mother to come to my bedroom where, after some coaxing, she agreed to lay beside me for a listen.

"Chris," she warned, "I only have a minute, I have to start dinner."

"Just listen," I assured her, "just listen."

For the next three minutes we lay supine—as if sunbathing atop my waterbed. Side-by-side, eyes closed, we silently studied "Art Groupie," Grace Jones' melancholic ode to art. The music was minimal, the bass was guttural, the vocals were sharp then soft then sharp again, and the lyrics were perplexingly matter-of fact. When it was over I gave my mother a squeeze, "See. I told you it was amazing."

"It's nice Chris," she answered, "do you want Thousand Island with your salad, or Ranch?"

In the months that followed, a portion of my upbringing would be handed off to Grace Jones, to Nina Hagen, Dale Bozzio,

Alison Moyet, Kate Bush, Laurie Anderson, Diamanda Galás, and Siouxsie Sioux. I adored my mother but in the words of a woman who should have been president, it takes a village. Under the watch of these wild-haired women—this sisterhood of singing stepmothers—my ideals developed, my boundaries broadened, and my hair grew into a wig.

Just a year earlier I went to class wondering how I could change—to become more like those schoolkids who the rest of us envied, and by the next year I wanted only to distinguish myself from them. The curious thing is: though they never wanted me in their scene, they were furious when I became my own.

One day in the quad of my new school, a boy I had never seen before spit in my hair as he walked past. I heard the quick discharge then felt the warm wet drizzle as it slowly snaked down a tangle of backcombed hair to my scalp, and then I saw shoulders bouncing laughter as three boys walked away. I wound-up a math book and threw it at their backs. The toss mostly missed—on account of sports—but they got the idea.

"I'm gonna kick your ass, I'm gonna kick your ass," the ringleader notified me. I sat down my remaining books to prepare for my first teenage fight.

"Throw a punch," he insisted—four or five times. I wondered why I needed to throw the first punch if *he* was intent on kicking *my* ass, maybe it was some sort of a 'Ladies First' policy.

"Do it Fag, hit me," he persisted.

After a couple of minutes it became apparent to both of us that he was waiting for one of his friends to intervene with a 'Don't even bother with that fag, he's not worth it'. Finally, someone from the crowd of thirty yelled-out, "Watch out Brayden, he knows karate!" which appeared to be the discouragement the boy needed to hear.

"Forget it then," the spitter announced, then he and his

friends all gave me disapproving 'karate is cheating' glares as they walked away. The crowd dissipated, an asymmetrically redheaded girl with gigantic eyes and an oversized coat stayed behind.

"You know karate?" she smirked.

"Apparently," I replied, "I wonder if I know judo too?"

Liz was two years older than me and the school's only other new-waver, we were best friends from that day on. Like me, Liz had just moved here, after getting in trouble at her old school—some sort of scandal involving marijuana, another girl, and titty lube. Liz's mom—embarrassed by the scandal and tired of a daughter who mocked her—sent the impertinent ginger here to live with the father and his new wife (and former secretary). Apparently the new arrangement wasn't going well, on several occasions Liz's new mother had laid-down the law, and my new best friend had casually kicked it out of her way.

The newly formed pair of us ate our lunches together everyday, usually cigarettes and milkshakes. Liz was old enough to drive and she drove an aging orange VW bug that always smelled of pot, and sounded of Depeche Mode. On weekends we drove to Giddyuptown—our version of NYC. We watched punk and new-wave bands play in little venues on the strip of the city that catered to our peacock-haired kind. Driving to our second or third show, I split a doobie with my new friend—it was my first time. I felt fine but a little thirsty so we stopped at a convenience store, as stoners do. Somewhere between the slurpee machine and the burrito freezer I fell...into a crack in the space/time continuum (there should have been a sign, like WET FLOOR, warning customers it was there.) I spun around looking for my friend—to tell her to watch her step, there was a dimensional anomaly floating about—and when I stopped, the room didn't. Little bags of chips and boxes of crackers, snack cakes and tubes of mini donuts kept whirling all around me, like I was stuck on the 7-Eleven ride at Marriott's Great America. The caloric whirlwind filled me with fear, and the fear doubled me over with laughter. I stayed bent over, laughing, not in real time but more in rapid snapshots of time, until Liz found me and we slowly walked our inappropriate laughter back to the car.

Minutes later we were at the club, sitting on a floor around a stage where a punk girl was singing something about something, I watched her flit about. "Are you alright?" Liz asked, noticing my shifty eyes darting left and up and right and down.

"Everyone's looking at me," I answered.

"You're just paranoid," she laughed, "it's the pot."

"No, really. They know I smoked it. They're staring at me."

"Relax," she patted my indian-bent knee, "it'll pass...it will, I promise."

I closed my eyes and took a deep breath to settle my paranoid egomania, *no one's looking at you, stupid,* I opened my eyes.

The girl—the singer—is squatting now at the edge of her shallow platform, still singing something about something but with her big face four inches from mine. She is bright white with spotlight, I am too, she winks at me in a theatrical manner then waves her microphone in front of my mouth as if waiting for a contribution that I forgot to rehearse. I add nothing so she rubs the sides of my hair—the short bits of an otherwise foot-tall mohawk, the spikes cast pointy shadows into her neck (if only they could pierce). Her brightness grows intolerable so I look away, around the room. A hundred people with two hundred eyes look back, collectively, staring at me as the children would in *Village of the Damned.* Liz's eyes are there too, round with horror and glassy with delight. I don't really like pot.

Several months into our new friendship, my mother announced that Saddle Burger's regional manager was going to manage the location himself, and we were moving back to Puddin Foot, the little farm town we had moved from earlier that year. My sister had a new gal-pal—a lightly mustached lady named Gwenda—and would stay in Twisterton with her new 'friend' while she finished her last years of high school. For the first time in my life I was sad to leave a town. Liz was my first best friend, and we had become weekend fixtures in nearby Giddyuptown's oddly impressive punk and new-wave scene. When I told my friend I was moving she promised she would drive to Puddin Foot to pick me up on weekends.

A few weeks later Mom and I were moved into our new apartment. I felt sick at the thought of going back to the school that I had escaped almost a year earlier. No one there had missed me, no one would be lining up to tell me how much they liked my colorful new hair and clothing style, no one would welcome me like a mastermind returning from the underworld. Puddin Foot had barely tolerated me when I tried to fit in, now that I was determined to stand out it seemed unlikely I'd make it through the next three and a half years of high school without being dragged to somebody's barn, tied to a post, and given a make-under.

Just as she had promised, Liz came to pick me up for a weekend—it was the weekend before I was to re-enroll in my old school. I went to my mom's room to give her a kiss and tell her goodbye. Liz stood in Mom's bedroom doorway with a "Hi, Mrs Madrigal," in an awe-shucks tone that she used to win-over reluctant parents. Mom answered with a "Hello Liz, would you mind waiting in the car, I need to talk to Chris."

"Listen," she said, in her 'Listen, I'm about to be a bitch' tone, "Listen, here's twenty bucks for you to get a haircut. When you get back from Giddyuptown I want all your hair cut off and I want it back to your natural color."

I appreciated the beauty tip, but, *excuse me?*

"I mean it," she continued. "Your grandparents live in this town and I don't want them to have to listen to a buncha assclowns talkin' about your hair. Maybe in Giddyuptown people can walk around with their hair like that, but this isn't Giddyuptown."

"Are you serious?" was all I could think to say.

"You're damn right I'm serious. I'm sorry but this jagwagon town is fulla jagoffs…"

"And that's my fault?"

"No dipshit, I'm not sayin' it's your fault. But I'm not havin' the same Gong Show bullshit here you had in Twisterton—And I'm not gonna argue about it—If you wanna go to Giddyuptown with Liz today then don't say another word—And don't come back until your hair is normal."

"Normal," as if *that* were something to strive for. I had tried to be a normal kid, and I failed. And if I hadn't failed, the success would have killed me. Here, it was *normal* to get married and have two children before the age of twenty, is that what she wanted for me? It was normal to work a mind-numbing job and then to come home and drink until you passed out. Is that why she praised my childhood creativity—so I could find more creative ways to be normal? My hair, my clothes, they weren't just a passing fad. The style might change when I'm twenty, thirty-five, fifty, but the sentiment will remain: *I don't want a normal life, I don't need to fit in.*

When I was "normal" people made fun of me covertly—with the underhanded lob of an improvised explosive device. I prefer people to make fun of me to my face. When I look like this, the worst people can't help but reveal themselves, I see them coming like tired old warships and my shields are up—I'm bombproof.

I didn't think of this then, I was too pissed. I did want to ask if she remembered getting beaten by her mother for ratting and spraying her own hair in the junior high bathroom when she was in school. Or if she remembered the times I came home crying, nose bloodied by someone I'd attacked for telling me my heavily made-up, biker mother looked like a whore. I wanted to grab her by the back of the head and push her nose into the hypocrisy, as if it were a wet spot on the carpet. But I took the twenty dollars instead, walked to the parking lot and into Liz's car.

"Oh my god, that fucking bitch, that *fucking* bitch!" Liz repeated the latter a third time as she pumped her upper body by quickly pulling and pushing on the rigid steering wheel, churning her big red hair into an angry muppet. "You're hair is so fucking cool," she continued, "I'm not letting you cut it. That fucking bitch!"

"I'm gonna need to find a place to live then," I said, half kidding.

"My friend Jeff will let us stay at his apartment. He's moving out and he won't care if we crash there. I've fucking had it with my dad's secretary-slut wife anyway, let's just fucking move to Giddyuptown."

In the thirty-five minute drive to Giddyuptown, Liz and I hashed out the plan: we would live somewhere, and we would get jobs somewhere. And so, with a foolproof plan in place, I never went back home.

"Thanks for watchin' my drink, the line at the powder room was awful—you'd think Montgomery Clift was giving handys at the urinal." I didn't know who Montgomery Clift was, but the thought of Sloppy Joe-Ann using a urinal made me uncomfortable.

"I think I'm gonna get myself a fresh one, can I get ya a Coke or somethin?"

Why did I have to watch it if you were getting a fresh one, "Sure," I answered (my two hundred dollars were long gone, the prospect of starvation loomed like a buzzard and I wasn't turning down any offers.)

Thirteen days after I left home I called Saddle Burger Rodney—the assistant manager, he said my mom was worried and thinking about calling the cops. I fed him a story to regurgitate to her: that Liz was pregnant, I was the father, and we were getting married (surely my two-kids-by-seventeen mom would be sympathetic to a teenage pregnancy.) Rodney and I'd had enough sex-wrestling that he knew I was lying, but he relayed the story. Mom wasn't mad, she said I should call and we would work it out. She invited Liz and me to dinner at my grandma's house, everyone hugged and welcomed Liz to the family and Mom gave me two hundred dollars. "Listen you turd, I want you to promise me you'll use this money to go back to school." I knew a baby would be a full-time job, but I promised her I'd get my education. "I know you'll be good parents," she assured me and my lady, "because I had *my* kids very young and I did a *damn* good job raising them."

Once I was sure the story stuck—and that Mom wasn't reporting me as a runaway (sometime near the end of Liz's first trimester), I decided it was time to abort the pregnancy yarn.

"*I have a collect call from Chris*, will you accept the charges?" the operator asked.

"......................Yes, I'll accept," Mom replied, after an awkward pause that let the operator know she didn't appreciate being put on the spot.

"I have some bad news, Mom," I prepared her, "Liz fell in the shower and she lost the baby."

Mom took the news well. "That's a bummer, Chris," she said, "Will you tell Liz I'm sorry?" (I would.) "God works in mysterious ways," she continued, "and sometimes everything happens for a reason," stringing clichés into sentences and pretending she wasn't an atheist with no interest in becoming a thirty-two-year-old grandmother. I thought she might finish by insisting I move back home but the topic never came up.

Liz and I had no furniture until we found a card table, its chairs were plastic buckets turned upside down. We ate dinner there, undelicious foods flavored by candlelight (the apartment still had electricity but we worried that illuminated windows would give us away.) My roommate told me dinner table tales about growing up the way she did, in a house where divorcing parents were even less interested in her than they were each other. I told her about the years I spent sitting in a weed field because I was too old to sit indoors. Something scary happened to Liz when she was eleven— something she wouldn't want me to share here (the story was just for me and the flickering candle, no one else.) "Your turn," she then demanded, "tell me something scary that happened to you."

I thought for a moment, poking a plastic fork around baked beans. I knew what the story would be but was unsure where to begin.

"How old were you, start there?"

"It was last year."

"Where were you?"

"At Rick's [Playroom]."

"Oh shit," her big round eyes widened, titillated by the prospect of villainy at the gay bar, "what happened?"

"I told you about the first time I went there, with Rodney."

"He left you there…"

"I told him to. I didn't wanna go home."

"How'd you get home?"

"After the bar closed and everyone left, I just sat outside their front door. It was cold so my knees were inside my shirt and I was trying to figure out what to tell my mom."

"She was pissed, huh."

"Always."

"So how'd you get home?"

"Well, I was sitting there for an hour or so—I think my eyes were closed—and then someone said, *Hey*."

"Who was it?"

"Some guy, in an El Camino. I couldn't really see his face but

134

he asked me if the bar was open and I said *huh-uh*, and he goes: You need a ride?"

"You didn't get in the car with him. Please tell me you didn't get in his car."

"I needed a ride!"

"Not Smart. What happened?"

"I remember: I opened the door to get in but there was stuff on the seat, garbage or whatever, so he pushes it onto the floorboard and then I sit down."

"You know who has dirty cars? Crazy people."

"Your car's dirty."

"My car's disorganized, there's a difference. What happened?"

"He asked me where I was going. I told him and he said he used to live out that way."

"Was he a hick?"

"Hickish. He had a baseball cap and sunglasses, he was hard to see."

"Why was he wearing sunglasses at night. Was it Corey Hart?"

"They might have been regular glasses, but tinted. I don't know, it was dark."

"He's a creep. Continue."

"So we're driving, and I'm assuming we're going the right way but you know me and directions."

"I know."

"Then he reaches into his pocket and pulls out some chaw and asks me if I want a dip."

"Gays don't dip."

"I know. So then he asks me what kinda bar that was."

"He doesn't know?"

"I guess not. I just say: they play music. And then he wants to know if I think it's a gay bar."

"What the fuck?"

"I go: I don't know, coulda been."

"Well is it or isn't it?" he insists.

"I guess it is."

"Well do you go to gay bars or don't you?"

"I go wherever."

"Wherever huh, okay, wherever," he leaves it at that.

We drive a few miles in silence, in the only car on the highway. When we hit bumps the garbage in his car rustles, and intermittent signs make a whooshing sound—those and chaw spit are our radio. I doubt I said that to Liz.

"You look young to be'n a bar."

"I'm twenty-one."

"Liar."

"I will be twenty-one."

"So'll my newborn."

"You have a baby?"

"And a wife."

"Oh."

"Why, you thought I was a fag?"

"Hm-mm."

"No, I don't look like a fag?"

"Hm-mm."

"You do. You look like a fag."

I slide my foot around the floorboard trash, resting it on what I am sure is a tire iron.

"But you wanna look like one, right. S'at why you wear yur hair like that?"

"I just like it."

"Yeah, you like havin' fag hair?"

I wedge a toe under the metal bar, tipping it upward, nearer my hand.

"S'at iron in yur way?"

"What?"

"Here," he leans rightward and reaches a big arm across my knees, it grabs the tire iron and lodges it behind the seat. "S'at better?"

"Yeah…thanks."

"Holy shit, you shoulda jumped outta the car."

"At fifty miles an hour?"

"Okay maybe not. What happened?"

"My daddy use ta kick my ass for actin' faggy. You ever get your ass kicked?"

"I've been in fights."

"Ever been tied up with a rope and had horse shit rubbed in your face."

The door handle is black and nearly unseeable against the black interior. "Probably not."

"Ever been hit with a shovel til you passed out?"

"Hm-mm."

"Think that'd leave a scar on your head?"

My keys, they're sharp, I reach into my pocket. "Probably."

"You're damn right it would. If my daddy saw me with yur hairdo, he'd've buried me under the chicken coop."

The keys make a little jingle as I position one between two fingers. "You had chickens?"

"Faggots go to Hell."

"Chickens are cool."

"They go to Hell where razor-dicked demons fuck em in the ass everyday until they jizz inside your pureed guts…"

I slide the house key/fist from my pants pocket. "We didn't have any chickens, but my grandparents did."

"And then the next day they fuck you all over again. S'at sound like fun to you?"

"They had cats, and some chickens."

"Think about that: a demon usin' yur own pureed guts to lube his dick when he fucks you, in and out and in and out."

"Chickens and rabbits."

"Razor Dicked Demons, that's what my dad use ta say. Man, he woulda hated your hair. I like it though. I think you little gays have a lot more courage than they did when I was growin' up. You think so?"

"I um, I guess so."

"I don't want my kid growin' up a fag, but if he does then I hope he's loud and proud, you know what I mean? Hey, I think this is your street, right?"

"Oh, yeah—that's it, this is my street, right here."

"What! He didn't kill you?"

"Nope!"

"Then it's not a scary story."

"It *was* scary!"

"No it's not. Finish your beans."

When the money Mom gave me ran out, Liz and I started shoplifting our food. We weren't very good at it—stuffing things in our waistbands that slowly fell down our pantslegs—but it worked for a while. We hooked up with other kids from the downtown music scene, kids who were also interested in a free apartment with electricity and running water in the second-floor corner unit of an unmanaged tenement. Stoney moved in with us, Liz said his mom kicked him out after finding a letter he'd written about being bisexual. He was a sixteen-year-old with a big smile, a nervous laugh, and a headedness so thick it'd stop a bullet. But there was a charm about his sluggish mind, like watching a baby trying to make sense of a spoon or a drunkard trying to urinate away from his own shoes. Stoney's dim wit and all-american style made him an odd fit in our group, but the qualities reminded me of my stepbrother Vanne so I was glad he was there. Scooter stayed with us on weekends—sometimes longer, he had a lazy eye and a stalker-like fascination with other people's boyfriends. Scooter loved to dance, and Muleskin—the podunk town where he lived with elderly alcoholic parents—was too long a commute from Giddyuptown's nightlife. Scooter was bitter and kind of a dick (making fun of people until they cried) but also smart and undeniably funny, and he had a car. Some of the other kids in our group would move in for a few weeks, and others would disappear. Sometimes someone's irate mother would show-up, demanding to speak to an adult. "My mom just passed away," Liz would explain, "and my dad's out shopping for tombstones. Can I give him a message?"

"Here's yer soda," Sloppy Joe-Ann announced on his return from the bar, "I had them put a cherry in it for ya, you like cherries don't ya?"

I did.

"Good, good. I thought about feeding it to ya but thought that would probably be too forward?"

It would.

"Living on yer own huh, that's gotta be expensive, are ya workin?"

"No, I'm still looking," I lied.

"Well what're ya doin' for money, sugar, can I ask?" Joe-Ann showed his concern by touching my cheek with a soft hand that smelled of something I'd later know to be face powder. "I know it's none of my beeswax, is that too personal?"

It was. "My mom gave me some money when I left," I said instead.

The truth was the money was long gone and we couldn't live on shoplifted food alone. Within a month, four of us—Me and Liz, Scooter and Stoney—decided to try burglary, I knew Saddle Burger like the back of my penis so that was our first mark. We arrived around 3:00 AM, when justice surely slept. Stoney's dad gave him an old truck with the advice "Don't tell your mother" and "sometimes the ignition doesn't start," it was our getaway car.

We parked in the lot of the Futon Palace next door then climbed onto the Saddle Burger rooftop. I had been on the flat roof of a Saddle Burger before (to clean the grill vent) but this roof was thick with cooking grease, every surface covered in half an inch of the oily restaurant muck. We may have been poor but we were vain and we liked our clothes so, standing on the top of the restaurant, we all stripped and threw our outfits to a jumbled pile on the comparatively clean parking lot below.

Naked Stoney shimmied down the grease vent, landing on the grill. He tried the front and back doors, confirming that both required a key, so we all shimmied our naked selves down the greasy vent. I knew the cash drawer was hidden in the walk-in refrigerator—under the lettuce, I went there; the others had their assignments. Stoney filled a garbage bag with meat and corndogs, Scooter did the same with bread and condiments, and Liz shopped the vegetables ("You boys *need* to eat vegetables," was her reason.) After I bagged the cash, I searched for any other valuables: a cassette player, Ajax, toilet paper.

Ten minutes later (with bags expanded and character condensed) we tried hoisting each other back up the long slippery vent, but even athletic Stoney couldn't climb it; without a door key we were trapped. After a confused moment we dropped our get at the front door and did a naked run around the restaurant, frantic for anything hard enough to break the glass. I found first, and slammed the ice cream machine's heavy steel blade into the double-door. The glass cracked from my first whack so I pounded a dozen more. On the final blow my hand slipped, slapping a karate chop onto the sharp edge of the door's remaining glass. I saw blood pouring like a stream of urine onto the restaurant's cement floor, then I saw the gash. It went into the pinky side of my hand, two inches above my wrist, long and deep enough that I could have hidden my Carmex inside. I looked at the laceration then I looked at Liz, her big eyes were somehow bigger and their concern made me feel faint. The others grabbed our bags and we all climbed through the hole I'd made, careful not to graze our genitals against the jagged glass.

"We have to get him to a hospital," Liz pleaded as we made the naked sprint to our truck in the parking lot next door.

"Wrap it in a shirt," someone said.

"SHIT, our clothes!" Stoney yelped, his greased butt bouncing as he ran to retrieve the pile of shirts and pants and shoes waiting like overly obedient pets behind the ransacked restaurant. When he bent forward to pick up the clothes my groin contemplated an erection, but my hemorrhaging hand decided against it.

Though the night was warm enough for momentary nudity, we all froze stiff when we heard the sound of one, then two sirens crying "Crime! Crime! Crime!" through otherwise silent streets. After a quick thaw we shouted, "Run Stoney, Run!" as the dithered boy—naked, but for arms full of clothes—spun clocklike, then counter-clocklike, in confused jailbound circles.

Three cop cars pulled into the Saddle Burger parking lot just seconds after we all flattened nakedly into the back of Stoney's truck. "I'm not going back to jail," Scooter threatened in an insistent whisper. "Shut up!" the rest of us replied.

An hour, maybe two hours later the last cop car pulled away

from the crime scene, never curious enough about the lone truck in the neighboring parking lot to investigate the shivering fleshpile inside its rusty bed. We waited another minute before peeking outside our white Ford bunker, slathering on clothes and driving me to an emergency room. Dressed like cat burglars we told the doctor a Pyrex pan exploded while we baked a tray of 4:00 AM biscuits. "Okay," he said, interested in neither the shuck nor the jive.

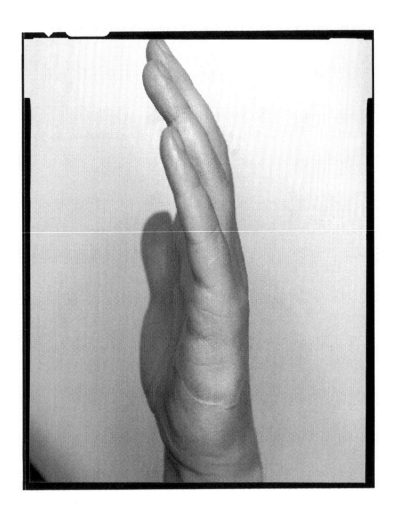

We feasted on corndogs and chicken-fried steak sandwiches. When the food and cash ran out we hit a few more Saddle Burgers in Ewe Neck and Owl Head and other neighboring towns. Our friends came over and they feasted too. We told people we won the food in a grocery store lottery, only a few knew the truth. We confessed to Kiki Augustine when she rejected our lottery explanation. Kiki was a smart girl, sixteen years old and the only rich kid in our clique. She lived with her parents in a big beautiful house that I had seen only from the outside. The pretty girl drove a new sportscar and had her shiny straight black hair cut in an expensive salon, the lustrous locks hung to her jaw on one side and to her eye on the other, the back was shaved nearly to bald. Hers wasn't the most outrageous hair in our group, in fact it may have been the tamest, but Kiki was punk at her roots and everyone knew her petite frame harbored a tasmanian devil, a cartoon cyclone of fists and knees and teeth. She was fearless, and if there was going to be more action—she wanted in.

Scooter showed up on Friday, as he usually did, only this time he brought something extra. While friends ate in the kitchen, and others slept haphazardly (like Nan Golden models, on unsheeted mattresses and other, less comfortable corners of the barely furnished apartment) Scooter ushered Me and Liz, Stoney and Kiki into the bathroom.

"What is it?" Stoney asked, as Scooter pulled a shoebox from his little suitcase.

"It's a shoebox, stupid," he answered.

"Oh wow," simple Stoney marveled, impressed by the little cardboard box.

Scooter removed the lid and began unwrapping its toiletpaper-mummified bundle, our chins slipped when he revealed the revolver inside.

"It's my dad's," Scooter boasted, "it's a .38 Special."

The only other gun I had seen was the little pearl-handled one my mom kept in her purse after she left Mickey. It seemed like a toy compared to Scooter's. "Is it loaded?" I asked.

"No, I don't think he has any bullets for it. I couldn't find em anyway. But we won't need them."

"For what?" Stoney asked.

"To shoot some bitches!" Kiki told our dim-witted friend, picking up the gun and causing each of us to duck as she pointed it around the bathroom.

"Stoney," Liz said in a careful, maternal tone, "we've been talking about maybe going to Custer's when they close, and taking the money from them before they take it to the bank." Liz had worked at Custer's Indian Imports across the river in Simmerdown Town. She knew they kept the back door open while they cleaned the store, and that they had thousands of dollars in the register.

"Well what do we need the gun for?" he asked.

"Cuz they're not just gonna *give* us the money, stupid," Kiki replied.

"Quit calling him stupid," Liz defended.

"I'm not doing it," Stoney objected, shaking his blockhead.

"Leave then, pussy!" little Kiki ordered.

Stoney reached for the doorknob, scurrying us to shield the gun from view of the open door. "And keep your mouth shut!" Kiki warned with a slap to the back of his numskull as Stoney walked out. "I'm glad he's gone," she finished, "he woulda fucked it up anyway." The rest of us held in the bathroom until we had sorted the sordid details—we would do it, and do it soon.

"My mom gave me some money when I left," was the only explanation I wanted to give Joe-Ann.

"Well that's good sugar, yer mom sounds like a sweet lady."

"Uh-huh."

Resting a plump hand on my knee, Joe-Ann asked, "You know it might be hard to find a job at yer age, have ya thought about that?"

I had.

"Well Phyllis and I know lotsa people here in Giddyuptown. Would ya be interested in being a bar-back or somethin' like that?"

"That'd be great [I had been in a bar every night for the last two months anyway], I'd love that." I was excited enough by the prospect to overlook the intimations of intimacy his flirtatious finger drew on my knobby knee, somewhere under the small table.

"Oh, but you know what?" a look of concern souring an otherwise sweet conversation, "You'd hafta show 'em an ID that says yer old enough to work in a bar."

"How old is that?" I asked, knowing fourteen wouldn't be the answer.

"Maybe eighteen, do ya have a fake ID?"

I didn't.

"That's gonna be a pickle. You know, they don't ID the performers, would ya ever consider doin' drag, you could make a little spendin' money."

"Are you serious," I asked, raising a manicured eyebrow at the preposterous suggestion.

"Why not, you have a beautiful face. You'd be amazed at what a little make-up can do."

"Do you mean like lip-sync and stuff."

"Yes," she chuckled, "unless ya know how to twirl a baton."

I laughed a little too.

Me and Liz, Kiki and Scooter drove Liz's bug across the river to the strip mall where she once worked. We had Scooter's .38 and he borrowed his dad's shotgun too (neither was loaded but they were guns nonetheless.) Usually a chatty bunch, we drove the first fifteen minutes in complete silence—each waiting for someone to say 'this is stupid, we should turn around'. Even lionhearted Kiki was mummed, sitting quietly in the passenger seat, the warm wind whipping whimsically through her newly dyed electric-blue hair. I sat behind her, not caring that the bug's open windows threatened my big, carefully teased hairdo (I had a gun in my lap and armed robbery on my mind.)

Half way to Custer's Indian Imports, with the whimsical wind in full rollick with my Robert Smith locks (I hadn't really copied The Cure coiffure but the singer did happen to own the look, if I'd chopped some bangs into it then Siouxsie Sioux might have owned it, and if I'd added a diamond necklace then it could have been Elizabeth Taylor's), a car pulled alongside us, keeping pace with our little Volkswagen bug and vandalizing our collective silence with adolescent laughter. We all turned to the right, curious about the hilarity in the next lane. We saw four girls, cheerleader types in an expensive sports car, looking at us and laughing convulsively as if we were a dozen clowns comedically crammed into a miniature car. We'd all seen laughter like this before—in junior-highs and shopping malls, it was how the bitchier bunches of teenage girls chose to assault the kids who were the most noticeably different from them. And we were different inasmuch as we looked different, and we didn't harass people for their differences. We— the four of us and our friends—sculpted our hair (not the small tasteful sculptures you might find on a bookshelf, but the large variety designed to bring civic pride to a public park), we used gelatin or egg whites or whatever form of stickiness was rumored to have the greatest hold. We wore scissor-hacked sweaters as though they were Milanese couture. "We are art," we thought, "we should be wired with alarms and encased in glass." We stood at the intersection of lowbrow and highbrow—where the shit hit the fancy.

The four girls stayed along side us, each using a hand to point at our blue and pink hair, and the other hand to curtain their exaggerated laughter in a mockery of discretion and modesty. "Oh My God, Look At Their Hair," they shouted, laughing and bouncing in their seats like husky children with mouths full of ice cream. We watched them taunt us for one or two hundred yards, pulling their car unnecessarily close to ours. Then—with a synchronicity that seemed rehearsed—Kiki and I reached for our guns, each of us confident the knee-slapping girls hadn't anticipated we were packing heat. Kiki's skinny arm and long revolver reached so far out her window I could have tight-roped it into the driver's seat of the neighboring car, and my shotgun seemed to sit just inches from the faces of the bitches in the backseat. It took a second for the four girls to process the dilemma before them, and another second for their laugh-squinted eyes to round with horror, and one more for their screams of laughter to fully transition to cries of terror. Each girl's outstretched index finger—the finger she'd used to point-out our uproariousness— was quickly joined by her hand's remaining fingers and its full palm in a defensive gesture, as if to deflect bullets in the same overly optimistic way Janet Leigh had pitted her palm against Anthony Perkin's knife. Then, in a final act of self-preservation, Aubrianna (or Terrifany or whatever the driver's name) jerked the wheel, driving off the thoroughfare, coasting the sportscar of screaming girls to a full off-road stop.

I didn't know the sad details of how my friends had been tormented in the many years before I knew them, but I knew they had—no oddball Oklahoma kid hadn't. It was, in part, the perpetual ridicule that had banded us together. We knew the girls weren't injured, the car hadn't crashed or flipped or exploded, it only stopped. There are few defenses against the invincibly ignorant; we felt we'd found one. For the rest of the drive we celebrated, we loudened the music and laughed till we thought our ribs might snap. We thought we might travel the interstate looking for cheerleaders and other troublemakers, 'Satan's Flamers' would be a good name for a vigilante highway gang, we decided. Oblivious to Columbine and Stoneman Douglas and all the epizootic shootings that would bloody the roads ahead, it was good to share a moment of revenge. I was happy too because Kiki and I were alike. Without words, without hesitation, we both went for our guns; Kiki was fearless and so I knew I was too. From now on when I was physically provoked—assaulted as lone Oklahomos often are—I would rise up. Without words, without hesitation, I would attack from all angles, *Crouching Tiger, Hidden Drag Queen* style, unleashing a tasmanian cyclone of fists and knees and teeth. (Some day I may thank my mother for this particular trait; she gave my sister a car, and probably gave me an appreciation for shag haircuts, the capacity to binge on revenge, and the potential for incautious courage. But today wasn't that today, today I gave credit to Kiki.)

We drove around Custer's and parked in the rear. Liz knew they left the back door unlocked to carry loads of empty boxes to the dumpster. We would hide in the storage room, she explained, until she could hear who was working (one employee had been in the military and she thought he would rush us—armed or not; if he was there we would abort.) We pulled pantyhose from our pockets, tugged them over our brightly colored heads, and entered the building. We found hiding spots—each of us tucked between the room's many empty boxes—and we listened to the muffled voices in the next room.

Maybe it was fear, maybe it was nerves still acute from the highway incident, or maybe it was the humor of seeing each other with stocking-squished faces—the nylon legs flopping like dog ears at the sides of our heads, whatever the reason, we had a moment of shared clarity and we laughed loudly and uncontrollably, we were ridiculous. "Who's back there?" someone yawped from the showroom floor. Liz's big round eyes popped forward, pushing perfect spheres into her hosiery mask, Kiki pumped her rifle as if readying an imaginary bullet, then we all jumped from hiding spots—toppling stacks of boxes—and barreled for the back door. We ran to our car and sped away. That was Wednesday.

Friday, near 3 A.M.

"Turn right, up here."

"Where?"

"Here!" Scooter grabs the wheel; the car swerves accordingly. A car honks, Liz punches Scooter in the arm.

"Oww!"

"Don't touch my fucking steering wheel."

"Sorry, I'm hungry."

"We're all hungry."

"What about here?" I ask from the back seat, hungry too, but half-hoping the answer will be no.

"Pull in over there," Scooter points to the small parking lot of a business that is too unlit to identify. Liz listens, and we glide into the empty lot with the hot lights of her conspicuously orange car already doused. Talklessly, we look through a wire fence into the windows of an insomniatic neighbor; on this dark street, their fluorescent-lit glass glows like the last ember in an abandoned fire pit. "I forgot my glasses."

"Did you forget the gun too?" (Crime makes Scooter bitchy, so does hunger and housework and mornings and laundromats and drag…)

"Fuck off."

"Stop it, both of you."

I reach into my jacket, the gun's still there.

"Should I keep the car running?" Liz asks.

"Yeah. We'll be fast." Scooter opens his door. Mine requires the twist of a wrench and takes a little longer.

The walk from our parking lot and across the neighboring lot is over before it began, as if sprinted by someone who hadn't a clue he was capable of olympic speed. Scooter opens the glass door before I remember to ask about a plan, I don't know what to do.

"Good morning," a middle-aged mexican lady says, she is short and plump, offering the kind of smile that can only be summoned by the thanklessly overworked.

Scooter walks to the counter then bends forward as if studying the sweet contents of its glass case. "What are you getting?" he asks me, demanding that I play my part.

"This looks good," I say, gesturing toward a donut of some variety.

"Jou wan this?"

"Umm maybe. I'm not sure."

Scooter shoots me a "make up your mind look," his wonky eye burrowing bullets into my indecision.

"Yeah, I'll take that one."

"Wait!" the little lady in the paper hat insists, "I have fresh, jou wait, I get fresh."

Yes, I would very much like to wait.

Scooter doesn't though; when the donutress turns and walks into the gut of her bakery he jumps the counter. He's now on the employee side of it, poking fingers into the register. "Do it!" he barks.

It, is point the gun. I point the gun. I point it at the woman.

"Don't" she says, as if I might shoot her, "please don't."

I look at the face of the startled woman; she looks at the barrel of the unloaded gun. Then I see her feet, sensible shoes inching backward, half-stepping toward the back door. "Don't move," I insist, but she doesn't listen, maybe she doesn't realize she's moving, her wide eyes are fixed on the gun but her frightened feet have a plan of their own. "Don't move," I say again, shouting now, "Get On The Floor!"

This time she hears me, her feet hear me. She looks at me and I look at her; she looks like my grandmother, my father's mother. My grandma's english was barely that. She called me *mijo* and made tortillas from scratch. Her house was small but pretty, it seemed a shrine to a painting of weeping Jesus that loomed large at the end of a dark hall. Some nights I'd sleepwalk from my sleepingbag bed to the end of that hall, to urinate into a potted plant at the bottom of the shrine; secretly she must have thought me a demon. If she's watching now then she knows she was right.

"Listen to me. We're not gonna hurt you, I swear to God, we just need the money and we're leaving, I promise. Lay on the floor and don't get up until we're gone. Okay?" I say these words in a softer voice, so that she might think a nice person has her at gunpoint.

"Okay," the woman says in a language recently learned. She eases herself to the ground, as if on bad knees, "okay, mijo."

"Grab those," Scooter yells, about a tray of donuts, his hands busied with the register's money drawer. I take the tray and we reverse-hop the counter, we run out the door and across a lot and into Liz's car. She peels out of the parking lot, as best as an unmaintained 1970s VW bug can, then drives too fast down a short road and onto a long highway.

"Did you get it?"

"Yeah."

"How much?"

"I don't know."

"Fifty? Five hundred? How much?"

"Just drive."

"Hey…"

"What?"

Liz's big eyes are theatrically lit by her rear view mirror, "Don't look, but…is that…a cop?"

Scooter and I twist exorcist style, our faces immediately inflame in a patrol car's headlights.

"What do I do? Shit! What do I do?"

Scooter and I shove money and donuts under the seats, no

151

cop would think to look there.

"What's he doing?"

"I don't know, just be cool."

"I'm getting off the highway!"

"No, that's suspicious, just drive."

An exit approaches, Liz swerves the car to meet it, the cop car follows.

"He's still behind us. Fuck! He's still behind us."

"Go into a neighborhood…we'll pull into a driveway and turn off the lights."

"You think we're gonna lose a cop, in this piece of shit?"

"If my car's such a piece a shit then why didn't you drive?"

"At least my car has oil."

"What's he doing?"

"He's still there."

"Should we eat the donuts?"

"There's like twenty donuts."

"How are we gonna explain twenty donuts?"

"I can't eat, I'll puke."

"There's a stop sign, should I run it?"

"Stop. Just stop."

We stop at the sign. The cop arrives a second later, his siren sounds and his lights ignite, showering us in criminal colors, our faces horrify as if the sirens have alerted us to some radioactive breech. The cruiser drives past us and speeds off, into the road ahead.

At home we count the money, eighty-seven dollars. Liz and Scooter smoke a joint to settle themselves, I hate pot—I am unsettled. I eat a donut but it isn't sweet. It's the least sweet donut I've ever eaten. I follow Liz into the bedroom.

"How was it?" she asks.

"Not like I thought it would be."

"No?"

"I thought it'd be cool, you know, like Patty Hearst robbing a bank."

"She's hot."

"I don't wanna take guns any more."

"Were you scared?"

"*She* was."

"The lady?"

"Yeah."

That wasn't the end of our crime spree, but it was the beginning of a policy that formally forbade the toting of guns.

I told Joe-Ann none of this; aside from statutory sex I imagine she had no interest in crime. She and Phyllis drove Scooter and me home from the bar. The middle-aged drag queens told us about their long, cross-dressed careers. Phyllis had been doing drag for fifteen years, Joe-Ann for twelve. They were celebrities in Oklahoma's gay bars from Giddyuptown to Cowboy City. They lived comfortably off moneys made from squeezing into Outsize Outlet's shiniest evening dresses and working only a few nights each week.

"First place gets two hunnerd dollars," Joe-Ann told us, "second place gets a hunnerd. If ya don't like it—you can just chalk it up ta experience, but if ya like it..."

"*and* if you're good at it," Phyllis interjected, about the weekly amateur drag contest at Yellow Brick Road that, with their help, they were sure we could win.

"and if yer *good* at it, then we could help ya get more shows."

Scooter could dance—he danced constantly, incessantly. And he loved attention, annoyingly so. "Don't make me do this by myself," he pleaded (in the guise of a command), "you know you need the money."

"I can get money," I lied, "I'm gonna get a job."

"Where? You're like nine years old, who's gonna hire you?"

"I've had a job before."

"Oh please, your mother was the manager. No one's gonna hire you with that hairdo. Maybe if you wear a hat. Be a chef, they wear hats. How about a beekeeper. Or a Pope, are you gonna be a Pope?"

Truth was, Scooter was right. I had no idea how I would make money, I had tried nothing and was already out of ideas. "I could use the money I guess."

"Shit yeah, a hundred dollars."

"I thought it was two hundred," I corrected.

"The *winner* gets two hundred dollars. I've seen you dance, you better budget for a hundred-dollar paycheck."

"You're a dick."

"Tell you what," he negotiated, "if you do this with me I promise I'll fix you up with Jimmy." (Jimmy was Scooter's sidekick some weekends. He was tall and prissy and kind of a tease. Sometimes, as a joke, he acted like a stripper who was giving me a lap dance.) "Okay," I said, "I'll do it."

Phyllis hit it off with Scooter immediately—both were bitchy queens. Without the formality of a baptism, circumstance decided she would be his drag mother, and Joe-Ann mine. That night in our squatted apartment, new drag-mother Phyllis Cheesesteak put make-up on her new drag-daughter Scooter for the very first time. And Sloppy Joe-Ann—my inappropriately amatory drag-mother— put make-up on me. "This is pink powder," she explained, "you make this face," (looking like she had a sour penis in her mouth), "and then dust it onto the balls of your cheek."

"You mean like this," I asked, mimicking the face.

"That's perfect," she proclaimed—as if I'd just mastered the

Speak & Spell, rewarding me with a kiss on the forehead.

When our powdery new faces were complete we stood together and tiptoed them to the bathroom mirror, to see ourselves for the very first time. There is a ubiquitous truth about gay boys and drag. All I have known (and I have known many: from the stringy-haired, hook-nosed swamp witch to the clown-faced queen with make-up so harsh it looks like a second-grader drew it), all were resplendent in their own eyes. "My eyes are so smoky and symmetrical, what straight man could deny them?" she wonders. "My skin, it makes porcelain seem crude—like something you'd hammer into pots and pans; and I honestly had no idea I had these cheekbones, I swear they've been injected with something! I am radiant," she thinks, "not like light, but like goodness itself." But, having said that, *I was really pretty*. Scooter was pretty too, but I was resplendent.

My drag-sister and I stayed in the bathroom mirror, frozen like Narcississys, until we were pulled away. We hugged our proud new drag-mothers and promised them we would get wigs and costumes in time to perform in the amateur contest at Yellow Brick Road, just two weeks away.

Scooter and I went to bed in our professionally painted faces (art isn't something you wash down a drain.) From floortop mattresses we talked about the songs we might lipsync. He decided Klymaxx was a good choice for him, and that Nina Hagen was a terrible choice for me. I said I'd give it some more thought. Scooter's new drag name would be Fabrielle Fontaine, or maybe Cristal Von Cartier. For mine, I was leaning toward Motherfucker Teresa, or Lieutenant Betty Valentine.

The next day we went shopping. We tried on a dozen outfits—lamé dresses and fluffy fur coats, exciting the salesgirl each time we added another "I think I'll take this one" to the pile. Once our piles were as hard to carry as bales of hay, and the salesgirl re-insisted, "Why don't I take some of those to the counter for you," Scooter screamed "Now!"

An expression of terror was shared by everyone in the room, then we ran our loot out the front door. The short-legged sales girl ran behind us—the clomp of her clogs pounding the pavement like a running of the bulls, and then she stopped to breathe and to scream:

"Come back here you fucking faggots!"

Unfortunately for her, running is a sport all smalltown gay boys mastered, especially those whose ruses were as short on the nuances of sophistry and chicanery as ours were. So, arms full, we ran to the next block where an excited Liz revved her VW Bug's engine and opened its doors. We jumped in, burned rubber, as best as her old bug could.

I'd like to say we felt guilty about the things we stole—the dresses, the gloves, the shoes—and that we didn't run home and model our new outfits like six-year-old finalists in the Glitzy Miss beauty pageant at the Tampa Ramada; I'd like to say we didn't go 'shopping' at the wig store later that night.

We'd been to the wig store twice before, but never after dark. Last time I tried on a dozen of the brunettes and Scooter tried most of the longer blondes—shifting the little chinese lady's voice from sharp to shrill when we didn't purchase.

"Why try so many you no buy?"

"We're just browsing," we apologized.

It looks different at night though, scarier. For all we know the little chinese lady sleeps on a cot in the back room, waiting for desperate drag queens to crash through the front window. And we are in drag (we thought it best to try the wigs with make-up on, and in a dress), wearing temporary wigs we bought at the Salvation Army (mine is missing some hair in the back and Scooter's smells like a fishtank.) He parks his car in front of the store; it's a part of town without much night traffic so we hope no one will see. I look into the store's front window, trying to remember which wigs are my favorite, but the closed store is lit only by streetlight so it's hard to be sure. I wonder if the chinese wig lady is crouched in the blackened corners inside, a throwing star in each hand.

The sound of Scooter's trunk startles me, it sounded like a chinese lady cocking the hammer of her old war pistol. He pulls out the barbell and gives it to me.

"You do it, you're dressed better for it," Scooter says, wearing a butterfly-shaped sequin top and a pair of black tights—they match the black gloves that cover most of his hairy forearms, a headband holds his blond hair on because the wig's elastic cap is all stretched out. I'm wearing a fluffy waist length fur coat and a black vinyl mini skirt that looks like alligator and smells like a tire, and silver shoes that don't really match. My black wig reminds me of Cleopatra, if she were missing a chunk from the back.

"How am *I* dressed better for it?" I ask.

"Because you have a coat on [I suppose that's true, it is kind of cold]. Besides, I drove."

There are black metal security bars over the store's glass door, so I'll have to break the display window instead. One of the wigs I want is there—I hope the falling glass won't damage it. With both hands on the barbell, I give the window a tap, then another. "Are you serious," Scooter interrupts, "Girl, you're gonna have to do it a lot harder than that."

"I'm just feeling it out," I explain.

I take a nervous breath and thrust the barbell into the window like a sword into a dragon's belly. A spider-shaped crack instantly appears, we both look behind us to see if anyone is watching.

"Again," Scooter says.

I hit the window a second time and a large piece of glass—the size of a frying pan—falls to the ground.

"Again!" Scooter screams, as though I were bashing some masked assailant who'd just tried to rape us.

I reel back and hit a third time, a few more frying pans drop and then a piece as big and loud as a garbage can lid. I strike harder and again, throwing Scooter into a tizzy. "Do it Girl! Do it!" she screams, like an illegal dragracer's frenzied girlfriend cheering from the sideline. I swing the bar—batting the top of the window, the glass collapses like sides of glaciers crashing into the ocean; the sound is deafening.

"Girl you did it," Scooter squeals as I tap the last shard to the ground, high praise from my bitchy friend.

That night we played with make-up and teased and styled our new hair. Scooter gave me a dress for my vinyl mini skirt; I liked the skirt but didn't mind, it just looked better on her. Then we practiced lip-syncing until we fell asleep on fluffy piles of new clothes, each cradling an armload of black or blond synthetic hair wigs like proud mothers nursing shiny-coated litters of precious transgendered puppies.

CHAPTER 10

All the Fixin's

I thought: if I had worn a dress, or maybe if I brought more friends.

Scooter brought Jimmy and two girls from his hometown, they stood in front and were really loud. All three yelled for me too, but maybe without using their voices, and when they clapped for me it looked like their hands might not be connecting; Joe-Ann said queens were ruthless, but I didn't think he meant Scooter. Still, if I couldn't win first place I was glad he did, we were drag-sisters so his success spoke well of my bloodline. I did win a hundred dollars for second place, not bad for a night of work.

"You were so amazing, I can't believe you didn't win first place."

Liz was right, I should have won. "I think Scooter told Jimmy and those two girls not to yell for me."

"Oh my god, that fucking dick, that *fucking* dick."

"Yeah, but alotta people clapped for me, huh."

"Totally. I was screaming; did you see me?"

A lot of people did clap for me. When I walked out—before the music started, wearing only black pumps, a pair of lace pantyhose, a dance belt, and a man's dress shirt tied in a knot in the front—everyone seemed a little confused. But then when I sat down the big boom box—the one we stole from Saddle Burger—and pushed the button and "Fame" started to play...I think they totally got it. Anyone can just come out and lip-sync, but this was conceptual, like I was Irene Cara auditioning for a Broadway show. It was probably too avant-garde for first place, I decided.

Phyllis and Joe-Ann were right: no one ID'd me. When Scooter and I said we were there for the show, the tough-looking lesbian at the front door just pointed us to the dressing room. The same thing happened at other bars too, by the end of the month we'd high-heel it into a bar like we were storming an embassy. Some bars had amateur drag contests two or four times a month—we entered all of them, and within a couple of months we were booking regular paid shows. Liz got a job too, at McDonalds, so (after they padlocked the door of the apartment we'd been squatting, and we cut through the thin part of the back kitchen door with a serrated knife to rescue our clothes) we got our own place. Liz was underage, and me—more so, so her dad cosigned. "This is the last thing I'm doing for you," he warned, "and I'm only doing it for your mother." Some of our friends stayed with us too, but the place was really Liz's and mine.

Our apartment building lived on the edge of a half-dozen residential streets, each with houses that were much nicer than our unit would suggest. Our place was fine but the houses on the neighboring streets were stately old brick behemoths, two and three stories tall. At night we'd walk up and down the sidewalk, admiring our new neighborhood—its big houses and old money—pretending we were a part of it. One house had wrought iron chairs and a matching grey marble-topped table sitting on its front porch, we thought how nice it would be to sit there in the morning, drinking coffee.

"Do you think we could carry the chairs?" Liz asked. We could. And a little later that night we carried the table too.

"You know this is wrong," she huffed, as we stumbled away with the heavy marble table, "we should put it back."

"You're only saying that because it's heavy."

"And these are our neighbors."

"Larceny is the greatest form of flattery."

"I don't think that's how the saying goes."

"This isn't about you."

"I'm sorry, I was being selfish."

Most of the houses had furniture on their porches, as if the families had more wealth than their giant homes could contain. Many porches ran the entire length of the front or side of the big old structures, often enclosed but always unlocked. Around two or three A.M. we'd drive Liz's old orange bug, park a few houses down, walk up to a porch and take what we wanted. Glass side tables, brass planters, the painted bust of a young woman with long tendrils of cement hair. We took a rattan sofa from one house (our friend Wally and I had to run alongside the car to keep it from sliding off the top), and a large potted plant, then we went back to the house next door. It was one of the largest houses, scaled in blackish-brown shingles and buttressed with brick columns that seemed stout enough to withstand a canon blast from the Northern Union. The red brick was nearing black too—the color of canned beets in heavy juices. The doors and shuttered windows were white wood, not bright white, but white artfully airbrushed with decades of mercurial dirt. The side of the house clutched a screened porch in the grasp of its powerful brick columns, the enclosure was as big as our entire apartment. We peeked through the screen first. "Look at that carved table," we said, "look at those floral chairs!"

The screen door was unlocked, which was surprising given the copious treasures inside. This porch was carpeted with old rugs and full of furniture and pillows, even a desk, there was a candelabra and books on a big low table. It was dark and hard to see but the furniture seemed less outdoorsy than the wrought iron and wicker things we'd found outside other homes. "This kinda seems like the *inside* of a house," I whispered, "are you sure it's a porch?"

"It's a porch, but we never open the windows," a voice answered that was neither Liz's nor Wally's.

"Have you got a light?" it asked.

"Yeah," Liz answered, with a nervous chuckle, handing over her Bic.

The girl was about Liz's age—sixteen or seventeen, sitting in the middle of a sofa, lighting a cigarette and lit by lighter light, and wearing a loose nightgown that floated several inches above her knees. Liz looked at me with eyes widened as if to say "Oh My God," (not *Oh My God we've been caught*, but *Oh My God she's cute*). The shiny-haired girl took two puffs then dropped the still lengthy cigarette into an empty glass. She spit on it and we were all quiet enough to hear the sizzle. "I'm going to bed," she said, standing from the couch and walking toward an open doorway, "take the floral chairs, I don't like them."

"We can do that," Liz answered.

"Have you got any pot?" the girl asked from the doorway. Liz rushed to her, pulling a joint from her cigarette pack and presenting it to her in an upturned palm, a tip of a head, and a little bend of the waist—like an eighteenth-century gentleman presenting trinkets to a lady.

We decorated our new apartment, we didn't just furnish it— we decorated it. I had been decorating my rooms since I was in the seventh grade, working at Saddle Burger. I'd spent the summer watching soap operas and was inspired when Dorian Lord Callison redecorated her *One Life To Live* Llanview penthouse, giving the daytime program its first modern interior. I took my burger earnings to the mall and bought colorful glass vases, two geometric art prints, and the abstract bust of a woman's head. My mom said they were very nice, but the restrained enthusiasm revealed disappointment that her twelve-year-old son hadn't returned with a football-shaped tablelamp and a Babe Ruth/"The Sultan of the Swat" bedspread. I told Liz I wanted this apartment to be mysterious, witchy. I loved Stevie Nicks on the cover of her *Bella Donna* LP, draped in a cascading kaftan of white gossamer—like the hippie granddaughter of the Bride of Frankenstein. I imagined her mountaintop mansion would be trussed in fabrics too, with lamps and chairs and even the coffeemaker swathed in chiffon throws or fringy shawls. Like Gizi's house.

A few years ago, when mom was still married to Norm (in our Puddin Foot "farm" house with the June bugs and tarantulas), there was a dilapidated shack behind our property. I was never sure where our property ended—there was no fence. I found it one day when I took two of our dogs to a creek behind our house, about ten minutes into the large area of woods and overgrowth that extended from our back porch to infinity. The creek was a little trickle of water running through large flat slabs of boulder, on semi-warm days the rocks heated from the sun and felt good on my skin. While the dogs drank the creek and hiked the rocks, I lay on a particularly inviting slab of stone, dropped my pants, and masturbated to the thought of Decker—my sister's boyfriend. Maybe I thought about how his jeans looked as he bent over to pet Edwina, or about his eyeteeth that sat higher in his gumline (which I saw only when he smiled because he was happy to see me). This was before we slept together so I didn't know how happy to see me he really was.

After I finished I pulled up my pants and called the dogs and we headed back toward the house. We walked forty, maybe fifty feet when Edwina turned and barked. I turned too and saw a tall man with his back to me, standing at the edge of the trees only twenty feet up the creek from the slab of rock I had just molested. I recognized the shirt, the corduroy pants—it was my stepfather Norm. And if he had been standing in that spot, facing that direction for two minutes or more…he had watched. Edwina barked again and my mother's new husband turned around and began walking toward our house. Surely he heard my dog bark, surely he saw me standing there, but he never turned his head the forty-five degrees to face us. He never waved. He only walked, mechanically, toward the house. I froze for a moment—imagining what he would tell my mother—and then I ran full-speed in the opposite direction. I ran back to the creek, over it, and into the woods that lay beyond. I had never gone into the woods on the far side of the creek, not knowing where our property ended I just imagined the creek to be the property line. But if Norm was going to tell my mom that I traipsed around the open countryside—masturbating on innocent trees and unsuspecting rocks—then I didn't want to be there.

Edwina found the shack, barking me and Milton (our beagle) to her location. Milton barked too, in his effeminate manner; Edwina rolled her eyes as if to say, "you bark like a cat." The dilapidated two or three-room shanty was surrounded by gnarled trees, and thick with overgrowth. The walls had the strange prickly texture of old, sunbaked paint that had begun a slow curly peel away from the underlying barnwood—as if a persistent magnet were trying to suck the lead pigment from the exhausted paint. The room on the left side had no doors and was missing its roof, allowing decades of rain to rot a seven by seven-foot hole into the floor below. Edwina continued barking at the hole, into an underground storm cellar that was filled with feet of stagnant rainwater and was now more of a well. Frogs lived in it, and Edwina and I thought we saw something larger…maybe a leviathan.

"If that dawg falls in you'll have a helluva time fisheen'm out."

I looked up, startled by the unfamiliar voice. An elderly woman wrapped in a shawl stood in the doorway, a dead rabbit in her hand. "That yer dawg?" she asked, in a primitive Oklahoma twang.

"Yes, ma'am. Is this your house?" I asked, though not really sure it was anybody's house.

"Yep, fer now anaway. Yer dawg like rabbit?" she swung the dead thing for Edwina to smell.

"I guess so," I answered, "I don't think she ever saw a rabbit before."

"You live aroun' here?"

"Yeah, I live on the other side of the creek."

"Then she saw a rabbit before."

"I guess so," I conceded. "What happened to your roof?"

"Twister got it," she (Gizi, it was a hungarian name) said, "took my chickeens too."

Though we had moved to Puddin Foot almost a year ago, this was the first neighbor I'd met, in fact hers was the first house I had seen on these dirt-roaded outskirts of our small town.

Gizi had a husband and a son. She was married to a russian man who died of cancer a quarter-century earlier, but she was certain he died of a 'broked heart'. I don't remember if it was my first or my second visit to the little, black-haired woman's house when I asked about her son.

"My daddy's daddy's daddy come from Hungary. *Mitya,* that were my husband's name, you know like nice-ta-*meetya,* he were a Rusky. His name, *Mitya,* it meaned sumbuddy that love th'Earth, n'my mama liked that. Mama'n her mama'n her mama were all practitioners—you know what I means, they practicioned at wershippin the Earth'n the Mist'n the Moss'n stuff like that—ya know what I means?"

I nodded, to be polite.

"Course you duz. Anaway, Mitya were a Rusky'n moved to America, near Blackburn, aftern the war. I lived near Blackburn too'n we met'n got married in 1948, I mean '49, no '48," she decided, after a quick calculation on most of her fingers. "That nex year we had a lil baby, a lil boy. Mitya, he were a cordwainer by profession, so we packed'n moved to Fort Prairie'n he opent a cordwainery'n we lived upsterz. Sumtime, 'bout that time, Mitya's new customer dint like his shoes. Mitya give'm his money back'n the man tooked it. An' then three'r four days later folks'n the shop nex door says the man told'm my Mitya were a Commie."

"What's a commie?" I asked.

"You know—a Communist, becuz he's a Rusky. This were about the time'n Russia tested the A-bomb'n Truman'n McCarthy was tellin everone Ruskys was unamerican. Anaway, people started ta askin if we wuz commies, n'then one night sumbuddy throwed a mason a gasoline through our winda. We wuz asleep, n'when Mitya woke up the fire were already half up the sterz. He tried ta woke me'n the baby but he couldn't stir us. He curried the baby downsterz'n comed back'n curried me. Burnt my arm."

Gizi pulled the shawl from her shoulder to show me the marbled skin that was peeking out the sleeve of her shirt.

"We never did woke the baby."

"Do you mean he died?" I asked.

"Yup," she answered, the sadness of the word polluting her casual expression.

Without much money, Gizi and Mitya fled Fort Prairie, into the barely populated Puddin Foot hills. The little house was three rooms then, before the tornado took the roof off the second bedroom. She said her husband was diagnosed with cancer just a year later, and then he died soon after. But Gizi knew it was the sadness for his dead son that killed him. That was the first time she used the things her mother had taught her—she asked the Earth to set things right with the person or persons who threw the mason jar through their window. She cast other spells too. Ten years later she hex'd Byron De La Beckwith after the court failed to convict him for the murder of Medgar Evers. And two months ago she hoodoo'd Crow Hop County's building code enforcement for trying to condemn her house.

From the outside Gizi's house looked like something that should be condemned. And the roofless room with the rotted floor and cellar full of water smelled like an outhouse, or maybe that was the smell of the outhouse. But the other two rooms, though small and crude, had a beauty about them. They were full of things that looked like somebody had made them. The dish strainer had wood pegs—all of them different, and the tablecloth had a pocket from where it used to be a dress or an apron. There were stacks of quilts, Gizi made them and sold them in town at the Country Rendezvous. Pieces of not-yet-used fabric lay on half of the room's available surfaces: the chairs, a plant trolley, the foot of the bed. Cottons with tiny flowers (maybe old bedsheets) cozied the top and sides of a small Frigidaire, burlap from old feed sacks hung on a hutch and others were positioned as little carpets on the floor. Delicate rectangles of old brown and beige laces clung to lampshades like giant moths seduced by the light.

I told Gizi about my mother and her new husband, and how much I wished they would break-up. "We never spend any time together because Norm is always there," I complained, telling her that when Mom and I talked—he had to listen, and when I kissed her goodnight—he'd stare at me like I was out of line. "Even on Mother's Day," I explained, "I wanted to give her my present in private but they sat on the couch with his arm around her the whole day." My new friend said she didn't think it was right that someone would come between a boy and his mother, "A boy needs his mama'n a mama needs her boy," and that she would say a little prayer about it later that night.

It was a couple of weeks later that the swarm of June bugs besieged our dining room window, and a month after that when they left and Mom kneed Norm in the testicle and told him *it was over*. The next day I ran to Gizi's shack, I hadn't seen her for most of the summer but had to know if it was her bewitchment that ended my mother's marriage. When I got there the house was gone. The hole in the floor was still there, and next to it was a pile of rubble. I guessed the building code enforcement had condemned the place, and knocked it down. I kicked around the debris and found some pieces of a quilt, which I kept, and an old photo of Gizi—she looked years younger but it was her. I took the photo too, and the next day I went back and left a note in a zip lock bag, weighted by a stone at the edge of the rubble. THEY'RE GETTING A DIVORCE, it said, THANK YOU.

After Liz and I finished decorating our new apartment, we called my mom. My mother spent Sundays at my grandparents' house, sun tanning in the warmer months and making dinner for them in the colder ones. It had been a year since I left home and I hadn't seen my mom in about as long, I wanted to invite her and my nana to come for a visit.

"Giddyuptown's a forty-minute drive and I can't afford to spend the extra money on gas right now," she explained, "they're predicting oil prices could skyrocket with the troubles in the middle east."

Since my mother hadn't had to feed me for the past year, I wondered why she couldn't use some of the money she'd saved on groceries to buy a tank of gas. "Okay," I said, "maybe you can come next year." Mom gave the phone to my grandma.

"Chris, is that you?"

"Hi Nan."

"Are ya bein' haved, Chris?"

"I'm behaving, Nan."

Nana told me she and Arlis (her husband) were having new friends over for Thanksgiving dinner. The holiday guests were a respected couple in Puddin Foot, they owned the local appliance store and were once given a plaque from the Maytag corporation. (When I was younger my nana would introduce me to her friends with a "Chris is an Ar-*Teest* [artist], show em' somethin' Chris,"…"Like what Nan?"…"Nevermind him, he's shy.")

"Chris, why don't you come too," she invited, "when's the last time you had a home-cooked meal?"

"Long time."

"And bring Liz if you want. Do ya wanna come?"

"Yeah…" I hesitated, reluctant to return to a town that suddenly felt like a south american prison I'd escaped, "yeah, I do."

"Well do ya really, or do ya?"

"No, I do. I'll bring Liz too. It'll be fun."

We had another friend living with us, I explained. "Bring him too," Nana said, "tell him we're having turkey and stuffing and all the fixin's."

Thanksgiving day, Liz and Wally and I woke early—excited to be expected somewhere. Liz wore make-up (something she rarely did), and I wore a hat (something I never did). Mom said my grandparents' new friends were old-fashioned and asked if I wouldn't mind doing something with my hair so I piled most of it into a newsy cap. Wally slicked his mohawk back (something he did for job interviews), and he and I wore vintage ties that we bought for the occasion.

On the ride to Puddin Foot I told my friends that my mom was a terrific cook, "I hope she made a peach cobbler, I swear it's the best thing you ever tasted." Neither of them had parents that wanted them home for the holiday; we all agreed that my family was pretty cool.

It was strange driving into the little town where I had gone to junior high. We drove past the Saddle Burger where I used to work, and a few blocks that way was the trailer where I peeped a couple having sex. "That's my old house right there," I pointed to the place where we rented the back room to Saddle Burger Rodney. If we turned left and followed the curve we'd pass by Decker Abbott's old house, where I spent the night with my sister's ex-boyfriend.

We pulled into my grandparents' gravel driveway, their petite house whiter and more welcoming than I remembered. Lace curtains gussied the front window, a garnish of bushes along the porch hadn't been there before. Liz reinforced her lipstick—smacking her lips without really knowing why, and I rearranged the portion of my black hair that stuck out the front of my cap. Wally fumbled with a pumpkin pie.

"Should I hand this to your mom or to your grandma?" he asked as we unfolded from Liz's little car.

"I don't know, my mom I guess."

"Which one's your mom?" Wally persisted.

"The hot one," Liz answered.

"Don't be gross," I warned.

I knocked on the front door, and we three straightened ourselves and shared a quick 'this is it' look—knowing it would be several hours before we could be ourselves again.

My mother opened the door wide and I saw a group huddled in the kitchen—hovering like co-workers around a birthday cake, or anyone who knows a feast is nearby; *This will be fun,* I thought. Then she stepped forward a bit—into the doorway, blocking our entry. Not smiling or reaching to hug me, just standing.

"I thought you were doin' somethin' about your hair," she said, without a 'hello' to me or my washed and combed friends.

"I wore a hat," I answered, pointing to my head.

Mom stood a moment—her in the house, us on the porch— saying nothing. Then she stepped back, but only to close the door just inches from the brim of my newsy cap. It wasn't a slam, just a dispassionate shut, as if she had turned away an unwanted salesman. I stood another moment, staring at the closed door, uncertain what had happened. I looked at my friends who only reflected my confused expression. And then I remembered: the childhood prank calls my mom instigated to my unsuspecting grandmother, causing her to faint in front of my aunt June-Ida . . . and her winter morning dares, "Chris, I'll give you five dollars if you jump in the cold swimming pool" . . . and how she chased me and Mona through the house, tossing lit matches at us while we laughed and screamed.

Mom was joking. Oh my god, she totally got me. I knocked again.

"What!" she said, in a tone usually reserved for a boyfriend just before she slapped or otherwise humiliated him (like when she answered the phone and it was Bucky with the odd teeth calling for the third time in an evening, after the novelty of dating a black man had worn off). This time Mom had opened the door only six inches, but the contempt in her eyes was unmistakable, it was no joke. I said nothing and only stared—me at her and her at me—until something that felt like a gas-bubble (or some other flux that I wouldn't have expected until after the meal) ascended my chest and catapulted itself past my teeth and gums. YOU FUCKING BITCH.

The words hung in the mesh of the screen door, like smelly cheese stuck in a grater. We paused for a moment—staring at it, wondering how it would ever come clean.

CHAPTER 11

Frank Anne

If I drink the rest of the tea then I can piss in the empty container. But then I won't have anything left to drink. I hadn't even heard anyone since yesterday so maybe I should ration the rest. I decided to take another look around, maybe I missed something—an old vase or a bowl.

Under a plastic cat cage—the kind you'd take on an airplane, a box labeled PIX & PAPERS hooked my eye. I couldn't urinate in it but thought it might pass some time. *So this is what they look like*, I thought, *that must be her mom*. She was pretty, but looked like someone who wouldn't hesitate to call the police. A photo of her brother, I assumed, wearing swim trunks and sitting in a deck chair, *there's no way I'm not taking this*. I peeled the cellophane from the page and plucked the photo—had the thought that it was wrong— then decided it wouldn't be in a box in the attic if anyone really cared about it. I looked around some more, found a thermos, it smelled faintly of coffee. I unzipped and pointed myself inside its narrow metallic interior. It filled quickly, *I can't believe how little a big thermos holds*, I pondered, and also, *the next person who stows-away up here will think that the thermos 'smelled faintly of urine'*.

I took the photo album back to my sleeping bag and box of crackers. Opened it, saw an elementary school portrait of Kiki wearing a plaid blouse with lace trim. A piece of ribbon tied in a bow around her neck, under the collar. She looks like one of the girls in the title sequence of the early episodes of *Facts of Life*, laughing but not getting more than a line or two per episode. "I don't know, Natalie, you better not let Mrs Garret find out," something like that.

Another photo: a string of preteen girls all lined-up for the camera, a great big house behind them (probably this house as seen from the backyard). They're all holding hands, like a chain of paper dolls. Kiki's impossibly shiny black hair is unmistakable, cut in a short bob to the bottom of her ear. It's her birthday; she's wearing a silver paper hat and fighting back a laugh. Her dad is behind them, just to the right, waving to the camera with barbecue tongs. I wondered why anyone with everything would become so insurgent. (Driving here, a cop pulled us over, told Kiki she was doing sixty-five. "That's a fuckin lie," she shouted. The cop stepped back and hovered a hand over a holster. "I'm sorry officer," Kiki added, "I have Tourette's. Faggot!")

I'll take a nap, I decided, *that'll pass some time.*

Liz and I let our friend Felix stay with us. He was a little older than me, maybe sixteen, smart and soft-spoken, with Xymox's mushroomed-out hair and a mortician's buttoned-up wardrobe. He left home when his mother slapped him for saying he was gay; his frail physique and refined manner made her slap sound crude and vulgar. We made-out once on my bed, but nothing else. I'd also once made out with Delta Dyke on my bed. She looked and dressed like Rodney Dangerfield—with a wino's big red eyes and a pudgy face that seemed hand-wrought in clay, as a first draft—and had never kissed a man (she confessed this from the foot of my mattress as I tried to sleep.) Delta was thirty-five—maybe older— and a bouncer at the lesbian bar Yellow Brick Road. She had a crush on Liz (they met when Scooter and I performed at YBR) and would bring us bags of groceries whenever she visited. Nearly everyone in our group had made-out with everyone else at one time or another.

Delta wasn't the first girl I'd kissed, that was Sherie—a bossy stoner with muddy mascara, and thick legs in frayed jeans—who told me, starting Monday, I was her boyfriend. For several weeks the big girl flattened me against a gymnasium wall so we could kiss. She wasn't objectively unattractive, but the tongue-work was misogyny-making, like frenching your grandma (if your grandma wore feather roach clips in her smoky hair). Sometimes Sherie would wipe her lady fingers against my trousers, a fish looking for a worm. She'd rub around a bit, causing my organ to go concave. I probably should have said something to set her straight, but my twelve-year-old tongue hadn't the spine to say that my penis was very gay.

I've had a recurring dream about the pushy girl. In it, she is older and thicker and straddling me like a bull riding a cowboy. As I lay trapped on my back in something like a chicken coop (a John Waters contribution, I'm sure), Sherie's big ass bucks violently up, then displaces a theatrical puff of chicken feathers each time it falls violently back down, her gelatinous jugs tumbling synchronistically. When the dream seems unending I nervously ask "babe, are you close?" to which she always unsucks her dry stoner mouth from a big tumultuous bong to screech, "I Said Tickle My Tits!"

I thought of Sherie while Delta Dyke and I kissed, I believe it's what cured her of any lingering longings for men.

A few weeks after Felix moved in with us his slaphappy mother visited, announcing her arrival with the persistent bang of small knuckles on the apartment door. When Felix refused to leave with the irritatingly knuckled woman she contacted the manager of our building, telling them we were an apartment full of runaways. The following afternoon we found a typed letter taped to our front door.

TO ALL OCCUPANTS IN APARTMENT 37: IT HAS COME TO OUR ATTENTION THAT THERE ARE NO ADULTS LIVING IN THIS UNIT. WE HAVE ALSO HAD NOISE COMPLAINTS AND RUMORS OF TRANSSEXUAL PROSTITUTION. PLEASE VACATE SAID PREMISES BY THE END OF THE MONTH OR WE WILL NOTIFY THE GIDDYUPTOWN SHERIFF'S DEPARTMENT.

Liz was tired of working at McDonald's and considering moving back to Maine to live with her mother, to finish high school. Scooter and I had been driving to Cowboy City once a month to perform at an underage club called Crash Box. "You boys should move here," Phyllis and Joe-Ann told us, "there's lots more money doing drag in 'the City', they *love* drag here."

The Crash Box crowd did love drag, they idolized the performers in the same way the city's butcher kids loved choreographed wrestling and monster trucks. And Phyllis and Joanne were center stage, like Undertaker and Grave Digger in a dress.

Scooter and I had a small following in Giddyuptown, many were friends and we could get shows a few times a week. Only, the crowds were small and so tips were small too. When we drove to Cowboy City to perform at Crash, we'd each make a hundred dollars in tips alone. If it had been three months earlier I wouldn't have considered leaving Giddyuptown, since I had just gone back to high school.

On the first day at my new school I sat in the admissions office, waiting for a printout of my class schedule. Kids pushed against the closed door's large glass window—their faces stacked like british mods in a bright red phone booth. "Oh my god, look at his hair!" or "Hey Rooster!" they'd shout through the glass partition (apparently a mohawk resembles only a rooster to Oklahomans of the 1980s. Why not "Hey Saturn-head" or "Hey Patti-Labelle-when-she-was-in-that-band-with-Nona-Hendryx.")

I was held in the office until third period when the administrator asked a girl to escort me to Geometry. She and I juggled a polite conversation as we traversed the halls, trying not to fumble the chitchat each time a "Cock-a-doodle-doo" was screamed at me down each corridor. At gauntlet's end, my chaperone pointed me to a door; I walked through.

"Yes?"

"I think I'm in this class."

"Yes, I can *see* you so you *are* in the class. Are you supposed to be?"

I reached a schedule in the math teacher's direction; he briefly inspected the paper and assigned me to the room's only open seat. I sat as the teacher stood and walked to my new desk.

"Mister Mudreegull," he mispronounced, "here is your book, please take care of it."

"Thanks," I mumbled, looking down at it to avoid the eye-contact of every student in the room.

"One more thing," he added, "please leave my classroom until tomorrow. I'd like you to go home and wash and comb your hair and come back looking clean and presentable."

I no longer have a true visual recollection of the teacher (sometime in my twenties his voice, his face, his puritanical mannerisms were replaced with the evil Doctor Zachary Smith from TV's *Lost In Space*, so surely there are similarities) but I remember looking from my new textbook to him to ask, "You want me to get up . . . and leave . . . right now?"

"Yes, I certainly do," he replied. "Everyday, I make certain my hair is clean and my outfits are presentable, and my students are conscientious enough to do the same. So, young man, please pick up your things and leave my classroom until you are fit to be around other civilized people."

Every student watched—bug-eyed and silent—as I picked up my notebooks, my class schedule, my things. I handed the math book back to the teacher who still hovered over my desk. "You must feel hopeful now," I said, "berating an already berated student right in front of your class, so everyone can see what a team player you are. Maybe now they'll stop calling *you* fag?" At least that's how I remember saying it—it may have sounded more like "Whatever."

I went to the office and told them what happened, they said they couldn't force teachers to let me into their classes. Two more teachers refused me entrance: the History of Democracy teacher and the Driver's Ed guy. The Art teacher said I could come to his class during those hours so I spent four of my seven periods there. I also stayed in the art room during lunch, after I had a fight with a kid who had been harassing me daily. He'd call me a fag, and this time he punched me in the back of the head while I carried a tray full of needed food. I flew at him like a knife-wielding octopus, a spinning spiral of pseudo judo, landing on top of him—chest to chest—on the ground. With my face hovering two inches over his I closed my eyes and closed the gap, kissing the basher hard and long on the mouth, partly to humiliate him and partly because he was cute (I'd have opened up a can of lick-ass if the crowd had given us some privacy.) An unfamiliar teacher dragged me to an office where the vice-principal instructed me to avoid the lunchroom because the cafeteria monitors complained my appearance was disruptive. So for the next few months I did drag shows three nights a week, came home at 2:00 AM, scrubbed the thirty-year-old woman off my fifteen-year-old face, and then slept until my alarm blurted it was time to get up, get dressed, and pretend I was getting an education. Three months later I admitted I would never graduate taking four hours of art everyday. I quit, and this time for good.

"Hey faggot, wake up." Kiki stood over my sleeping bag, holding a tray of food—soup and a sandwich. "Why are you looking at my photo album, I look like a dick in those pictures."

"You were so cute," I said, "what happened?"

"Cocaine, bitch!"

"Is this your brother?" I asked, showing her the photo of the cute boy on the deck chair.

"That's my cousin, and he's not a fag so forget it."

"Then can I keep the picture, as a consolation?" I bargained.

"If you don't jack-off with it."

I ate my sandwich—dipping it in the bowl of soup—while Kiki searched for split-ends and told me something about her mother thinking she heard a mouse in the attic.

"I'll be quieter," I said, "but it's really boring and I need something to piss in. Can you bring me an empty milk gallon or something? And I'll have to take a number-two soon, I think your cooking's giving me diarrhea."

"Too much information!" Kiki shouted as she climbed down the ladder, disappearing into the attic floor.

After the eviction Liz moved back to her mother's, and Reuben (my boyfriend of four months) and I needed a place to stay. Reuben was dour around my friends and seemed jealous of the attention I got when I performed. (I know only awful people think others are jealous of them so I admit I might be awful, but me aside…that bitch was jealous.)

One of the clubs I worked—a semi-weekly gig at a trashy little underground bar (not just metaphorically, it was below ground, a basement with a disco light) that catered to drunks, punk kids, and transient transsexuals—was one of my favorites. It paid only twenty-five dollars but, in a time when most gay bars expected queens to wear beaded gowns and perform to Barbara Streisand or Diana Ross, it was the only one that didn't mind if I dressed in a spandex jumpsuit and lipsynced to Grace Jones or Nina Hagen (for a broad on a budget, those wardrobes can overlap.)

My friends liked it too, because they never carded, and because it was the only place where people of all ages mingled, and

where people of all sexual orientations could be seen fagging it up at hours long past night. After the weekly shows we'd go to IHOP, taking up two or three tables for an early A.M. pancake breakfast.

"You were amazing," Delphine said, "I can't believe you can dance in those shoes."

Darlice and Delphine were sisters who always came to my shows. We bonded when Geoff Shurte—a wild-eyed kid who spent time in a sanitarium—sprayed us with mace and hit us with a bat. An hour earlier I was performing a duet with the korean queen Señior Rita when jilted Geoff flicked a lit cigarette into Darlice's unnaturally large and largely flammable hair. I jumped off the stage and did a competitive-dance-worthy kick into his scrawny chest (leaving what I am certain is a permanent mark in the shape of the heel of a vintage silver pump). Geoff was known to be a troublemaker, he was quickly debarred and we finished our song. When the club closed (after Paraliza Minnelli sang "New York, New York" from an electric wheelchair) I walked, arms full of make-up and costumes, out the front door and into an unseasonal cloud of defensive spray. Semi-blinded and thoroughly choked, we fought Geoff and his bat and his can of spray until the police came. Afterward, four or five of us went to Delphine's studio apartment to flush the hot pepper from our eyes, the two sisters were regular fixtures at my shows ever since.

"Why didn't Reuben come tonight, where is he?" Delphine asked, though without much concern—she wasn't a fan of my boyfriend. "Home, he had a headache."

We all ordered, about a dozen meals. My new best friend Bonnie and I couldn't decide so we split two orders. Bonnie was a red-haired (tinted to burgundy with vermillion hi-lites) Rubenesque beauty, a faint universe of freckles gave her porcelain skin the allure of a light craquelure, she wore band shirts with stirrup pants and ballet slippers, and she had an old soul (not old like a veteran vampire, but elderly like a sassy grandma). Her maturity was most evident in the sincerity with which she listened to my problems, and made sure I had plenty to eat, and in her unrebelliousness—like when she slathered teenage affection on both her parents in unapologetic gobs. Bonnie fantasized about renting a white horse and riding it into a Stevie Nicks concert—up to the stage, we bonded over our devouring preoccupation with the singer. My friend had a highschool boyfriend but had also been fantasizing about sex with women; pie-curious, I guess you'd say. Halfway through the breakfast Bonnie leaned to me, whispering into my ear.

"_Don't_ look now, but isn't that your red dress sitting at the table behind you?"

Still in drag, I pulled out my compact and pretended to retouch my lipstick—using the mirror to look at the queen sitting at the table behind ours.

She was a sad little thing, knobby and frail, sitting at a table all alone. She glanced from side to side as she sipped soda through a straw—presumably expecting an order but appearing as if waiting for an estranged lover who might never come. The boisterousness of the three tables my friends and I occupied made her solitude seem lonely by comparison. It was odd that she had chosen a table in the restaurant that was so close to ours, not knowing any of us but giving the impression that she wanted to be nearby. She wore a curly black wig, familiar looking, like one of the short frizzy ones I blindly grabbed when Scooter and I broke into the wig shop (one I never wore because it wasn't very pretty). Her make-up was harsh, _first-timer make-up_, I thought, with bright white highlighter on her cheeks and poorly blended raccoon eyes. Her lips were much too dark and unfortunately her heavy blush matched. _No matter_, I thought, _proper make-up wouldn't have helped_—it wasn't a face God had intended for drag. She wore little white gloves, their daintiness made her big bony shoulders seem absurd. The dress though, it was nice. A big, red 1950s tulle prom gown, _my_ prom gown.

"It's Reuben," Bonnie whispered, "oh god, it's Reuben."

I looked again, harder, with less denial.

182

The girls scooted so I could slide out, then hushed as I walked the seven feet from my table to my boyfriend's. The closer I got, the more he twisted his neck, pretending not to notice my approach. Then, "Surprise," he said, facing me with a nervous smile and misaligned eyelash, pretending the crossdress was something he had done for me. "<u>THAT'S</u> <u>MY</u> <u>DRESS</u>", I answered.

That was the first strike against my boyfriend. The second strike: Reuben went out dancing all night while I was bedridden with strep throat—a disloyalty Bonnie and I felt was unforgivable. Then—a month later, after the eviction notice—he and I spent two nights with my sister and her girlfriend Gwenda. The couple lived in a rundown one-bedroom house in Twisterville, Mom suggested I call Mona when I told her we couldn't move into our new apartment until the first of the month. I hadn't spoken with my sister in the year since we both left home, but I called and she agreed we could sleep on her couch for three nights, if I gave her ten dollars per night to cover *electricity and other expenses*. "You'll have to bring your own food," she said, "we don't have any extra." That night we slept on the lumpy sofa of her dirty, cat urine-scented livingroom; the next morning we folded our blankets, speaking only in polite whispers. Gwenda emerged from the bedroom's blanketed doorway first—mumbling an uncomfortable "Hey" as she passed by us on her jostle to the kitchen, then she ran back into the bedroom sharing an excited whisper with my sister. A few minutes later the two large women walked back to the kitchen and slammed some things around.

"Chris, can you come in here please," Mona said in a tone that reminded me of my mother.

"What's up?"

"Did you eat a can of our soup?" she asked, pointing toward Gwenda who was angrily holding an empty can like it was a hidden microphone or a receipt for heroin.

"Nope," I answered, before yelling, "Reuben, did you eat a can of soup?" into the next room.

"I haven't eaten anything," he shouted back.

"Wasn't us."

"Then how did an empty can get into the garbage?" Gwenda asked, tiny beads of perspiration appearing on her mustache.

"Dunno," I said, "but it wasn't us."

"You're a fucking liar," my sister said, "you owe us a dollar."

"IT WASN'T US."

"You need to get out of our fucking house, you thief!" Gwenda ordered.

"You need to get a fucking razor, you monkey-faced bitch!" I replied.

I'm not sure if it was Mona or Gwenda who threw the first punch (I tend to disorient in fights) but I do remember my three hundred pound sister standing behind me, pinning my arms behind my back while her three hundred pound lover punched me in the mouth. Then I remember leaning back into my sister's generous chest for leverage and raising both legs to kick Neanderthal Gwenda in her troglodyke face.

After we left, Reuben told me he ate the can of soup. Strike three.

Without an apartment, without a highschool career, and without a boyfriend I was free to leave when Scooter said he'd leave his parent's house so we could take our drag careers to the next level, Cowboy City. 'Della' (one of the queens who lived in the city and worked at Crash) said we could stay with her and her hag 'Dicksy' until we got a place. So, for almost two weeks—while Scooter prepared himself for our move, I lived at Kiki's parent's house, hidden in the attic like a cross-dressing Anne Frank. *The Diary of Frank Anne*, they'll call it, if they make a musical about that period of my life. Or maybe *Diarrhea Van Frank*, if she doesn't find me a place to do my number-two.

CHAPTER 12

Edge of Sixteen

Five gowns, a leather jacket, a futuristic silver pantsuit. And my 'Stevie' dress—a *mass*, or was it a *mess,* of black chiffon, it needed more jewels sewn to the chest but there would be plenty of time on the road. Three wigs—no four, hip and butt pads, and a robe for the dressing room. Something to arrive in, should be stylish without looking like a costume. And shoes. My boy clothes all fit into a backpack, my girl clothes most definitely would not.

It wasn't what I expected, nothing like the bus I imagined Fleetwood Mac toured in. It was more of a camper, or an RV I guess you'd call it. Something a husband and wife would drive to Yosemite, to celebrate his retirement and rekindle their waning libidos.

"How do you girlz like it, isn't it divine?"

"It's gorgeous, so much nicer than I imagined."

"When Mizz Kittenz tourz it's the *only* way she travelz," Mizz Kittenz often referred to her female self in the third person, "and PS, don't even ask how much money I've saved on hotels, literally hundredz of dollarz."

"It's as nice as a hotel," Scooter lied.

"Can I try-out the bathroom," I asked, not exactly sure how that might work.

"It's as nice as *any* hotel, like The Plaza on wheelz," Mizz Kittenz boasted, folding open the bathroom door, "PS, you may need to flush twice."

I closed the door and sat, hoping Mizz Kittenz' incessant talking would drown-out any unpleasant noises. I wondered how much time I would spend in this water closet over the next three weeks, to escape the sapless drivel of the eternally chatty. Then I flushed, twice. While I've never been to The Plaza, I bet their toilets can sink a turd in a single flush.

The RV looked nice though, adequate. I'd eventually realize the three-quarter scale of most things—the stove, the dinette, the beds—ensured not only the illusion of space but also the denial of comfort. Still, it was better than a car.

When Scooter and I moved from Giddyuptown to Cowboy City we were rewarded for the decision. In Giddyuptown we had to hustle to book shows in the local gay bars; now we were recruited—guaranteed weekly work at the popular club Crash Box. From Thursdays' regular shows through Sundays' amateur contests, the underage dance spot was packed with Cowboy City's weirdest and gayest kids, and all of them loved their drag queens. If you were a regular performer there—a 'Crash Box Bombshell'—you were practically a celebrity in this town with a level of fame somewhere between the local news's roving reporter and a popular hostess at Dennys. If you performed next door however, at Crash Box's strictly twenty-one-and-up sister club Mangles, then you easily had the celebrity status of the roving reporter, and maybe the weather girl. There were only three queens who held that position, the 'Mangles Angels'. They were the midwestern/transvested equivalent to Charlie's Angels, and the envy of every lesser queen in the state. Scooter and I both had hopes of working at Mangles, at least as guest entertainers, but we were years away from a legal drinking age and knew their front door ID'd everyone, performing or not.

There were plenty of other drag bars in the city too, probably a dozen weekly shows. 'Tawni Eclaire' had a show, she was a muscular, hundred-year-old version of Angie Dickinson with hair like cotton candy and skin like beef jerky. She was a legend in this state, and a few others. Tawni was one of the few queens in town who'd had *work* done, plastic surgery to look more like a caricature of a woman. Her new face's new cheeks were enormous (possibly the transplanted buttcheeks of a drunk driver), and her new lips looked like an old vagina. The facially refurbished queen invited me to do a performance at her martini bar, on the little three by five foot stage. I was third, sandwiched between Gussy Dupp and Miss Clairol. Tips were generous and applause sincere but it wasn't for me, I needed space. Tawni's nemesis was an equally aged, equally well-known queen named 'Mizz Kittenz'. I heard the two old-timers had been lovers, sometime in the 1960s I think. Something scandalous had happened involving a conniving houseboy and forbidden seduction. A wig was snatched, gowns were slashed, and secrets were reported to the IRS; the two never spoke again.

I met Mizz Kittenz at her drag bar The Kat Klub, Scooter and I thought we should get in drag and go watch her show—to network. We sat in the front row so Kittenz would notice us, and she did.

"Oh my my my, who are theeeeze precious little kittenz?" She stuck the microphone into our faces, it smelled of gin.

"Girlzzzz, aren't you divine," she continued, clawing her pressed-on fingernail against my cheek, "and darling, your cheekbones are purrrrfect. You both must come to Mother'z dressing room after the show. Will you do that for Mommy?"

We nodded, still networking.

"Do you promise?"

We nodded some more.

"Well they don't talk much but they certainly are pretty."

Five or six queens performed (none as pubescent as Scooter and me) in the one-room bar, which really looked more like a cement-floored garage. Folding chairs surrounded three sides of the plywood-platformed stage and its small runway, the chairs were probably the sturdier construction. They served alcohol, but I doubted they did it legally. Aida Fajita cried real tears during her ballad, and Melissa Manchaser took an unchoreographed tumble off the stage, performing the end of her song in pantyhose that had a bloodied knee. The dressing room was the corner of the garage behind the stage, walled by a black curtain that also served as the stage's backdrop. Between shows we stood next to Mizz Kittenz' make-up table (which I am certain was my grandmother's folding dinner tray) while she retouched her face, she glossed her lips without removing the cigarette that dangled there. The other performers eyed us nervously—as a ladies' volleyball team might eye the leggy scandanavian ringers brought in to win the big match.

"Hello Ladiez, where are you girlz from?"

"Giddyuptown," we answered in unison, "but we live here now," Scooter finished.

"Are you performing anywhere?"

"Crash Box," in unison again. Scooter shot me a 'one-at-a-time' look.

"Oh sure, nice gig. The emcee'z a dear friend of mine, when she'z sober I mean. Would you girlz be interested in performing here next week, it only pays forty dollars but tips are good and the drinks are free."

We made more money at Crash, but that was only one or two nights a week and we moved here with nothing so weren't turning down any paid gigs. "Sounds good," Scooter said. "Really good," I added.

I was nervous about living with Scooter, he was as vicious as he was funny and a year of drag had only brazened his bitter personality. (I didn't know it then but his nasty attitude was the groundwork for becoming an internet troll, which—decades after this chapter—I learned was his career, albeit unpaid, up until the time he died of complications from bookstore sex.) Maybe Della and Dicksy would get the brunt of it.

Della DeLorean was a regular at the underage drag bar Crash Box, a 'Box Bombshell', performing at the teen tabernacle every Thursday night. She took her name from the legendary 1980s sports car, though 'Julie Jalopy' might have been a better fit. Della would take a running charge at the audience then—just before colliding with the crowd—she'd stop on one foot (demonstrating her precision braking system), then lift both arms over her head in a slow hydraulic simulation of the DeLorean automobile's unique winged doors. She was an idiot. Her career was mercifully shortlived, I prefer to imagine it ending like her namesake's—in a late `80s drug trafficking scandal.

Though Della and her hag Dicksy (a doughy straight girl who thought she had some rank in the gay bars because of her association with the auto queen) agreed that we could stay with them for a couple of months, they began acting put out by the third day. Names were written on food. Could-you-keep-it-downs were issued whenever we laughed in our bedroom or rehearsed new routines. A juice glass was left outside our bedroom door with the note YOU FORGOT TO WASH ME taped to its side. And the couple rolled their collective eyes every time we came home late—interrupting their candlelit meals, shared-blanket movies, or other affectations of a sexless marriage. *It's only temporary*, I reminded myself (I'm sure they did the same), *Angela will be here soon.*

Angela Butchynne had a famous father—if you lived in Giddyuptown and were of a certain age. He was a popular columnist for the local newspaper and had once run for mayor. His daughter was older than I was, and a senior at the high school I briefly enrolled in before dropping-out when the teachers refused to let my "distraction" of a hairdo into their classes. Angela had a hairdo of her own—a three-foot long blond rat's nest, teased and sprayed until it frightened children. She had a hooked nose and smeared-on black eyeliner and red lipstick, inspiring classmates to nickname her Broomhilda, and not affectionately.

After school Angela would invite me to her parents' house, still decorated in the tasteful shag carpets and asian screens of the 1970's—when they'd entertained the city's socialites. A large family portrait in the foyer suggested her parents were a generation older than mine, though I never met them. Angela used the microwave (an invention I hadn't seen before) to melt cheddar cheese into onion rolls, serving it to us with mayo, it was the best thing I had ever tasted. "Do you wanna come over for a cheese sandwich?" she'd ask in her hoarse, mannish voice. The answer was always 'yes', and as the cheese melted our friendship solidified. On the fourth or fifth visit, Angela's father came home from work, looked at me and my hair and called Angela to the bedroom.

"We have to leave," she said, "my father doesn't want you in our house."

We gathered my schoolbooks and quickly exited. "He thinks you look like a punk," she confessed, "he doesn't want me to talk to you anymore."

"What a dick," I recognized.

"No, he just doesn't want me to get mixed up with the wrong people."

"People who backcomb their hair, I guess. He would hate my grandmother."

"Don't be like that."

But Angela was, however briefly, a rebel. Her father's lack of appreciation for my early fashion sense stoked a forbidden friendship: shared lunches, shoe shopping, dancing, and ultimately a vow of 'best friends forever'—like the new-wave fag and hag version of the Montagues and the Capulets. Angela would graduate in three months then meet me in Cowboy City. We'd get an apartment and eat cheddar cheese sandwiches, everyday.

After Scooter and I had done our third or fourth night at Mizz Kittenz' show bar, she cornered us as we packed our garment bags. "Mother'z taking her show on the road," an unfamiliar flicker of excitement in her tired eyes, "PS, don't tell the other girlz, but I've told the clubz in Wichita, Springfield, Little Rock, all about you two and they're *very* interested."

"Wow," we said.

"Exactly. It's nothing like this shithole of a town, they'll roll out the red carpet for us. These clubz know how to treat a queen. Will you come, tell Mommy you'll come."

"Shit yeah, we'll come," Scooter blurted—sharing none of my trepidation about spending time alone with Mizz Kittenz.

"How long would we be gone?" I asked, brightening my eyes and smiling as to not seem like a wet blanket.

"Not long, a week. We'll take my tour bus, you'll juzt die when you see it, I'm talking five-star luxury. We can take the interstates almost the entire way. I usually go for two weekz, but juzt one this time—I have to be in court the following Monday." (Court? I hoped it wasn't for strangling young queens and dumping their bodies along I-44.)

Our first tour with Mizz Kittenz wasn't exactly Liberace at Madison Square Garden, but it was impressive to the easily impressed. Scooter and I felt like visiting dignitaries as locals lined-up to give us their dollar bills. Some of the clubs were dumps, but some were nice—really nice, and we returned from our eight-day genderbender a thousand dollars richer. A few months later Kittenz asked us to tour again, mostly the same clubs, and a couple of new ones. Each time, we came home more seasoned and with more money.

When Kittenz told us about the fourth tour, "It'll be the biggest one yet," she promised, "we're adding clubs in Topeka and Kansas City, we're gonna blow the roof offa those mother fuckerz!"

"Bitch, I can't go," Scooter told Mizz Kittenz, "I've got community service four days a week until September [a little mix-up involving stolen credit cards], can't we go in six weeks?"

"Girl I'd wait for you if I could, but Mizz Kittenz has billz to pay."

Scooter looked disappointed—like a drag queen who just got bumped from the tri-state tour.

"Don't worry baby, Momma will take you next time."

I thought about not going but also had some billz to pay. When Angela moved here we got an apartment. We went out every night, quickly spending the money I made winning amateur drag contests around the gay enclaves of Cowboy City and performing the weekly gigs at Crash Box. Angela looked for a job, she even considered stripping—in middle school she had done gymnastics and was still limber for her size. "We could cut the crotch out of a leotard," I suggested, "and you could twirl ribbon on a stick—like the gymnasts do."

Between drag gigs, when the money ran out, we'd sleep all day—her alone, me with a boy I'd met the weekend before. Angela woke one such day, heavy make-up still on her face but not where she had intended it, and hair looking like something spiders spun while she slept. "I'm going to the store," she said, or rather coughed, and without any money. "She looks like Sid Vicious' girlfriend," a boy said, the one lying next to me. When Angela came home from the mini-mart she had a fresh pack of cigarettes, two burritos, and a guilty expression.

"Where'd you get the money for that?"

"I just got it."

"What do you mean you *just got it*."

"I mean I don't wanna tell you where I got it."

"*Angela*, did you shoplift?" She was a good girl from a good family (a virgin even, due to the poophole loophole) and would never have shoplifted.

"No, don't be stupid."

"If you don't tell me where you got them I'm gonna to throw 'em in the toilet."

"One of the burritos is for you."

"The toilet!" I stood, demonstrating my resolve. Then I began a slow, menacing walk toward her—like a man about to flush a girl's burrito.

"Don't you fucking dare," her eyes and mouth widened with fear and excitement, just as they might have in infancy, playing 'peek-a-boo' or 'I'm gonna get you' with her father. She turned defensively, as if her back were an impenetrable wall. I lurched, clamping my arms around her from behind. "No, No, No" she screamed, like Nancy Spungen caught in a bear trap. My hands seized the paper bag.

"I SHOWED HIM MY BOOBS, I showed the mini-mart guy my boobs!"

Angela moved back with her parents, realizing she wasn't ready to be on her own, she joined the military and became a realtor, then moved to the suburbs and raised children; I moved to a smaller place. Cowboy City had two fag-friendly high-rise apartment buildings, I moved into the one that would rent to an underage teenager with a recently met gentleman cosigner. Even though mine was only a studio, I felt somehow superior to everyone living street-level below. It must be something left over from a more animalistic version of my species when early-man felt (as bears and gorillas must) that they bettered their contemporaries if they possessed the height advantage. *In a fight*—some unevolved part of me thought—*I can surely trounce the residents of mere one and two story apartment buildings, if it comes to that.* I was however still poor, living only on drag income, so I felt only as superior as one who hopes for a sale on ramen noodles can feel. Occasionally, when I was bored with noodles, I would take a 3:00 AM stroll across the parking lot to the dumpster behind a steak house. After a little digging I would walk the remnants of a steak dinner home, rinse off the coffee grounds, and enjoy part of a steak on the picturesque balcony of my high-rise apartment.

THE GLAMOURISH LIFE

With Scooter at community service, Mizz Kittenz invited two more queens on our junket. The new line-up included:

'Lena Cuisine', a plus (possibly multiplication) sized beauty with a natural va-va-voomness about her. She'd just been through a bitter divorce from 'Poly Grip'—a much older queen who had also been Lena's drag mother and her co-owner in Big Wig, a failing wig shop. The break-up was well publicized on the Kat Klub's bathroom walls. Mizz Kittenz fired Poly after the elderly queen threw a Mint Julep on her ex, during Lena's heart-felt performance of "I Will Survive."

'Black Opal' was, as her name suggested, an opal. Also, black. Very black, she had a tattoo on her wrist that no one had ever seen. She was a charismatic (er, spastic) queen who flailed big arms violently during the most intense verses and choruses of all Patti Labelle ballads, as if she were swatting a swarm of invisible wasps in a desperate fight for her life. "Somebody help her," I wanted to scream, "they're killing her!" She sweated profusely through her beaded gowns (the unwashable kind you buy in the India tent at

the county fair) prompting most of us to call her by her initials, B.O.

'Marsha Mellow' was white, very white (so white she once called the cops on Black Opal). Marsha had enhanced breasts; they were, like her personality, perky. She was also simple-minded and quick to tears. Scooter made her cry once when he noted that dancing during her performances, with her face pointed to the floor, made it seem she'd lost her keys. He nicknamed her "Sienna Therapist," which also made her cry. Marsha wasn't naturally charismatic (her first drag name was Jan Riggs) but audiences liked her because she was pretty in the usual way. They forgave her awkwardness—performing every song with an undercurrent of confusion, like a woman with nowhere to turn. A rumor said Marsha had modeled for *Kitten With A Dick* magazine, and then (under the name 'Cookie Jar') starred in the late '70s transsexual fisting flick *Caught with her hand in the Cookie Jar*. She since found God and supplemented her drag income working part-time as a motel laundress (probably to be near the bibles).

'Guyrene' could spin like Tonya Harding and scream like Nancy Kerrigan. Her high-kick was as mean as her loud-mouthed personality. Like me, she started very young—beginning her drag career performing unspeakable acts in backrooms and bathhouses. And she was a thief, regularly seen wearing other peoples' jewelry. "My grandmother left me this necklace," she'd insist, "she was a showgirl." The only thing Guyrene valued more than other queens' jewelry was their humiliation. She'd shove a sister down the stairs if she thought it would get her a laugh, and it usually did.

Me. I was the youngest and only underage queen on the bus, a rhinestone in the rough. I also thought of myself as the smartest and prettiest of the bunch. "She looks like a model," I thought I heard one of them say, or maybe it was "supermodel." My drag had blossomed into something a little witchy—casting spells and collecting tips from the four corners of a dance floor. Usually to songs by Kate Bush or Stevie Nicks. Maybe Sheila E. if I felt like showing some leg. Or Ann Wilson if I felt like showing some Heart.

And *'Mizz Kittenz'*, the emcee and headliner, and a *Legend* according to the rhinestones on the back of her custom denim jacket (if God got chilly, he'd have a jacket like that.) By most accounts, she'd had only one serious relationship and it was with a rival queen, any other trysts were tricks or tricked. Her moodiness was widely attributed to the fear of spinsterism that any unwed drag queen feels as she approaches manopause—the age at which one's high-kick fails to reach above her knee. In our line-up, Kittenz always performs last. "It's like sex," she said, "the climax goes at the end."

Kittenz usually drove the RV. On the third day Lena did, though she was a tight fit behind the steering wheel. The four hundred and a quarter pounder swore she was on a diet, eating only "cottage cheese for breakfast and salad for dinner." She gained forty pounds since the break-up of her marriage and was in danger of outgrowing her caftans. But the "salads" were eaten from a casserole dish, and were mostly croutons, bacon bits, and chunked cheese.

"I thought you were on a diet?" Guyrene asked.

"I have to eat *something*, you want me to get anorexia?"

"There's about 250 pounds between you and anorexia."

"You need to shut up, I'm eating a salad!"

"That's not a salad," insisted Guyrene.

"If you put Ranch on it then it's a salad, *bitch*."

"Guyrene, leave her alone," Kittenz warned, "she's been through a lot."

"Alotta Ranch."

"Hush."

We ate half our meals on the road, the other half at truck stops or RV parks. Twice we ate at restaurants and, though only Marsha was in drag (she was permanently in drag), the entire table was a spectacle. I was grateful Guyrene, Black Opal, and Lena were so large because a table full of loud-mouthed queens with my small frame would surely have been subdued by the locals. When not eating we were styling wigs, beading dresses, or engaging in a little *titty boo*—our slang for dish. Lena Cuisine, we learned, loved riding a horse (Guyrene asked where they buried it.) Black Opal didn't understand why anyone would want to ride an animal, astonishing country gal Lena.

"Girl, you've never ridden a horse before?"

"Uh, No—I have a car."

Marsha, we learned, had giant balls. She said tucking her testicles was nearly impossible and she wanted to get rid of them but couldn't afford the surgery. Someone nicknamed them her 'detesticles', which made her cry.

"Why are you crying, sweetie?"

"I just don't think it's funny."

"We're not laughing *at* you, we're laughing *because* of you," Guyrene explained.

Black Opal put an arm around the doltish queen, "Girl, I like big balls. You need to be proud of those things."

"How big are they?" Lena asked.

"Really big," she sniffled.

"Can I peek?"

"Lena, you *peaked* years ago,"

"Guyrene, be nice."

"I'm not showing them to anyone"

"I don't understand, didn't you show them to the whole world in your porno?"

Three, maybe four queens gasped at Guyrene's announcement. We all knew of the movie, but we never spoke of it. Marsha flipped her hair in front of her face, crying into it like it was an ash-blonde hankie. I used my finger to split an opening down the middle, exposing her snotty nose.

"You're gonna get your wig all dirty." I said, using my dinner napkin to wipe her face. "Are you wearing this one tonight?"

"Yes," she whimpered, "is there snot in it?"

Black Opal leaned in, "Ooh yeah girl, there's a big ole booger in it. That's nasty."

I dried Marsha's eyes and then we washed her wig. "I wish Opal would wash her dress," she whispered, "it smells." After a week in a crowded camper I wasn't exactly Chanel No. 5, but yes—it smelled.

In Wichita, Guyrene performed in a pair of Daisy Duke shorts that would have been cute if not for the bullet hole in her leg. Still, the crowd approved and she picked up a hustler. The boy came on stage, using his mouth to tip her a dollar bill on which he'd written I WANT 2 SUCK U. He was eighteen or nineteen, named Rocky or Rocko, and missing a front tooth. Lena called him 'Rock Bottom', but not to his face. He rode with us to Topeka where his grand-mother lived. The streetwise kid walked around the camper in a pair of red briefs with an outline illustration of a hot dog in a bun over his crotch. The text above read 'Bone Appetit'. The girls all giggled as he squeezed past them, except Mizz Kittenz—she got a hunger in her eyes that looked deadly serious and made me uncomfortable. When Guyrene and Rocko went to bed (hanging a sheet over their bunk), Kittenz asked, "Are you using protection?" and Guyrene answered, "I've got pepper spray."

The RV had four small beds, two stacks of two. I was the smallest so I slept on the bench that surrounded the dinette. Kittenz slept on the floor, her troublesome back required a hard surface. In the middle of the fifth night I woke with a shout. I often woke up yelling—not the cinematic scream of a horror queen, but a "Hea Wasulha!" or some other passionate gibberish (like someone trying to shout *Stop, you ran over my dog,* but before the invention of language.)

"What's going on? What's wrong?" Kittenz asked, pulling the sleeping mask above her cat-like eyes. Without foundation, Kittenz' sallow skin startled me, her man face resembled a ransom note from years of plastic surgery. In drag she made a fairly attractive older woman, but her unpainted face was not designed for the RV park's bright security light.

"I'm okay," I said, "I just had a weird dream."

"Honey, you're not ok, you're dripping in sweat. Are you crying?" She wiped some wet from under my eyes.

"I don't know, I guess so."

"Let's go have a smoke," she said, "I don't wanna smoke alone."

Mizz Kittenz put on her fluffy robe, the one she wore backstage. I followed her to the front of the RV and out the passenger door.

"It's nice out tonight," we agreed.

"That must have been quite a dream."

"Yeah."

"Will you tell me about it, if it's not too personal I mean."

It was personal, but Kittenz and I had never really had a conversation before, not a real one. "It was about my mom."

"What happened?" she pressed. I answered, too tired to edit.

"I dreamed this guy Mickey beat up my mom . . . And I found her on our livingroom floor . . . In front of the big sliding glass doors . . . Unconscious but not really . . . Mumbling something incoherent . . . I grabbed a glass vase . . . The kind I used to buy at yard sales to give to her on Mother's Day . . . I grabbed it from the étagère . . . Then I knelt next to her . . . And I lifted the vase over my head . . . Then crashed it down on her face . . . I did it like four or five times . . . Her forehead had a big dent in it . . . Then it just started to collapse . . . First her forehead then her face . . . A section at a time . . . Like California [is supposed to, in an earthquake] . . . Into the Pacific Ocean"

Kittenz didn't say anything, she took a deep puff of cigarette.

"When I looked down again, her whole face had caved-in, like it wasn't a face anymore. It was more like a bowl full of face parts. Then I woke up."

"I see why you screamed."

"Yeah, it was pretty gross."

"Is your mom alive?" she asked, probably wondering if I had Norman Bates'd the woman.

"Yeah, she lives upstate."

"That'z nice. Do you see her often?"

"No, we don't really talk any more."

"Why not, can I ask?"

"I left home when I was pretty young. I haven't really seen her much since."

"Do you talk on the phone?"

"Not really. I went home last Thanksgiving and she wouldn't let me in the house, because of my hair."

"Your hair?"

"Yeah."

"How old iz your mother?"

"I'm not sure, early thirties."

"She must have been a baby when she had you."

"Yeah, she had me and my sister by the time she was sixteen or seventeen."

"Well that'z it, she was just a child, probably about your age now. How old are you? I heard you were only fifteen. Girl, iz that true?"

The question was one I had learned to avoid, for fear of getting thrown out of a bar. Kittenz noticed my eyes darting or my lip being chewed and decided not to press. "Babiez shouldn't be having babiez. Little girlz don't know how to be motherz. I bet she made lotza mistakes."

"I guess so."

"Maybe try to remember, she was just a kid herself. Maybe you wouldn't be so mad at her."

"She was in her thirties when I went home for Thanksgiving."

"That'z true. That was juzt fucked-up."

"Yeah."

Kittenz leaned in, "Can I ask you something?" she purred.

"Okay."

"Scooter told us that sometimes you ate out of a dumpster, is that true?"

"I guess, a long time ago."

"That's nothing to be ashamed of honey, that says you're a survivor. Hell, I've eaten outta some of the best dumpsters in the tri-state area."

"You did?"

"Oh yeah. You wanna know the secret to eating garbage: Sriracha, bitchez!"

Kittenz often wrapped-up a punchline with *bitchez!* "You're funny."

"Hilariouz. Tell you what. This year, why don't you have Thanksgiving with me. I'm a big ham so every year I cook a big ham. A few of the girlz don't have family around here so we spend the holidayz together. PS, it'z a hoot. Whaddaya think?"

That sounds nice, I thought. "That sounds nice."

"Good. Give me a hug and let's go inside. Mother'z freezing her titz off."

On the sixth day the toilet stopped working. We blamed Lena, who abandoned her diet to binge on the all-you-can-eat Continental Breakfast at the Patty Wagon cafe (after the bathroom blow-out we would refer to it as her Incontinental Breakfast.) Without a running toilet we urinated in the sink, anything else was done at RV parks, restaurants, drag bars, or—in an emergency—outdoors. The timing was awful, tonight we were performing in the biggest club on our tour. Kittenz and Guyrene had worked this club before, I hadn't. They said it was bigger than Mangles or any club in Oklahoma, all the great queens in the region had performed there, and more than a few Miss Gay Americas. The girls assured me I wouldn't be carded, "We'll all walk in together, they're expecting us."

I'd spent the last five days sewing beads on my costume, a floor-length layered confection of black chiffon. It wasn't a reproduction of anything Stevie Nicks had worn (I wasn't an impersonator), but I did feel it captured her essence. The other girls had planned their best routines for tonight too—it was going to be a big deal. When we played a club, we took it over. Most or all of their regular performers took the night off, it was just us. We always got in drag in the RV and arrived in costume (Kittenz thought it spoiled the illusion if we let them see us as civilians.) It's not easy getting six queens ready in a camper, especially with no working toilet.

"I'm going out to uze the little girlz room," Kittenz said, throwing on a spiky Tina Turner wig with her make-up only half done, "PS, if I'm not back in ten minutes, drag the lake."

Our RV was parked by a lake just outside of town. It was about five miles to the club, they'd send a car for us. Marsha and I teased and sprayed our synthetic hair in the bathroom mirror, I used my hand to wipe some schmutz from its surface. "If you leave fingerprints on the mirror Mizz Kittenz'll scratch your eyes out,"

Marsha melodramatized—she was like that, fearful I mean. Kittenz was in a mumpish mood though, sometimes she got that way before a big show. The old-timers took their drag very seriously, like every performance might be their last.

A black Town Car picked us up though some of the larger girls made for a tight squeeze, even in a full-size luxury sedan; I'd never had a club pick me up for a show, tonight was going to be special. We rode in more silence than any of us had heard in the last week. Mostly we closed our eyes, remembering lyrics and choreography. Marsha was probably praying.

"Okay, here we are ladiez," Mizz Kittenz announced, "it'z showtime!"

We were ushered inside, past the ID guy—no problem. High ceilings, cloth'd tables, three bars. The stage: big like you'd see at a junior high talent show. The place glowed with soft dim lights, *How natural we look*, I thought, and *I have to pee*. A little person in drag walked us to the backstage, her name was 'Millie Meter' or 'Minnie Stroke' or something like that, "but you can call me Smidge."

Smidge escorted us down a hall to the dressing area, one or two queens each in the string of private and semi-private rooms. All the clubs I had worked before stuck all their performers in a single room, usually a storage-type with walls lined in folding tables. You'd share a long, makeshift clothing rack if you were lucky, otherwise lay your garment bag across a stack of green-olive boxes.

Kittenz and Marsha shared a room, I shared with Guyrene, Lena and Black Opal had their own. Ours was long and narrow with all its walls completely covered in dark, dusty-rose velvet. Everything seemed old, like it had hosted the Ruth Wallis or Memphis Minnie impersonators of the 1930s and 40s. The long wall on the right had built in vanities complete with starlet lighting, all the wood was rose colored (painted a high gloss for easy wipe-downs) with a round, rose velvet stool at each station. The long wall on the left, behind us when we sat at the vanities, was a built-in clothing rack that ran the room's twelve or thirteen foot length. *Now this*, I recognized, *is class*.

After minutes of marveling and unpacking and then a strip down to my tights, Smidge returned.

"Music ladies, I need your music."

I handed her my cassette, "It's cued," or did I mean *queued*.

"Song?"

"Edge of Seventeen. Stevie Nicks."

"Love it, [pulling a long pencil—perhaps the length of her leg from knee to heel—from her bouffant wig and jotting something onto a clipboard]. Lighting?"

"Make it witchy."

"Got it," she finished, turning her tiny back to me and walking away.

Right now Kittenz must be drinking a whiskey sour, I thought. Before a show she drank them like kids drink Kool-Aid, with closed eyes and open throat, then a slam of the glass and a hard look in the mirror (that "You're a legend, Lady" look in her eyes). Marsha must be sitting quietly, as she did for her pre-show prayer. "Please Father, blesseth my performance, so that I might bringeth happiness to others. And blesseth my sisters, they knoweth not what they doeth. And *please* Father, blesseth this duct tape, for it doth holdeth my giant balls."

Kittenz was first—not to perform but to emcee, Kittenz performed last, <u>always</u>. After her usual jokes—funny to a new crowd but tired to us—she ran down the hall. "There's a hot crowd tonight," she said from the doorway. Guyrene shouted something sassy and Kittenz winked agreement and scrambled back toward her own dressing room. Kittenz usually ran backstage while we girls performed, to retouch her lips and slug another drink.

I was third in the line-up, right after Lena. I stood to the side of the stage, watching the big queen dance. For a big girl she could move.

"Let'z hear it for Lena Cuisine!" Kittenz barked through freshly glittered lips. "And how about that dress! Backstage Lena asked me, *Kittenz, do I fill out this dress?* And I said *Honey, you'd fill out a sleeping bag!*"

[Pause for laughs]

"I teaze, I teaze. Let'z have another big round of applauze for Lena."

[Pause for applause]

Kittenz introduced me the way she always did, with a "You're in for a real treat," and then a "She'z the prettiest thing this side of Christie Brinkley…"

"Get em girl," she said as she passed me on her exit.

I entered behind an unexpected puff of stage fog, the white smoke curling around me as I passed through. My cautious steps were timed with the song's iconic guitar intro, timed to get me to the center of most stages as the vocal began. I hadn't recalibrated for the size of this stage though, it was massive; I hurried my pace. The wooden stage was floor level, round tables with white cloths were four-deep in all directions. Beyond the people sitting at tables—six each, more stood—hundreds of them…maybe more, all of them wondering when I would trip and fall. The bright stage lights were disorienting from all directions, they probably wouldn't have to wait long.

When I was in the seventh grade, a few months after we moved to Oklahoma, my english teacher (Verna Lutz, or Verna Muntz or somesuch poetry) brought a boom-box to class. She was a short, mousy lady. Not to suggest she was timid or skittish, rather she looked like a mouse. Her shoulder length grey-brown bob was as thick and heavy as the turtle-necked winter sweaters she wore year-round. Stretchy brown pants were in a style and synthetic fiber that suggested she had never been asked to marry, and that was fine by her. Big, thick glasses (the kind you'd prefer to start a campfire) made talking to my teacher feel like a prison visit—conversing through plate glass. When the bell rang and everyone seated themselves, the woman pressed PLAY, and then began a slow seductive dance, gyrating her hips to Olivia Newton-John's "Magic." She'd lip-sync the suggestive lyrics to one student, leaning to him and tossing her heavy hair over his first-year-of-junior-high wooden desk. When finished with a boy, she'd wink through her bulletproof glasses, spin a little spin, and pump across the aisle to assault the girl in the next row. I counted the desks and cursed myself for not choosing one nearer the back of the room. When the song ended—bringing a close to her sensual routine (one I was certain her cats knew well), the teacher directed our seduction-burnt eyes to a list of songs she'd written on the blackboard.

1. *The Gambler*, Kenny Rogers

2. *What a Fool Believes*, Doobie Brothers

3. *Magic*, Olivia Newton-John

4. *Do That to Me One More Time*, The Captain & Tennille

5. *Escape (The Pina Colada Song)*, Rupert Holmes

6. *Babe*, Styx

7. *Night the Lights Went Out in Georgia*, Vicki Lawrence

8. *Sad Eyes*, Robert John

9. *The Rose*, Bette Midler

10. *It's Still Rock and Roll to Me*, Billy Joel

"Something for everyone," she said, the choice was ours. We would each stand in front of the class and lipsync one minute of one song. Lyric sheets were permitted, dancing was encouraged. "It will teach you to be comfortable when speaking in public," she promised. And "participation is mandatory."

I watched classmates stand up, one by one, and walk to the front of the class. The girls giggled, the boys played air-guitar. All of them, however reluctantly, had a good time. Then, "Chris Madrigal, you're up."

"What song will you be performing for us?"

I looked at the woman as if to say, 'Is this really happening?'

"How about Billy Joel," she suggested.

I wondered if punching through the window—cutting my hand on the glass—would wake me. It would hurt at first, I'd be startled, but then I'd sit up in bed and everything would be alright. I'm probably over-sleeping anyway.

"Okay." I replied.

I walked as slowly to the front of the class as movement would allow, a sheet of lyrics in my hand. I'd heard the song on the radio enough to know most of the words. Still, when the music played and Billy Joel began to sing, I did not. Instead I raised my bent arms, palms upturned as if to say, 'I don't know what to do.'

"Just feel the music," Ms. Lutz suggested, grinding her mannish pelvis to show me what feeling the music looks like. She started the song again, twice more, each time I began with my signature move of upturned palms expressing 'I don't know what to do.' The crowd watched with its mix of pity and 'we want our money back', as if witnessing a stagelit Janis Joplin slowly overdose.

"Ricky, Aaron," she said, "will you help him out."

"Sure thing," the happy, handsome basketball stars replied. The two flanked me—one on air guitar, one on air drums—both golden from summer swimming, we were only a month into the schoolyear and it was already the worst day in history (the eleventh of September, mark my words, worst day ever.) I looked at the nearest boy as if for amnesty, he looked downward, air-tuning his invisible guitar. The song started a fourth time and the boys bounced around me, laughing and playing solos where none were recorded. I stepped cautiously from side to side, mumbling something into a sheet of lyrics.

I've come a long way, I thought, fog billowing around me, standing alone on the biggest stage of my career. No friends in the audience to cheer me on, *I can do this.* I lifted my arms—swathed in chiffon just like the white wings of a dove, I sang a song that sounded like I was singing, "Ooo, baby, ooo," I said, "ooo."

My pupils responded to the bright light, constricting into focus. I began churning the dozen layers of sheer black silk into an angry ocean, until only the messy spirals of my blond wig remained buoyant in the tumultuous midnight waves. The crowd gathered, those from the back of the room migrating to the front. People came from the corridors outside the main room, till there was no one left standing in the hall.

I bent forward, arms outstretched, hands outstretched, spells spilling from my fingertips. The magic brought them to the edges of the stage, it reached into their pockets, and pulled out their dollar bills. *Not yet, not yet.* A kick and a snare took hold, shook me, shook my head—it bounced, dancing my hair, like a strand, in the wind, on the wig that was my own. Then I began again, like nothing else mattered.

"Take our dollars" the crowd seemed to cry, their bills waving at the edges of the stage like walls of wind-fluttered hyacinth.

Yes, I thought, now I will receive your gifts.

Gravity had lost its hold over me so I floated just above the dance floor to its perimeters, from dollar bill to dollar bill. Like Diana Ross, I reached out and touched somebody's hand, and then their dollar. One, two, three at a time. Some gave their bills then fell away, others wanted a hug. Every third or fourth person said something I couldn't hear over the music, the applause. I smiled through my lipsync and nodded my head as if to say, "I hear you child, I am here for you." *Another dollar. Yes, another hug for you.*

The song was ending soon. I wanted to say, "I need to step away, I have another spin to do," but they waved their dollars more furiously—don't forget ours, don't forget ours! I grabbed what I could, pinching it to the sheaf of singles in each hand. I'm sorry, no time to stop for the little shared moments. *They* would understand, the unhugged: sometimes, to be near me is to be unable to feel me, my Loves.

When the song faded the crowd cheered, stood and cheered. "More, More, More," they shouted, give us more! I waved goodbye as best I could with hands clutching fistfuls of their cash. Had I dropped any? Would the next queen give it to me or keep it for herself? Black Opal was up, she waited by the side of the stage as I exited. "Oh my god bitch, you tore it up!" *Yeah*, I thought, *I did.*

After the show Smidge came back to our dressing room, returning music from the ten o'clock performances and collecting music for the midnight show.

"Wayne wants to make a change in the line-up," she said (Wayne was the club manager), "he wants *you* to go last," she continued.

"Why?" I asked, "Mizz Kittenz always goes last."

"Wayne said the crowd really liked you so he wants you to close the show. If you have a problem with it, talk to Wayne."

"Does Kittenz know?" Guyrene asked Smidge.

"Yup."

My dressing-roommate mouthed, "Kittenz's gonna be pissed," behind (and above) Smidge's back.

A few minutes later Mizz Kittenz' head appeared in our doorway, "Have you girlz heard, there'z a change in the line-up."

"We heard," Guyrene answered, rolling her glittered eyes.

"I'm last?" I asked, knowing the answer.

"You're last," she said, looking at me as a neglected cat would a spoiled kitten, and then (if not for the clanking of rhinestones) disappearing down the hall.

We had forty minutes to kill between shows. After a quick relax I put on my mingling outfit—a bare-midriff black spandex dress under a black vinyl jacket with pointy, futuristic shoulders—and went to the bar. I didn't usually drink, but tonight I thought, *why not.*

"I'll have a white-russian," I said. The milky sweet made it one of the few drinks I could tolerate.

The bartender handed me the concoction. "It's on-the-house," he said, "you were amazing."

Then we should make-out, I thought. "Thank you," I said.

212

Two girls and a guy walked over, shouting, "We wanted to give this to you but you didn't see us," over the music, and handing me three dollar bills.

"One from each of you?" I asked.

"They're all from Jake," she answered, "he's shy."

"He thinks you're really pretty," the other girl added, "he loves your lips."

"Thank you Jake," I shouted, holding up the bills, "I'm gonna use it to buy more of this lipstick."

"What?" he shouted back.

"I'll use it to buy more of this lipstick!"

"Huh?"

"Nevermind. Thank you."

I sat at the bar for ten more minutes, watching dancers and absorbing compliments. *I'll have another white russian,* I thought, for the dressing room.

"Excuse me," a tap on the shoulder said.

"Hi Wayne." It was the bar manager. And another man.

"You need to come with us," Wayne said, in a tone not suitable for the performer who had just been asked to close the show.

"Where are we going?"

"Please just come with us."

"No seriously, where?"

"Do you have an ID?"

"Not on me. I think I left it on our bus."

"I understand you are underage. I need to escort you out of the building."

"I need to talk to Kittenz."

"I can't allow you backstage, and you can't be in the bar. I need to escort you out of the building. Now."

"My stuff is backstage."

"I'm sure the other performers will bring it to you. But I need to escort you out of the building. Now."

"What about my pay?"

"We're not paying you. You are underage and it's illegal for you to be on the premises. I need to escort you out of the building. Now."

"This is bullshit. I am getting paid."

"Please come with me or we'll forcibly remove you."

"Give me my fucking money."

Wayne and the bouncer grabbed me by each arm. I pulled my white russian hand free and threw the drink behind the bar, crashing seven or eight wine glasses, a '7-10 split' in bowling terms.

"You owe me three hundred dollars," I said, "I don't work for free."

"Is that when they called the police," Marsha asked.

"I don't know. They were already there when we got outside. One of the cops asked for my ID and when I said I didn't have it they put me in the car and took me away."

"Girl, were you scared?" Black Opal asked.

"I guess, but I was pissed."

"Honey, I woulda been livid," Lena added. "Livid!"

Truth was, I *was* scared. If a midwestern transvester wasn't safe on the street then a jailed one probably had the life expectancy of a gimped gazelle, or a time-travelling women's libber.

I'd been to jail once before, juvie really, after a drag show. Liz and two of her other friends, all older than me, wanted to go to the 18-and-up club where straights danced to music I didn't like. Liz had a fake ID, I didn't, but everyone said I looked older in drag so we went.

The doorman welcomed us to the club and said I should save a dance for him, so far so good. Inside, two of us danced while the other two got intro trouble. Liz was accused of stealing sunglasses out of a girl's purse, she swore she didn't do it but Liz did like sunglasses and had been known to lie. Bouncers removed us from the building, and then called the police when I began shouting that I hadn't done anything wrong and tried to push my way back inside.

At 2:00 AM the juvenile hall was mostly asleep. A group of staff talked for a moment, then one explained to me that they hadn't the facilities for someone like me. I was allowed a phone call which I made to Saddle Burger Rodney, and then given a blanket, a pillow, and a quiet spot on an office couch.

The next morning Rodney was seated in the back of an overlit room where I stood, hungover and smudged, before a juvenile court judge. Her Honor said I looked very nice, and that I should not return to the 18-and-up club, and that I could leave in the custody of the gentleman in the back row.

We went to Rodney's apartment where I showered, sniffed some poppers, and wrestled my adult guardian until we both came; Justice was restored.

No one told me anything when I arrived at the city jail. They just shoved me (gently), hot-rolled and handcuffed, into a cell already occupied by a sleeping prostitute. I waited for someone to interrogate me, a loose-cannon detective maybe (a bare, overhead bulb highlighting beads of sweat on my perfectly penciled brow); *this might be bad*, I thought. Would they know about the break-in at Saddle Burger, the stolen porch furniture, the guns pointed at the carload of cheerleaders? But other than a lady with a sandwich cart, and my hooker-with-a-tooth-of-gold cellmate using her gilded grill to gnaw a bologna on rye (and to explain that the bad thing about rapists is how they never pay; and that her boyfriend had a thing for whores, but *cain't no prostitute fellate your heart*), no one spoke till they let me out this morning.

"How did they know you were underage?"

"They didn't say. Where's Kittenz?" I asked.

"She had to use the bathroom. She's down by the lake."

We drove to the next town and parked at a truck stop. The bathrooms were padlocked, OUT OF ORDER written on the doors; there was a field across the street, it would have to do. We took a cab into town to do our show. Guyrene, Lena, and Black Opal wanted to party afterward / Marsha, Kittenz, and I did not. We three came back to the RV, jail had exhausted me, and Marsha needed to catch up on her crying. We two peeled off our hose and hair, washed our faces and prepared for bed. Mizz Kittenz had other plans.

"Why are you fixing your hair?" Marsha asked as Kittenz picked and sprayed the spikes of her if-Tina-Turner-were-an-old-white-man wig.

"I'm steppin' out," she said, vague enough to mean 'mind your business'.

Mizz Kittenz took her drink into the bathroom (something involving whisky, cream liqueur, cinnamon schnapps, and coconut rum...her own high-calorie/low-standards recipe for Death Warmed Over).

"Where is she going?" Marsha whispered. I raised my shoulders in reply.

Kittenz emerged from the bathroom wearing a one-piece swimsuit-like zebra-patterned bodysuit. It had long sleeves and no legs, with the otherwise sleek lycra stretched around her lumpy torso as it would a sackful of kittenz. Black leather boots reached her mid-thigh, leaving a gap in her outfit from upper thighs to upper buttcheeks. She had touched-up her make-up, insomuch as she had reinforced it in dark slapdash strokes, like she was painted for war. "Who left fingerprints on the bathroom mirror?" she asked as her long fingernails struggled with the buttons of her denim jacket.

"I guess it was me," I said, remembering the schmutz I'd wiped the day before.

"I run a tight ship here, and can't stand looking at myself in a dirty mirror. Pleaze clean it." She rolled a purple scarf and tied it around her forehead and then a fringy leather belt around her waist (the crown and sash of her ignobility).

"Sorry," I said, "I've been in jail."

Mizz Kittenz grabbed her cigarettes and then the camper door handle, "PS, don't wait up."

The door shut and Marsha and I turned off the light then peeked between the curtains. The elderly queen paraded across the truckstop's gravel lot—back, then forth, then back again. "What's she doing? Marsha asked, "Why is she doing that?" One of the rigs flashed its lights—on-off, on-off. Mizz Kittenz noted the interest and walked directly in front of the truck, stopped, then exposed a buttcheek as she bent forward to pretend to pull up her boot. The rig's lights flashed again—on-off, on-off. The invitation was clear, Kittenz unbent her rickety pose and catwalked to the long truck's passenger door, it swung open and she clawed her sixty-five-year-old self inside. Marsha grabbed my hand and squeezed, "I can't watch."

Words were presumably exchanged, hard to be sure, but not many; it didn't appear to be her first rendezvous in the cab of a truck. Soon Tina Turner's hair leaned forward, arced down, and—but for its bouncing spikes—disappeared below the windshield's horizon. "You don't wanna see this," I replied, closing the curtain.

"Can I tell you something?" Marsha asked.

"What?"

"You can't say I told you."

"Told me what?"

"I can't say."

"Say what?"

"That it was Kittenz. Mizz Kittenz told them you were underage."

"Are you serious? Are you sure?"

"Between shows, she told umm…Smidget?"

"Smidge."

"She told Smidge to send Wayne to our dressing room. When he got there she goes, 'I think we have a problem'. Then she tells him she just found out you were underage, like fifteen or sixteen or something. And that you didn't have an ID. She goes: I just didn't want your bar to get in trouble with your liquor license."

I leaned back, resting my forearms on the dinette.

"Are you mad?"

I picked at the nail glue on my fingertips.

"Oh Jesus, I shoulda kept my mouth shut. Are you mad?"… "Hey, are you mad?"

When the RV door opened, Kittenz stumbled in messy and drunk, "I said not to wait up for me." She took off her jacket, a wet spot darkened her top; she sat, smothering the stink of santorum behind her; she stared at no one in particular, something like redemption in her eyes (the eyes of a deserted matinee idol who just took a call from Louis B. Mayer).

"Did you have a good time?" I jabbed.

"Don't you dare mind your buziness," she sort-of replied, her hostility hampered by a hooch handicap.

Mizz Kittenz removed her belt and boots and then peeled off her eyelashes—one from her eye, one from her wig (no need to wipe-away her lipstick, the trucker had done it.) She began removing pins from her hair, now misshapen from the dirty hands of our neighbor. "I'll have to wash and set this later," she said (in case we were unclear about its recent soiling), then she sat at the dinette with Marsha and me, pushing baby-oil around the flaps of her face.

"Hey Kittenz. I was just wondering…"

Marsha looked at me, then to Jesus.

"…did anyone at the club happen to mention how they knew I was underage?"

Kittenz pulled more pins from her wig and dropped them on the table. "Why would they tell me anything? I'm juzt the headliner."

"Oh, I know. So, they never said anything to you, or you never said anything to them?"

A few more pins, "Watch yourself, Missy."

"Oh, no, I was just curious about right after they said they wanted *me* to close the show, I wondered if anyone discussed anything with *you* about my age or anything."

Kittenz pulled the wig from her head then stood, tossing her hair to the floor (Marsha ducked the wig, like a colony of bats might fly out) "You think you're hot shit? "Well, PS honey, I'm a *goddamn* forrezt fire…"

"So you didn't say anything to them about my age?"

Marsha pushed hair in front of her face, retreating into her blond bombshelter.

"I won't dignify that with a response but *No I Didn't!* I don't need to tattle to management, you ungrateful bitch. Do you know who I am? I wore the <u>Panhandle</u> <u>Princess</u> crown back when it *meant* something! Ever heard of class? That's what we had in my day. If class was cancer I'd be covered in tumors. I walked into a bar and thirty queens ran up to ask for my autograph / there was a different naked boy in my dressing room <u>every</u> <u>night</u> of the <u>week</u>! You know why? Because I've got *it*. Do you know what *panache* is, well Honey you better look it up cuz I've got it in spades! Do you think I was born yezterday? Don't let thiz bod fool you Mz Thing, I've got *wigs* older than you! <u>Custom</u> <u>made</u> wigs, not the mail-order mops you bitchez wear. And don't let this gray hair kid ya cuz PS, juzt because there'z snow on the rooftop doesn't mean there'z no fireplace below the basement! I'm a GD Inferno! Lightning and thunderboltz, baby! A tempest in a windstorm! You think you can compete with *that*? I've broken girlz twice your age! Trust me, every effing fucker who tried to upstage *Kittenz* is buried at the bottom of the litter box! Believe you me, I know how to fight dirty. Ever heard of ground glass in face powder? I have! I've <u>been</u> <u>around</u> the <u>block</u> a time or two! And more than once! Hell, I've danced back-up for Della de La Pierre! I worked with *all* the greatz, Norma Kristie, Michael Andrews, Charles Pierce! I know *what's what* Sister! They could write a *book* on the things I don't know! The greatest story never sold!"

"The greatest story ever told?" Marsha mumbled from behind her wig.

"<u>Shut</u> <u>up</u>!"

WEEDS No.2

I woke near nine, to the sound of the last trucker leaving the stop that following morning. Kittenz had migrated from the dinette's bench (where she passed-out) and was now sleeping in the RV's driver's seat, a fluffy robe her only blanket; I thought of bringing her another but decided otherwise. The remaining four slept in their beds, all snoring like little girls; it had been a long night. I sipped from a cup of yesterday's coffee then put on my pants, I'd delayed using the 'facilities' for almost three days and

221

now it wouldn't be denied. I found tissue in Lena's bra then opened the camper door as quietly as one could.

It was a trek into the field—to a spot where the weeds had grown high enough to obscure poopers from passersby. I stopped at one spot and pulled down my pants, then saw a lizard and moved on to another. *This will doo*, I thought.

Extramural excrement was not one of my strengths, just the thought of it jammed me up. When Mom and Norm took Mona and me camping I never went to the bathroom, number-two I mean. I did try a couple of times but no dice. But today, this was going to happen. I slid my pants to my calves and let the cool morning air freshen my testicles. Then I squatted like a baseball catcher for several minutes, until my thighs requested a more comfortable position. On a whim I removed my pants and planted both knees on the ground in front of me, then sat back on my ankles and heels. It was a clever position—my heels pulling my buttcheeks apart, why had no one ever recommended it to me?

Only the top half of my head rose above the weeds, I could see the RV from this vantage, and Mizz Kittenz sleeping. *Why should I give her a blanket*, I thought, she doesn't deserve to be warm. I should smother her with it instead. It probably wouldn't be hard, she's like a hundred. Everyone would just assume it was natural causes. "She had a long life," they'd say, "too long, really."

I don't know why she told the club my age, but *too bad* if she was pissed that I got asked to close the show. It wasn't my fault. And didn't I deserve it? I was good! The spinning, the churning, the magic. Still, I bet it hurt her feelings—she's been closing the show for a long time. Kittenz has a queensize ego (once—dressed like a cowgirl—I saw her wink into a mirror, "Honey, if you haven't winked at a mirror then you don't have a fringe vest!"), now that it's antique and fragile it definitely wouldn't withstand a blow as bludgeoning as public rejection. Bitchy as she was, if you squinted past the drunkenness you saw the transparency of her asperity. Last night, I did. I saw sadness through her anger as clearly as I'd seen ballsack through her tights. She was just a sad, old, big-balled lady (if everything goes wrong in life, the kind of lady I could be some day). I decided: *I should talk to her privately,* maybe when we stop for lunch. God, poop already!

There was a tree branch beside me, dead on the ground but lifted up by its arthritic tentacles. It was probably why I chose this spot—something to anchor me. I walked two of my fingers along the branch's knotty, irregular surface. When they walked to the end of a piece, they took a deep breath and jumped to another; made it, but just barely. I don't think Kittenz hates me. She invited me to Thanksgiving dinner. Why would she do that if she hated me? *It's just an argument,* I thought. Families argue, then they make up. So what if she fucked up. We all fuck up. I've fucked up. If she apologizes then I can forgive her.

I think she was right, about Mom being a child when she had me. If I had a child now, I wouldn't be a very good parent. But Thanksgiving, *come-on,* closing the door on me and Liz and Wally. Because of my hair! Guess what bitch, I'm not crazy about *your* hair. Does that mean I'd want you to spend holidays alone, *doubt it.* And why would you not visit me after I moved out? How much could gas cost? Why don't you skip a carton of cigarettes and go see your goddamn son. Please poop!

And another thing, please explain to me how you could hit me, with a belt, because I didn't say 'thank you' to your boyfriend for taking us on a ski trip. After Mickey! Did you really think Mona and I would be happy that you were starting-up with some other dude? Would this guy send me away too? Beat you up, hurt my sister, and set our house on fire? Are you really so stupid that you couldn't empathize with why we, *why I,* might not have liked your new boyfriend?

You know what? I don't really care any more. Because if I cared then I wouldn't already be over it—which I am. Did you know that mothers love their children because, in childbirth, their brain produces some chemical that dopes them into believing they feel love? So that they won't just abandon their babies in the wild. Maybe you just ran out of the chemical a little earlier than most, you did have a high metabolism. Maybe you were running on fumes and by Thanksgiving, it just pooped out.

(I felt a stir, below my stomach) And just to be clear, I bet Thanksgiving wasn't about my hair at all. I remember the way you ended things with Norm—attacking him for humming when he ate! Other men too, picking apart the little annoyances of their personalities. When you grow tired of men do you just decide that something about them is *so* unacceptable that you have to attack it? You have to cause a rift so big that they fall into it and disappear? By the way, did you do the same thing to my dad? Is that why you divorced him too? When the pages of your storybook relationships start to crease and yellow—from NORMAL use—do you become so intolerant of the imperfections that you have to douse them with gasoline. Dad. Norm. Me. Just books on the bonfire?

Well hey, joke's on you. I don't need to eat your stupid Thanksgiving dinners (definitely something stirring in my ass region), Christmas either. I have my own family now, I have friends, Mizz Kittenz *wants* me to come to her house for the holiday. Not because nature slipped her some chemical that tricked her into caring about me. But because she *really* likes me (not a stir, so much as a slide) and she doesn't care what my hair looks like. Which, FYI, looks great. Oh and PS, (This is it, I thought, pushing back onto my heels) I didn't love you because nature spiked my formula, *I loved you because I thought you loved me too.*

The words were like jalapeños burning my eyes. One faucet opened, and then another. Tears and terds poured out of me—a cask with too many spigots. *You fucking bitch,* I thought, *how could you lock a second-grader out of the house, how could you give me to Berniece when you knew she hated me, how could you slam the door when I brought you a pumpkin pie!* Eyes to ass, I pushed the blackness out of me, every way I could. *I hate you for not loving me. I hate you.*

I sat for a minute, *What the hell was that?* Then used the tissue to wipe my eyes, then to wipe the rest. *My first lawn sausage*, I thought, *not bad.* I sat on the ground—pantsless, parentless, and exhausted from the purge—then looked at the RV, *Kittenz is up.* I was glad to see her face, she was wearing her fluffy robe, *it's a nice robe.* She stood on the steps of the camper, *she's worried about me.* Her face panned the field from side to side, *yeah, she's looking for me.* I raised my hand and waved, not certain if she would see, but she did. She reached down, grabbing something—my suitcase. It wasn't zipped and something fell out, *Be careful!*, I thought. Then she threw the luggage as if a bomb was heard ticking inside, and she shouted, "Here'z your luggage. And PS,"…

"WALK HOME YOU UNGRATEFUL BITCH!"

I upped my pants and charged the RV but it was too far—I was too late, Kittenz put the paw to the pedal and sped away. I ran behind the camper, spit on by the dust of a dirt road as the vehicle shrank into the horizon. I ran until lungs and legs betrayed me and I just couldn't run any more. Then I stood in the street and cried like an eight-year-old who just lost his mother.

Thirteen Ghosts

You've Got Mail, and AIDS. By the end of the 1980s I had neither but they were all the rage, the world was changing and so was I. Maybe not in ways others would notice, but in ways that made it hard to sleep. I was a malcontent, dissatisfied with everything. My job—too trivial, my apartment—too american, my friendships—too detached. I was an intellectual with a ninth-grade education, a romantic with a fear of intimacy, an artist who envisioned clichés. I needed to find something to justify me— something to arouse an unpassioned life, but right now I'd settle for the packing tape.

Everything from my closet was boxed. All but two shirts, a *pair* of pants, a *pair* of shorts and a *pair* of sweats (or is it just *pants, shorts* and *sweats*), and some shoes. They'd fit a knapsack, the rest in the back of the van. I had no job lined up, no prospects, but how hard could it be for a gay with a GED to find work in San Francisco. The Village People might be hiring, I heard 'The Cop' left. I could be 'The Short-Order Cook', or 'The Stenographer' or something. Maybe 'The Candlestick-Maker', that has a nice old-world charm. Beau would be here in the morning, bright and early.

Or at least early (Beau wasn't all that bright.) He also wasn't motivated or conscientious or trustworthy. He was however my best friend.

The walls of my apartment were a sinister dark, a color I chose from the Aleister Crowley line at Sherwin-Williams. And the three gallons of 'Pearly-Gates White' latex that came with the place had been used to undercoat bad art. *She can keep my deposit*, I decided, then I won't have to fix the bathroom either. My dissatisfaction was most measurable at night, when I tried to sleep. Variations of 'This isn't enough' congested the mind as tangibly as mucus congests the nose, if only there were a nettie-pot for the brain. Like Madame Bovary, I had one kind of dream and another kind of life. And time, it seemed, was flying by. *Grunge music hasn't even started yet,* I worried, *and I'm already passé.*

Beau and I had been friends for a few years. We met while I lived in Giddyuptown and was driving to Cowboy City to perform at Crash-Box. My friends and I were still there the night after the drag show, dancing, when Beau offered, "You guys are the coolest people I've ever seen!" I immediately recognized his astuteness and invited him back to Giddyuptown. He was tall, skinny, blond, tan, pretty. A more feminine version of Cheryl Tiegs. He spent a week with us and told me a story about trying to smuggle a pair of his stepfather's dirty underwear past his mother and her husband. Despite much experience, Beau was not a skilled liar.

"What were you doing in our bathroom?" Trina—Beau's mother—asked.

"What?"

"Why were you in our bathroom?"

"Oh, I was just looking for some lotion."

"What's in the magazine?" she asked, gesturing to the one rolled like a suspicious burrito in his fidgety hand.

"What magazine?"

"The one rolled-up in your hand," Trina persisted.

"It's just a *Town & Country*," he explained to the couple—Trina and Larry—watching TV on the livingroom sofa.

"I know that Beau, what's rolled-up *inside* the *Town & Country*?"

"Oh, I'm not sure," he answered, "I just picked it up."

"Unroll the magazine and show me what's inside."

"Inside the magazine?"

"Yes Beau, *inside* the magazine."

"Oh, there's just stuff about towns and countries."

"Give me the magazine."

"Okay, but I need to go to the bathroom first."

"Give me the magazine, NOW."

(He handed the package to his mother)

"Beau, what are you doing with Larry's underwear?"

"What?"

"What are you doing with Larry's underwear?"

"Oh, I was gonna . . . have them cleaned for him. For Father's Day."

I told Beau about sniffing my sleeping stepfather's testicles, we were best friends ever since.

My wardrobe of thrift store clothes was packed, a career of drag costumes was not. Drag, as an occupation, was something I disclosed only case by case, but it's hard to deny your crossdress when you bend forward and there's a black sequin stuck to your white ass (if I charged a dime every time some sweaty guy chirped "What's this?" I'd have close to forty cents.) Some were excited to connect me to my alter ego as they'd been fans—gay communities are tight when cinched by a bible belt, it's easy to be well known. Other would-be boyfriends reacted as if I'd said I was a bankrobber or a professional baby-shaker. "I'm not just *any* baby-shaker," I'd try to explain, "I'm one of the best." My black chiffon Stevie Nicks dress, I had worn it many times since Mizz Kittenz stranded me at a truck stop, though never with as much excitement, I rolled it into a ball for safe travel. I didn't know if I would perform in San Francisco—if I needed the money, I guessed. I still did shows here and there, but supplemented a performer's fitful income with a more dependable gig as a telephone operator for the deaf. My nine-to-five was a fleeting romance with normalcy—a spasm of respectability in the eyes of Nana Pearl (and Uncle Sam).

"We're so proud of you Chris," my nana gushed, as though I'd just performed the world's first baby-safe abortion, "I always knew *you'd* be the success in the family."

"Thanks Nan," my sister would answer.

"And you too, Mona, you too."

The owner of the company liked me and I liked her, she made me the manager despite my status as youngest on staff. Ralph worked there too. He was tall and doughy, like an éclair turned on end, with hairy fingers. Like me, he was doing drag on weekends, though he was new to the scene and hadn't had the success I'd had. Ralph was funny and flirtatious, batting eyelashes still stained black from the night before. He would move with us to San Francisco, taking turns with Beau at driving the van. I was riding bitch.

It was an ill-fated performance of Sheila E's "The Glamorous Life" that inaugurated the end of my drag career. Phyllis Cheesesteak and Sloppy Joanne told some campy jokes and then introduced me, as they often did. Joanne gave me a wink, and Phyllis said *Get 'em, tiger* as we wriggled past each other stageside. It had been years since the night I met them, years since they first put me and Scooter in drag. While I'm sure I never told them, their weekly backstage presence had become a comfort in my mostly motherless life. It was, after all, only their willingness to mascara the eyes and blush the cheeks of a runaway that had given him—me—the means to eat. In fact I never eat a Philly cheesesteak or a Sloppy Joe without thinking of them.

I'd performed the Sheila E. song many times; the crowd knew it well. The routine was semi-choreographed with lots of kicks and spins, a hair toss here, a floor slap there. As always, I sashayed onto the dancefloor stage, stagelights bouncing off my shiny silver outfit as the crowd welcomed me with their claps and catcalls. I'd done it all many times before, only tonight—something was different.

I smiled at a boy, took a dollar from a girl, and ground my hips like they were first gear. It was all so familiar; still, something was wrong. Step—step—kick, I missed a beat so I winked at the crowd, but everybody knew from my coy little wink, this girl had a lot on her mind.

It wasn't the stage, I had pranced across this stage hundreds of times. It wasn't the song, songs never change. It wasn't the crowd and so that left only me. Tonight, as a verse turned to its chorus—as I prepared to rev it up, to kick my sparkly ass into high gear—I simply stopped. In my stoppedness I heard tinnitic tones instead of music, instead of an audience I saw sunlike spotlights. My legs locked and my lips fell out of lipsync. I was stuck.

In that moment, that endless moment, it was as if a silhouetted hand had pulled a meandering rope that tipped a precarious bucket that doused me in pig blood. Then, as the emptied bucket swung like time's pendulum overhead, I regressed. For a moment, an endless moment, I had never been a runaway, a showboat, a drag queen. I was just a kid, an awkward kid with skinny legs wondering how and why they were stuffed into fishnet hose and sequin shoes. With makeup masking childish confusion, I stumbled off the stage, barely able to walk in my towering heels.

"Bitch, what happened?"

"I, felt sick. I was getting sick."

"She's sick, back up, she's sick."

231

The backstage performers circled around me, one waved her purse to give me some air. "Here, drink this," another insisted, handing me her mai tai.

The moment passed and for the thirty minutes between shows the girls all mingled out front, dancing together and teasing boys. I stayed behind, wrapped in a long furry robe, sitting in front of a portable make-up mirror, studying my powdery face and curly synthetic hair.

When everyone returned for the second show I was ready, I knew the lyrics, I remembered my routine. Again, the sandwich sisters introduced me and I quickstepped a sparkly fringe dress onto the stage and the crowd clapped madly as fans would an injured quarterback returning to finish the big game. All was forgiven, but still, something was different.

The difference was: from that night forward I would perform each song with the gnawing knowledge that I had stumbled onto a path that could only be walked in high heels. I happened to look good in high heels and it was a decent life, but it wasn't mine... I'm not that girl.

I dumped a wooden drawerful of oil paints into a plastic sack then added a lump of colorfully paint-stained rags that resembled the bandages of a dying clown. I tied it closed and wondered if the fumes would ignite a fire. Paintbrushes were similarly sacked and then there were dozens of canvases—maybe hundreds—to wrap and box; had my apartment been packed by an art critic he would have thrown them all away.

I made art here and there (here by the bed, and there by the chair) since I moved into this apartment, trying to replicate the old-master paintings I'd studied in a shoplifted art book; I failed. Still, I once won a months-of-the-calendar drawing contest between the kindergarteners in my hometown, and you don't just lose talent like that. My teacher, Mrs Robertson, told my mother that I was the only child whose drawing used perspective; she was a white woman with heavy make-up and afro hair, and the first of my many art teacher crushes.

I wore painfully ill-sized oxford shoes to the City Hall award ceremony and Mom threatened to take me home when I attempted a cry. I squirmed in my plastic chair for half an hour, listening to my mother whisper her critique of my behavior, gritting my teeth and cursing my sadistic shoes. When the podium speaker finally called my name to receive a certificate, "Chris Madrigal...for...the month of May," the audience clapped as they had all afternoon, and then they hushed when I walked the difficult distance as if bow-leggedly traversing hot coals in slow motion.

I imagine my mother also said some nice things to me that day but I didn't give her the courtesy I gave acquaintances like Mrs Robinson, with her I catalogued only the insults.

After the art supplies, I boxed a collection of stolen underwear. There was a pair from nearly everyone I'd ever dated, even if we dated only long enough for him to lose his briefs. Some were labeled with the person's name, some were made anonymous by my lack of organization, all were hardpressed to fit into a single box.

I'd had a string of romances in Cowboy City, quartets really, but nothing that lasted. Maybe that's why I was disheartened, though it felt like something more. I dated Jules for a while, when I first moved here. I was at the underage bar when we met, the only place I could get in without wearing a dress.

Except for its backstage and bathrooms, Crashbox was a single room bisected by a wood divider and five or six stools. The area on *this* side of the divider offered two pool tables, three video games, a doorgirl with an attitude, and eighty kids with as many cigarettes. Most had fashioned their hair into something inconsistent with gravity, all had fashioned their fashion into something inconsistent with parental wishes. Every boy was accompanied by a girl, but rarely romantically; every girl held the couple's cigarettes in a box-shaped purse. The area on *that* side offered a neon-lit cement dance floor with a video screen at one end and dusty bleacher seating on the other, in between were the kids whose MDA regimens allowed them to dance to every song.

On this particular night I arrived early and stood near a video game, my hag was home sick so Ms. Pac-Man was filling in.

"Are you performing tonight?" an approaching girl whose name I don't remember asked, even though I'm not in drag.

"Not tonight."

"Do you want a hit?" she said.

"I don't do drugs." I answered, knowing it might incite conversation but saying it anyway.

"Oh my god, you're so healthy, I love you."

"That's the MDA talking."

Undeterred, she hugged me as if I were a family member boarding a flight that's scheduled to crash. "I love you," she reminded me, waving goodbye and dancing away.

Karlita, that might have been her name. I hate when people recognize me out of drag, shattering my sexy with a grenade of glitter; I found my footing and resumed my pose.

The crowd thickened since the last paragraph, another two-dozen hairdos had arrived. The boy with the eyepatch was there, he'd added a cane to the ensemble, like a gimp-legged Adam Ant. Inger and Ingrid were there, impossibly tall German sisters in Bananarama overalls, sharing secrets from behind a waist-length curtain of teased bangs. Through an opening in my own bangs I saw something approaching, two boys I thought, or lesbians maybe. Just as the couple reached me it happened. Drinking stopped, cigarettes snuffed, arguments ended. Me and the two lesbian boys and a hundred others changed direction, we moved like a school of fish, superbly synchronized without a leader.

It could have been the beginning of "8:15 To Nowhere" by Vicious Pink, or "Running Up That Hill" by Kate Bush, or "Looking From A Hilltop" or "How Soon Is Now?"…whichever intro, it was the gong that harkened a song—a song that converted a smoky shack into a charnal church. Shoulder to padded shoulder we crossed from *this* side to *that* side and we danced, writhing in the wild-haired worship of a judgeless god.

We were a collection of triangle earrings and studded belts, green hair with purple tips, and black mascara to our eyebrows. For five fevered minutes we—the alien outcasts on our own city blocks—danced as if returned to our mothership, we were home.

I left the dancefloor as Jules and his entourage arrived, he was mid-thirties—possibly forty, definitely a standout in our teen tabernacle. The mature man stood out not just for his age but also his beauty. With gently curling long black hair and an ivory linen suit he looked like a cross between a breezy Miami socialite and a crucified messiah. Jules was Cowboy City's most elite hairdresser, he ran full page ads of himself (surrounded by an over-blushed harem of reclining lady hair models) in the local paper; his three-dollar cover charge was comped by the door girl. As soon as Jules entered the club, he saw me staring and walked directly to me. Putting my face in his hands (as Jesus might a leper), he kissed me deeply in the mouth. "Come home with me," he commanded. "Okay," I obeyed.

The cocky coiffeur was Cowboy City's glitteratti, a mystery man with a legendary apartment. The 22nd floor penthouse had uplit curtains around big windows, and neon artwork on teal and magenta walls, it was an apartment decorated for late-night entertaining. Invitations to his after-parties were as enviable as the appointments in his expensive salon. The beautician's local prestige and Casanova charm were impressive to the city's many smalltown transplants.

"*Chris* is not your birth name," he growled, in front of a city-lit, 22nd floor window, "tell me your birth name."

"It's Christian," I confessed.

"Ahh, from 'Christianus'—a follower of Christ. I will call you Christian." With that, the celebrated hairdresser had restyled my name, restored its original length and natural curl. I would wear it this way from that point on.

Jules' demeanor was worldly, his eyes were searing. And his laugh—like his body fluid—was infectious, something the sexy svengali forgot to mention when we made-love on his livingroom's tibetan lamb rug. I was lucky though, escaping with only my ego sickened by an awkward introduction to his wife Shawndra the next morning.

Jules wasn't the only coin in the fountain, a few months later I was dating his best friend Leon. Leon looked like Jules (his eyes a little less intense, his nose not so carefully sculpted, his beard a bit more feral), I imagined the hairy pair might ravage me like two baboons ganging-up on a hyena; they didn't. Jules died a few years later, pneumonia or somesuch complication. His many friends made a commemorative panel for him when the AIDS Quilt came to town, I wasn't asked to participate but did consider starting an AIDS Pillow Case or a Syphilis Dust Ruffle to show my support for the sexually scourged. Five years further I learned that his wife Shawndra exploded in the Timothy McVeigh bombing. I wasn't necessarily filled with the rage that people even less personally affected by terrorism felt, but I did wonder who got the apartment.

Leon had a less glamorous job at Jules' salon, and a much smaller apartment. I spent the night at his house and he woke early the next morning. "I have to go to work," he said with a smile less bright than his friend's, "sleep as long as you want, you can lock the door when you leave, or stay here until I get home at five." I was touched—entrusting me with his apartment, "I'll be here when you get home."

The door shut and I listened to his footsteps fade into absence. I was alone in a sexy man's apartment and—for once—I had permission to be there, I jumped from the bed and looked around. What were his secrets, I wondered, where are his underwear? Under the bed I saw a suitcase, pulled it out, unhinged its latches, opened it up. Glossy magazine covers glistened like lost treasures dredged up from the sea. *'Teen Testicles'*, *'Boner Boys'*, *'Ding Dong Derelicts'*. I grabbed a handful of the magazines and then myself.

"Wait!" I thought. Not *"Wait! This is wrong!"* but *"Wait! I need lube!"*

I checked the bathroom first, then the kitchen—grabbing a tub of 'You Can't Tell Me It's Not Butter!', then I ran back to the livingroom where his bed was. *Not the bed*, I thought, I need space. I sat on the floor and arrayed two dozen of the magazines on the floor around me, like cards for a game of sexy solitaire. Then I dipped my hand into the tub.

"What are you doing?" Leon asked from the doorway, pulling his key from the knob.

"Huh?"

"My stuff, what are you doing with my stuff?"

"Oh, this stuff," I replied with a handful of butter substitute, "I wanted something to read."

I never stayed at Leon's house after that. The relationship fizzled like all of them would over the next year, two years, three. Every attraction felt like it would lead to something, but the something always turned out to be the next attraction. *Boys are like families*, I thought, *they don't last.* Not just them, me too—one in my trap, another in my sights, always. It's what you do when you fear starvation, you hunt. Sometimes it's hard to know what you're hungry for, so you reach for whatever is nearest. For me, dick was always nearby. But what my body really needed was a salad. Something healthy I mean. A healthy relationship? Probably, but not just. I needed depth that wasn't available in this kiddy pool of a life, I needed to grow up.

It may have been my deathscare with Jules that had me thinking. There were some summer mornings when I woke atop a muggy bedsheet, certain the swelter was the dreaded nightsweats. *Was I dying*, I wondered, as I scrambled a hand around my body, searching for suspicious perspiration. From the damp discomfort of my deathbed I thought about the people I'd miss, no names came to mind. I wouldn't miss people, I realized, but I was sad for the things I'd leave behind. I'd miss my record albums, my pornography, and the art on my walls. I also missed the things that hadn't happened yet: new inventions, celebrity scandals, mass murders. *Hellraiser* was a really good movie, what if they make a sequel and I'm not here to see it? And books...there were rumors of a fourth Katherine Dunn novel, *The Cut Man*, and I'd long dreamt of a Roberta Flack tell-all erotobiography, *The First Time Ever I Sat Your Face.* (Sitting on faces, I'd miss that.)

I amassed a great many things while in Cowboy City, all of them needed packed. *So many magazines*, I thought, keep a few favorites and toss the rest. "I need this Architectural Digest, it has that apartment with the gryphon statues and the black walls." My apartment's a dump, I decided, I want a place like this. I skimmed a half-dozen magazines, probably not fast enough. My next apartment will be designed in the manner of a windowless hideout for the smuggled treasures of an exiled aristocrat, I imagined. Two hours later the 'toss' pile had a Vanity Fair and an International Male catalogue, not sure where I got them. The 'keep' pile threatened to crush me if it toppled.

"I was paralyzed when a rocket-propelled grenade hit our humvee," an Iraq war vet will confide.

"Me? I lost my legs when a stack of Architectural Digests fell on me, it was really scary."

Nonetheless, I boxed them all. Packing tape. Wrote something with a marker. Five boxes in two hours, this wasn't going very well.

The phone rang, it had been ringing all day. Typically, young queens from the drag bar promising to write. None of them did, probably just as much my fault for not giving them an address. It was Sterling. We would have been best friends if we didn't each have friends we liked better. Still, we were close.

"So you're really doin' it?"

"Looks like it."

"Girl, don't leave me, I'll kill myself." Sterling was a stoner who really only used 'girl' in jest. He'd made a career of dating in-demand drag queens, including my drag-sister Scooter, and they'd rubbed-off on him (in more ways than the pornographic).

"You should just do it, kill yourself to teach me a lesson."

"What's the lesson?"

"Not to tell people they should just do it."

"Hey, remember that time," Sterling loved to play *remember that time*, "when you broke-up with that boy and he left a letter on your windshield that said he was gonna kill himself if you didn't want him anymore?"

"Yeah, that was funny."

"So funny."

Sterling and I had never really dated, though we sometimes watched porn together, and sometimes played 'monkey on my back'. (That's not really what we called it, I just didn't know a good euphemism for ass sex.) We were like the TV friends who make the pact: "if we're both still single by the time were forty then let's get married," except more like: "if we haven't picked up anyone by the time the bar closes then let's have ass sex."

"Angela called," I said.

"What does that fatty want?" Fatty was Sterling's pet name for Angela. The three of us were very close before Angela showed the mini-mart guy her boobs in exchange for two burritos and a pack of cigarettes then moved back with her parents in shame and defeat.

"She heard I was moving. She wanted to say good-bye."

I hadn't heard from Angela in a few years, since she got married and became a realtor.

"Oh, well that's nice that she called."

"She also wanted to know if I had fifty dollars to cover my part of an old electric bill."

"What! Are you fucking serious?"

"I know! She said her dad got the bill because he cosigned our electricity. She asked me to send him a check for fifty dollars."

"Aren't they rich?"

"Yes!"

"Didn't her dad kick you out of their house?"

"I know! Because he didn't like my hair."

"So that's why she called. After three years. For fifty dollars."

"Yes!"

"Girl!"

"I know!"

We talked for half an hour, until I announced that I had to go. I really did have a lot of packing to do, but it was the only phone call of the day that was hard to end.

"I love you, girl."

"Love you too."

"No I mean it, I'm gonna miss you."

"I'll miss you too."

The kitchen will be the worst, I thought, if I'm not getting my deposit back then I'm not cleaning the oven. So many boxes of cereal, plastic containers, packets of catsup. Why do I have a casserole dish, I'm not even sure what a casserole is. Actually it was my mother's dish. A couple of years ago, on my birthday, Mom and Nana came to see me. This was a year and a half after the Thanksgiving when she turned me and Liz and Wally away. Mom brought a peach cobbler—my favorite—and she left the dish. They didn't stay long. The ladies made some veiled and some naked insults about the style of my decor and the quality of my housekeeping, then Mom said something about traffic being heavy this time of year (code that I had fermented to a sour she could endure only a few hours at a time). It was the one time they visited this apartment, possibly the only time they visited any of my apartments in Oklahoma. I loved my mother, but only as much as she loved me. And that wasn't enough to sustain a relationship. She revealed the limits of her feelings for me on Thanksgiving, I decided; it was the anvil that broke the camel's back. Before that, I used to love her a lot more, but she plunged a plunger into my heart and let several quarts of it drain away. I didn't know it yet but I would see her only a few more times in my life—a funeral and a couple of Christmases in the 1990s. Then the relationship would just lie down and die.

I do wonder if she'll see this book, and how unfair she'll think the writing was. Pretty unfair, I imagine. She was actually wonderful at times, as a child I believed no mother and son had ever loved each other more. If *she* wrote the book it might have included some of *my* lesser moments, probably the time I visited on her birthday. I'd just started my drag career and decided what a treat it would be for my mother and my grandmother—Nana—if I came in drag, what mother wouldn't fancy a surprise like that?

Liz and I drove the long drive to Puddin Foot, me compounding my make-up and her telling me how good it looked, before accidentally running her car into a roadside ditch. We weren't hurt and my make-up was fine, and then a sheriff's deputy patrolling our dirt road offered a ride to my mother's house so we could call a tow.

"Where are you ladies from?" the police gal asked.

"We're business ladies from the East," Liz replied.

The crunch of driveway gravel announced our arrival; Mom and Nana came out—onto the porch, Mom holding a dishtowel and Nana clutching a cat. The women watched with confusion as the officer exited her cruiser. Their confusion multiplied when an unknown woman with excessive eye make-up then emerged from the vehicle's backseat, did a little twirl to model her purple Evan Picone business-executive skirt suit, and shouted "Happy Birthday Mom...it's me, Chris!"

I put the casserole dish in newspaper, and that into a box.

Where my relationship with my mother went, so went mine with my sister. I heard from her only once more, twenty years after this chapter. "Hey Chris, it's Mona," she said on my voice mail, in a voice that sounded like a butch old hillbilly. "Listen, Brother, I need money. They're trying to take my house. Call me back at— hey Gwenda, what's my number—call me back at..." It seemed she had forgotten not only her phone number but also that the last time we spoke she was pinning my arms while Gwenda punched me in the face for eating a can of their soup. By this age I no longer held with family, or excused disloyalties, so I didn't save the message or write down the number. I've questioned the decision however, at times, though never enough to try to see how the crisis worked out.

I don't regret not sending money to the two women, especially knowing what I think I know about their adult habits. But I do regret the slight it may have been to the little clarinetist—the childhood sister that I only vaguely remember—or whatever part of that sad little girl that might have survived the adult she became. If I knew six—seven—eight-year-old Mona's number I'd send money, I'd call.

I knew I couldn't take all my furniture, *but I'm definitely taking the floral chairs.* Half of my furniture was covered in sheets, not because I was preparing for the move but because that was the way I kept it (I liked my furniture to look like I was throwing a cocktail party for ghosts.) Some folks are relaxed by the sounds of songbirds or running streams, I prefer rattling chains and creaky hinges. And I like the somber scene bathed in lugubrious light: a candelabra, a torn silk shade, a dusty chandelier. The funereal affectations soothe a doleful soul. Plus, the furniture's witchy shrouds reminded me of Gizi's place (and helped hide ugly underlying upholstery). Not the floral chairs though—the ones Liz and I stole from a porch, I liked those the way they were. As I packed my apartment, my life, its sepulchral serenity sank into the floorboards and a brightly lit mess sprouted in its place; my new life hadn't even begun, and my old one was already destroyed.

I found a bright blue scarf with paisleys and fringe, I hadn't seen it in years. The accessory belonged to Dell (he tied it around his hair in a Paisley Prince styled turban), someone I knew from junior high. I was the dumbest person in my grade's accelerated learning program (that's not false humility—I just researched the spelling of *accelerated*), the program moved half my eighth-grade day to Puddin Foot High where I'd usually see twelfth-grade Dell in the highschool lunchroom, he was hard to miss. Dell was tall—not exceptionally, and fat—exceptionally. He was in fact the largest person in school, though many students had genuine confusion as to whether or not he was the largest man or the largest woman; I was among the uncertain. His long, wiry, stoner's hair frightfully framed an angry lapdog's face, he wore overalls and clogs to school everyday. I eventually learned that Dell's entire family was morbidly obese, which made it even less fortunate that they lived in Puddin Foot's smallest house. Dell had few friends and would seem to have been the perfect target for smalltown cruelty, though I never once saw a student make fun of the width of his size, the redundancy of his clothes, the bend of his gender, or his exquisitely unhandsome face. Surely they skewered him secretly, but never otherwise. I doubt this was because they were learning tolerance, but rather because Dell was one scary bitch. When his noisy wooden shoes clogged past you it was as if Leatherface had just rumbled across your path, you looked to the ground and tried not to draw his attention. This isn't to say that Dell was mean—he wasn't, in fact in school I'd never heard him speak. But there was a quiet quality—some component of his countenance, or element in his expression, or detail to his demeanor that made very clear: *Don't Even Think About It.*

I didn't know at the time but the imposing character happened to be close friends with Decker Abbott—the boyfriend my sister and I would later share. There was a secret circle of gays in Puddin Foot: Dell, Decker, Billiam, a guy named Fisher, and a lesbian (I messed around with three of them at one time or another…I'll give you a hint: it wasn't Dell or the lez), but I moved away before the circle had formally called me into the order. Instead, Dell and I became friends after I moved to Cowboy City, he moved here too—crashing (and burning) with me and Angela for the lesser part of a year. (Sterling stayed with us then too—after he briefly impregnated a previous houseguest [we called the unborn child 'Zsa Zsa Gabortion' because we were sure she'd've been fancy] but before he settled down with my lazy-eyed, hyper-competitive drag sister Scooter.) Dell was a maternal figure in our group, maybe because he was older or maybe because he longed to be a mother, or maybe we forced him into the role because it was one we needed filled; however it happened, it was nice to have him around. Dell became the archetype for someone I always hope to have in my life: a big maternal gay. I probably never told him so (before he was fatally heart-attacked), but I admired Dell and have never forgotten the extraordinary power he had to shut smalltown stupid down. This, with only the *Say something, I dare you* abilities of a face.

Other forgotten photos and lost mementos sprung like mushrooms from improbable places. I found my photo of Gizi, it had fallen behind a dresser. It was already in bad shape when I unearthed it from the rubble of Gizi's old house and it was worse now. Dirty and fading, it needed to be preserved. *I should scan this*, I thought, once flatbed scanners hit the market. I put her photo in an envelope with my only photo of Wally—he was laughing on a beach, I wanted to protect them like I would a birth certificate or the carcass of a dragonfly. Once when Reuben and I had a fight (I condemned him as selfish, he screamed I was inflexible. Maybe he was right but what I lacked in flexibility I made up for in rigidity; besides, I didn't believe his barhopping while I was home strep-throated deserved my elasticity), I stayed with Wally. I was having a hard time supporting myself at fifteen and unsure where I would live. Wally was a few years older than me, he played guitar and had dreams of riding a limo to the top of the charts. He kneeled beside the bed he'd made me on the couch of his small apartment, rested his head on the pillow next to mine, and said the sweetest thing anyone ever said to me.

"If you need me to, I'll take care of you."

I felt several people had played a hand in raising me (it takes a Village of the Damned to raise a child like me) and few had played their hands well. I say this because I felt it was done reluctantly, half-heartedly, and chiefly to satisfy legal obligations. (It may be the illogical child in me that harbors this belief, but he is the keeper of beliefs so I often defer in his jurisdiction.) By age fifteen, as I lay on Wally's couch, I had never considered that someone would do it voluntarily. And so, with only a mouthful of words, he increased my hope for humanity a hundredfold. Truthfully, I don't know if I heard the gesture then as I remember it now. I was dumb in the youthful way, and his beautiful words were likely like music to my nose—something I was poorly equipped to appreciate—but soon I would.

Reuben and I went back together, briefly, and Wally and I lost touch for a few years. Then I saw him in Cowboy City, out at the bar. We were mostly grown-up now and, though he had always been beautiful, he was even more handsome than I remembered. His hairy arms and calves were tan, he had been to a beach. His choppy hair had grown to his chin, it was thick and cinnamon colored, like pumpkin pie. We went for a midnight breakfast then back to my apartment—the one I'm packing now. He spent the night but we didn't sleep.

"I have to go back to Dallas," he said, "but I'm coming back next weekend, to see you."

Wally didn't come back, he didn't call. His mom called though, two weeks later when she called all his friends. "Wally's been killed," she said (in the timbre of an apology), "murdered." I told her how sorry I was, and I was, but for reasons more selfish than I wanted her to know. Old friends called too, each sharing a different detail from hearsaid histories of the crime; they delivered them throughout the day like pieces of slow-moving shrapnel. He was beaten, everyone agreed, then thrown off a bridge. Maybe a drug-deal gone bad, some rumored, but no one really knew why; the reason seemed obvious to me.

Darrold has ears like Alfred E. Neuman. He's excited about everything, skinny but strong, he has copperish skin and hair gelled in cactus spikes, his raspy voice seems inherited from some two-packs-a-day grandmother because Darrold doesn't smoke. I saw him pretend to smoke once, an unlit cigarette, he laughed with every puff. Darrold laughs at everything. It's not a nervous laugh, or a life-of-the-party type laugh, it's just an oddly raspy laugh that makes clear: Darrold is a happy guy. He tipped me three dollars every time I did drag, I always kissed him 'thanks' on the cheek and every time he giggled in reply. His apartment—the one I knew—was small and decorated with posters of race cars, he had a cat. I saw his apartment a few times, when I knocked on the door he'd usually swing it open wide to make a joke that wasn't funny until he added his raspy laugh to the punchline. This time he opens it only a few inches, looks down, and then opens it a foot more. He's wearing a robe over pajamas, the bottoms are Speed Racer; he is childish in a way that makes our visit even sadder. He says nothing until his cat runs outside because Darrold doesn't have the reflexes to stop it.

"Trixie! [Speed Racer's girlfriend]"

"Should I chase him?"

"He'll come back," he places a hand under his jaw when he talks, "come in."

"How're you feeling?"

"Like a...big pace."

"A what?"

"Pig...face."

"Cause you're swollen?"

His pig face nods a slow yes. The curtain is drawn but even in dim lamplight it's obvious that Darrold's excitable hazel eyes are cartoonishly black, they're teary with irritation and struggling to see through newly narrowed slots. His head is bandaged in peculiar lines and his arm is in an L-shaped cast, ruddy tissue is tamponed into his nose, and he persistently pivots his head leftward because an eardrum was ruptured in the assault.

"I hab to ray down."

"Lay down?"

"Mm-hmm."

"Do you need help?"

"I'm okay."

Over the years a dozen of my friends had been cornered and clobbered by boys or men or something in between, sometimes girls egged them on. That's how some missionary in the bible belt, though to them I suppose the belt is more of a whip. It seemed inevitable that a friend would die this way, only remarkable in that it hadn't birthed *more* deaths. Wally's mother said he would be buried in Giddyuptown, I planned to drive the hundred miles but my coal-hearted car died along the way. I suppose that was around the time I became a malcontent, when it became hard to sleep at night.

This is stupid, I thought, you won't get anything packed if you spend all night reminiscing. I pulled the sheets off the ugly wingback chairs and used them to wrap the petite floral ones. I think I won't call these 'the chairs Liz and I stole' anymore. From now on they're just 'the floral chairs'.

I hadn't spoken with Liz since I was sixteen. Until two weeks ago, she called. Hearing her voice made me realize I missed her, we should've stayed in touch.

"I wanna come see you," she said, "I'll be in Cowboy City, can I drop by?"

"Duh, of course you can!"

Two days later, at 6:00 PM, she rang the bell. *It's Liz, It's Liz,* I thought as I bounced down the stairs.

"You look great," she said, "you cut all your hair off."

"Most of it. You look really good too." She didn't though, her mismatched clothes and misshapen hair were gone, replaced with an outfit such as anyone might wear. We walked upstairs, me and Liz and Liz's friend.

"Oh my gosh, you still have those chairs," she said, of the floral pair.

"Yup, and there's the statue we *got* the same night." I was careful not to say *stole,* uncertain what the other girl knew of our criminal past.

"Chris and I stole those chairs from one of the porches in our old neighborhood, back in Giddyuptown," she explained to her chaperone. "That's crazy," the conservatively dressed young woman replied, sounding amused but looking at me as though I'd forcibly extracted a baby from an expectant mother.

"It's *Christian* now, I'm going by Christian."

I made coffee for us, my friend took hers with Sweet-N-Low, the other girl took hers without drinking it. Liz and I talked about old times, not the worst of it, but some. She laughed, but without the doubling-over that I remembered. Her eyes stayed focused, when they used to squint from the hilarity of the stupid things we had done. She seemed different. She wasn't like me anymore, she was now like this other girl. They were cut from the same cloth, and that cloth was khaki. I didn't recognize this creature from the beige lagoon, there was an insincerity behind her smile—it was artificially sweetened, like her coffee.

"Are you surprised I called," she asked.

I was.

"Well I'm glad I did. I've been worried about you."

"Worried? Why worried?"

"I was worried that you might not be spared from eternal annihilation."

"Did you say *eternal annihilation?*"

She did.

"Why, have you heard something?"

"As a matter of fact I have. I heard about Jehovah. Would you like to hear about him?"

I laughed a little, because she was joking. "You mean like Jehovah's Witness?"

Yes, she meant that.

I laughed again, uncertain what else to do. The two women stared at the laughter with an insistent blankness. Oh god, she's serious. *What would Katharine Ross do*, I pondered, quickly remembering the steak knife she stuck to Paula Prentiss in the coffee scene of *The Stepford Wives.*

"Chris, your friend Liz has secured her place in the Kingdom of Jehovah. She will not only survive the eternal annihilation, but is one of a select few who will sit beside Him and help govern an earthly paradise. Chris, or I'm sorry 'Christian'—you prefer your demonic name, does governing an earthly paradise sound like something you would enjoy?"

"Who are you again?"

"I'm Linda."

I sat quietly while Liz and Linda tag-teamed the conversation, my ass numbed by its duration and my brain numbed by its content. *She can't be serious*, I thought. I don't know what the con is, but there is a con going down here. Liz has tricked this girl and she's trying to trick me (the hypocrisy in her face looked like someone trying not to laugh.) Even if she is sincere, she is still a liar. This was an ambush, she could have told me on the phone that she wanted to talk about this nonsense. Instead, she was just like

Angela—pretending she called because we were friends. Angela wanted fifty dollars, Liz wants my soul. I bet she has a quota. Hypocrites, all of them.

It was Frank all over again.

JESUS CHRIST ON THE CROSS (DRESSER)

Frank was a handsome vacuum cleaner salesman in the Flow Queen sales office where I briefly worked as a telemarketer—a common career choice for the teenage highschool dropouts of Cowboy City. Each day I saw him my crush grew more crushing. It's like Hannibal Lecter explains to Agent Starling; "What do you covet? That which you see everyday."

I've always had an unflinching gaze and on most days it was directed at Frank. I've been told my stare projects confidence, but I think they failed to interpret the cowardice: I stare in hope that my eyes will relay the want my mouth is afraid to speak. And so when Frank entered a room my voice climbed up inside me like some hypothermic testicle; I only stared.

The man's tan skin looked as though he'd spent so much of his youth surfing (or playing shirtless frisbee in the park) that the amber tint had lasted well into his promising sophomore year at the Flow Queen corporation. His tall and unselfconsciously muscular body made a cheap suit look expensive. He reminded me of the models in the GQ magazines I kept near my bed. I bet he could have been a Calvin Klein model if the modeling requirements had been less stringent.

Each day I dialed numbers from pages of the city's thick phone book and watched Frank through a big pane of glass; this interior window separated comfortable sales offices from the stuffy, cubicle-lined closet where we—the barely employable—sat. Our small team of phone solicitors (pretending to take a survey on consumer spending habits) asked about the personal finances of anyone willing to answer. At survey's end, if we felt the target could afford a $900 vacuum, we'd offer to send a free camera or gold necklace to them, as thanks for their participation in our questionnaire. Whenever the elderly or otherwise gullible individual agreed to the gift, we'd send a vacuum cleaner salesman to deliver the worthless trinket to their home.

My granny-grifting boss was an evangelical type, holding early morning meetings to boost morale and morality among the staff. He sported a brand new Cadillac and velvet blazers (and not in the ironic way that I imagine I'll wear them one day), and she—his wife—donned big crystal-studded, purple-tinted sunglasses and flamboyant fur coats well inside the Flow Queen offices. Both squeezed several gaudy rings onto many chubby fingers. The power couple spoke to the telemarketers only if it could not be avoided, and with the same air of ascendancy that I imagine Jesus had when speaking to Matthew (or Jerry Falwell with his Laotian pool boy). We were—to them—worth our weight in salt, but they loved an audience so the unpaid twenty-minute prework lectures were mandatory, though I probably would have gone just for the free donut and opportunities to see salesman Frank.

One o'clock each day I ate a sack lunch at my desk (finding the gray cubicle to be at least as entertaining as the sand-colored stripmalls of Cowboy City). Thinking only miserable thoughts, I chewed a mouthful of meat and cheese sandwich, the subsequent swallow choked me as I turned to see handsome Frank in the swivel chair next to mine.

"You okay there buddy?" the swarthy salesman asked, looking directly into my asphyxiated eyes.

"It's ham," I whispered, lacking the breath to name lunchmeat in normal tones.

"Oh yeah?"

My passion for Frank (greater than my need for air) stifled the remaining choke, it and mayonaise allowed a clumsy swallow. "Yeah."

"Well hi Chris, my name's Frank."

"Hi, my name's Chris," I answered.

"Chris, I was just wondering: if you're not busy tonight..." he asked this with the no-nonsense directness of a well-seasoned salesman, "would you like to go out for dinner?"

"Okay," I considered choking again, "sure."

"Write down your address, I'll pick you up."

The rest of the day was a poorly mixed cocktail of nervous nausea and horny excitement. I'd have settled myself with a hasty masturbation in the employee bathroom but wanted to be in top form that evening. I sped home and showered, then combed my hair into a style closer to Frank's. I'm sure the door belled at a time that was as sharp as Frank's starched collars, I answered dressed in my only button-down shirt—hoping a conservative outfit might camouflage the many differences between us.

"There's some place special I'd like to show you before dinner, if that's alright?"

My father surprised me with two weeks at baseball camp—I haven't been much for surprises since, but I was touched by Frank's forethought and told him it would be fine. We drove in his well-kept, air-conditioned car—a car I could get used to. Frank talked a bit about life in a way that seemed deeper than the conversations other first dates had rendered, he was older and surely more mature than the people I knew.

"Here we are," Frank announced, puncturing a silent stupor that had overtaken me as I watched him drive.

We stepped from the cool car into the tail end of a hot day then walked a parking lot toward a large building's open double-doors. "What is it?" I asked.

"A surprise."

People piled into the arena, rushing down aisles to countless seats surrounding all sides of a platformed, blue-carpeted, huge center stage. 'A surprise,' I thought, 'for me.' Everyone eventually settled and the ambient buzz quieted, then lights dimmed and a suited man with an impeccable coif of hair claimed the podium.

"I can't *tell* you," he began, "how it *p'leases* me, t'see s'many *fine faces* here on this *very* special night." The crowd ignited—hands clapping and smiles plastering their many fine faces, as if the vocally twanged, middle-aged gent had just introduced Cheap Trick to the stage. "Give *yurselves* a hand," he insisted as a large video screen lit with every detail of his overly confident face, "*you* did the work!"

I applauded, proud of the work I had done.

I don't recall the moment, but there was one, when I realized the man in the Men's Warehouse attire—the one shouting now, and gesturing wildly—was a Baptist preacher; I couldn't remember the last time I'd been to church. And then there was another moment when I realized the fervored and frighteningly well-attended event was his annual assault on sodomy, a homicide on the homo side of sexuality.

In retrospect, with regret (in regretrospect), I know I should have stood up. I should have slapped my date and shouted something obscene at the room, maybe shat on a bible. I should have done this for myself, and for all persons of perversion. Instead I only sat, cloudyheaded and stonefaced (probably in anticipation of the stones that would surely be pelted at my face), fogged in disbelief when a young, pleasantly faced lady in a pretty floral dress who'd been silently sitting beside me leaned in, as if to share a good word. "Hello Chris, I'm so glad you could come. I'm Missy... Frank's wife, would it be alright if I pray for you?"

There are times in a decent man's life when he wishes social stigmas could be set aside so that he might punch a woman squarely in the face. I'm not a decent man but I did want to knock the bitch out. Instead, a youthful lack of self-control muttered a befuddled "okay." The four ill-considered letters caused eight surrounding people to rise, forming a standing circle of joined hands to jail the still-seated me. And then they prayed, begging an ancient baby—a magical messiah—for my salvation. The synchronous prayers were loud, any one of them would have been loud had they taken polite turns, but together they were stentorian. The volume came not only from my circle, but also from the countless other prayer circles that popped up like blisters throughout the auditorium.

Three or four of the Baptists in my blister became increasingly excited, some even cried as their prayers devolved into long streams of adolescent gibberish. "They're speaking in tongues," Frank's pretty young wife boasted into my hideously homosexual ear. (As a child I'd heard Sunday school rumors of a miraculous phenomenon of zealots speaking in tongues. And the frenzied Tourettic ramblings of this prayer circle might have been impressive if they had thrown a little Aramaic or some other dead language into the convulsive monologues. But theirs was messy and awkward, I suspect one gibberished man may have belted out a few lines from the *BJ and The Bear* theme song before he'd finished. But I suppose that, in the end, God doesn't subtract points for the quality of your tongues, you get credit just for pretending.) When the prayer blister popped, lots of teary-eyed strangers told me how much they loved me (which apparently was quite a bit according to a cheery gal in a sign-sized "Steer Clear of Queer" tee shirt) before they seeped away.

As Mr and Mrs Frank and I walked to the car she asked in her prim midwestern-ness where I'd like to go for dinner (homosexorcisms are hungry work). I explained that I was expecting a long-distance phone call and should probably go home. Missy generously offered the front passenger seat but, feeling the date was not going as well as I had hoped, I opted for the back. For twenty minutes of the twenty-minute drive I was too annoyed to enjoy the temperature-controlled environment, instead I contemplated the lace-trimmed scrunchee clutched to the back of the intrusive woman's hair. Scrunchees were the hallmark of Oklahoma's well-dressed ladies, here: the elasticized fabric surrounded a babyblue praying-hands hairclip, making a handsome ruffled halo for the lord's prayer. As hair retention devices go, it seemed overkill (does a caucasian woman's thin hair need both a clip and a scrunchee?); but as midwestern hair jewelry goes, it was just right.

I envisioned the puritanical Mrs Frank—still fevered from her good deed—rushing home to lie missionary under my date (her spiritual scrunchee softly bumps against a chintz headboard, an aspirational word like "Imagine" or "Holywar" is stenciled on the wall above it; she blurts 'oops-a-daisy' into a hankie as she cums.) The car mercifully halted in front of my West 22nd Street studio apartment. We all walked to my front door where big hugs were given as if to say, "we aren't afraid to touch you," (much how, I imagine, hugs were given to AIDS patients as Popes and their camera crews visited the hospital rooms of parish pariahs; a cynicism I wouldn't have entertained prior to this misanthrope-making date.) Whatever part of an erection I got from his hug was siphoned away by the hug I got from her, a total wash. Even worse, and the really offensive part of her entire intrusion into our date, was that she seemed legitimately sweet. She smiled as she spoke to me, resting her hand on my shoulder so I would be certain to recognize the sincerity. She was attractive, if not overwhelmingly then at least enough to have modeled in shopping mall fashion shows (maybe not swimsuits, but definitely aprons), and perfumed in something that smelled like butterfly farts; she was attentive and warm and terribly hopeful about my afterlife...what a cunning disguise. Maybe if I tied her to my radiator while I ass-raped her husband she'd have to admit that I was really the good guy here.

"Can we pray for you before we go?"

"Ok" I muttered, as they lowered heads in prayer (the laziest form of charity).

I've never understood the religious obsession with homosex. I hear if you dig deeply into a bible you can find a tiny reference to some man-on-man action, but what about those less obscure sins, like the bible-billboarded commandments (ten of them, I think). And how about lust and gluttony and greed and sloth and wrath and envy and pride—the Seven Cardinal Sins. Why don't I hear about churches tricking *slothful* people into annual wars on slothfulness? Maybe it's too hard to get them off their couches.

It's curious though, when *hetero* insists *homo* is a choice, how would they know? Did they have options, among them homosexual urges that they opted against? If so, that's called *bi* you stupid idiots, I myself am *gay*. Had it been a choice: dick's great, I might have chosen it. But the choice was never offered to me, it wasn't a matter of preference. I *prefer* pizza but can still eat calzones; *pizza* is a preference. I can however not eat peanuts. For me, eating peanuts would be like eating arsenic, I am not biologically equipped for that particular food. *Pizza* instead of *peanuts*, for me, is not a preference; it's a requirement. Likewise, dick instead of vagina, for me, is not preference; it's a biological demand. If I were to attempt to eat vagina my eyes would water, my gag would reflex, my dick would limp and I would vomit. Right there, in the poor girl's open lap, I would vomit. The unhygienic mix of vomit and lady parts would probably produce a new STD, some incurable supervirus that wipes out all mankind. Homosexuality is nature made, and even if it weren't then it would still be none of anyone's business. Consensual coupling is never unnatural, judging it is the abomination, and if you still object then beware my supervirus!

Despite Frank's sexual/spiritual intervention, my erotic and theistic orientations are wholly intact. I've always been atheistic (or at least agnostic; dystheistic if I believe the bible) but I rarely concerned myself with issues of faith, it was actually my date with Frank that cemented my religionless resolve. As missionaries go, Frank, his wife, that preacher and their religion made a terrible mess of my conversion. Among its many mistakes, the sloppy salvation was steeped in dishonesty (if I ever make a meaningful change in my life—a haircut, an orientation, a religion—it won't be on the recommendation of liars.) I do however maintain a jot of hope for an afterlife, I'm too vain and gluttonous to die gracefully. And in desperate moments, if I need to pray, I direct prayers to a transgendered deity I call 'The Miracle Queen'. She's a leggy thing, with opalescent make-up and frosted Crystal Gayle hair; she wears beaded gowns year-round. They—my cats—say she created Adam from dirt then forged Eve from a rib she removed from Adam, and then hatched gays from another rib—that one the plastic surgeons removed from Cher. I'd wager I've had as much assistance from my God as Frank's had from his.

Moments later Frank said "Amen" and the silent prayer was over (eleven seconds of silence, how could I possibly fail now?) The couple looked pleased, satisfied they had purified the putrefied. "God doesn't hate you," Mrs Frank assured me, "he hates what you are." Each said good-bye, waving farewell to me and my rotted erotics, and then walked away—hand-in-hypocritical hand—to their air-conditioned life.

Whenever I saw Frank at work in the days and weeks that followed he seemed to barely recognize me, maybe a brief hello as we filed into the Monday morning morale/morality booster; within a month he was ignoring me altogether. And when God closes a door he always opens a pothole…

Soon after, two police squad cars seized our office parking lot. The cops, heavy on questions and light on discretion, stormed the receptionist and asked to speak with me. The armed men were escorted to my cubicle where Frank and the other salesmen watched through the adjoining office's glass partition while I—for the worse part of an hour—answered unfriendly questions about my star-fucking, pot-smoking friend Sterling and his cross-eyed, cross-dressed boyfriend Scooter who apparently used a stolen credit card to call me at work. The police wanted to know what I knew of the pair's late-night burglary of a dress boutique, including its cash, credit card receipts, and armloads of beaded evening gowns. I explained I knew nothing of the LGBT caper but apparently any inquiry by armed police and all rumors of homosexuality make you something of a heretic in the Flow Queen corporation. Four days later I was told that vacuum sales were slow and I would be let go. I never dated Frank again.

"Ahem," Liz cleared the silence from her throat.

"You've given me a lot to think about," I replied.

"I'm glad, can I call you, so we can talk some more?"

"Well I'm moving…I don't know what my new number will be. Why don't I call you?"

The women exchanged a look of nonsuccess then stood and straightened their khaki slacks. "It was a pleasure meeting you *Chris*," Linda added, reaching for my hand.

"You too," I lied, "and it's *Christian*."

I never did give Liz my phone number, but she learned my email address decades later. I read the message with teenage excitement, it was sweet and probably sincere but I didn't reply. I did type a message—I'm a nostalgic fellow and I miss old friends, but ultimately I couldn't push the button. If she reads this then I hope she understands it's only that I'm still not interested in governing an earthly paradise (I already have so much on my plate), and also that my computer's new email filter junks all Viagra ads, Nigerian princes, and everyone who's slated me for eternal damnation.

Beau drove the first day. He wore a mechanic-style baseball cap and had torn the sleeves off a shirt—living-out a trucker fantasy he'd probably had as an effeminate child. Ralph picked clear-coat off his fingernails, nervous about the move. *This is my family now*, I thought, and San Francisco will be our new home. Yes, Ralph will only stay for five months (then he'll steal my drag costumes from our storage unit, move back to Oklahoma and undergo sexual reassignment surgery) and Beau will only stay for a year (then he'll burglarize my apartment while I'm at work, and also move back to Oklahoma), but I don't know that yet, I'm happy.

We drove I-40, stopping only to sleep and shower. Beau and I shared a motel bed, Ralph was a big girl and needed her own. By the second day we drove largely in silence—each surrendered to our own excitement, our own fears, our own regrets. I thought about the people I would miss, it was a short but pangful list. I thought about the ex-boyfriends I would never reunite with, about my favorite thrift store and the IHOP by the drag bar, and about a mother I might not see again. I considered stepping a foot over Beau's and stomping the break to the floorboard. Ralph's pretty face will reshape the windshield but I'll have my life back.

"This is gonna be cool," Ralph grinned, all finished picking his nails.

"Yeah," I remembered, "it will."

As the interstate shrank my confidence swelled, for the next hundred miles I imagined the things I would do.

Art school, I'll definitely go to art school. I could major in painting, then photography—I've always liked fashion photography. If I work as a paralegal I'll save my money, I may need it if I'm fired for ineptness and escorted by security out of the building ("It's just a formality," they'll probably say.) No matter, I'll start a business selling vintage and antique clothing on-line, if the internet becomes popular; *TheFrock.com*, that'd be a good URL. Celebrities could shop there: Heidi Klum, if she becomes a model. And Dita Von Teese and Loretta Lynn. Maybe I'll sell Anne Hathaway an Oscar gown, if she gets nominated for something; I wonder who Anne Hathaway is? Up-and-comers like Tom Ford and Zac Posen could shop there too, and I haven't even heard of Zac Posen yet. I could even provide wardrobe to feature films; *A Single Man*, *A Series of Unfortunate Events*, *Alice In Wonderland*,

Dark Shadows, those would make good movies. Maybe an editor at *VOGUE*—a Sally Singer type—will email to say the magazine loves my store, she may want to fly to San Francisco to interview me. Something like that would be great in their December, 2005 issue (I hope she doesn't print that I panicked, pretending to be hearing impaired when her first email asked for my phone number.) I'll branch out, do some fine art photography; I've always wanted to take photos of hideous monsters wearing couture gowns (à la the Real Housewives.) Maybe I'll start my own art and antiques gallery; *Madrigallery* has a narcissistic sound to it. I'll date around, probably too much, and eventually meet someone I can convince to start a band with me. *Werewuss*, that sounds like a band no one will ever hear. We can start our own clothing line too; *Lady Brothers*, that's a dumb name for a label.

On the third day—near the end of the day—we knew: tomorrow, we'll get there tomorrow. We bought burgers and drove with them on our laps, too kinetic to eat in a parked car. Beau's order was missing its sack of fries, but turning back wasn't an option so we split the other two. When seven crept to eight o'clock I saw the sun succumbing to the horizon on the slab of interstate just ahead. It was impaled by a pointy mountaintop, squirting a ring of theatrical light onto our windshield; this is what Photoshop filters will look like, I thought. Then, as the sun set—on the van, on the story—I had the idea: I should write about this. I'll write a book about my life, the rocky start of it anyway. *Oklahomo*—that could be the title (if I have a boyfriend in San Francisco I hope he suggests it.) It'll start in a weed field...the story of a boy with a hole in his heart and a pistol in his purse, looking for family, whatever that may mean. And if he doesn't find one here then that's okay, there's a bridge just ahead.

I knew just how I'd end it too: I'll end the book with something about having had a premonition—a premonition about how to end the book.

OKLAHOMO

une plus merci:

There are thanks at the beginning of the book, and one more important one here, it's for Oklahoma's drag queens—those I have watched, worked with, dated, befriended, known. (My book avoids calling them trannies—a word that offends some today, though back then we certainly did. Only we used it in the way that God intended...about one another, to one another. *Tranny*, to us, was *transvestite* affectionately shorthanded, it never doubled as slang or slur for *transgender;* we had another word for that.)

My earliest memory of Oklahoma is a sometimes mean, often oppressive place for a kid like me. And then I found a gay bar. To an impressionable teen the glittery performers were something magical—casting sequined spells that had the power to change my opinion of a time and a place. I used no real names but if anyone recognized something of herself in my book then I hope she wasn't offended. I would have limited my story to how talented you were but that just wouldn't sell books. And if your inclusion seemed only half true then you were probably merged with some other queen in editing, but rest assured—you were the pretty half.

And for Scooter (the drag queen with whom I'd been professionally inseparable, like siamese sisters joined at the wig) and all the girls who've moved on, into the clouds, to that great pageant in the sky: Miss you, girl. But I bet you look really natural up there, in all that soft light.

christian madrigal:
>CTMadrigal.com<

Lives and writes in San Francisco, as well as the historic 1870s neo-gothic 'Hendel House' in Reading, PA

Also works as a vintage clothier with a clientele that includes Heidi Klum, Dita Von Teese, Tom Ford, Anne Hathaway, Zac Posen, Loretta Lynn, photographer Cindy Sherman, and 3-time Oscar winner Colleen Atwood through his site, *The Frock* (thefrock.com)

Designs demi-couture clothing with accomplice Robert Glassford for their web-based atelier, *Lady Brothers* (ladybros.com)

Has provided wardrobe for film and television including: *A Series of Unfortunate Events* (2004); *Nine* (2009); *Dark Shadows* (2012); *Into The Woods* (2014); *Alice In Wonderland* (2010); and Julianne Moore wardrobe for *A Single Man* (2009)…

Was interviewed by *VOGUE's* Sally Singer for an article about his vintage couture collection that ran in their December 2005 issue, other publications include: *Glamour, In Style, Eve, Elle, Harper's Bazaar, Marie Claire*…

Is opening a fashion market for merchants of the modern macabre, *The Church of Satin*, in 2020/2021 (thechurchofsatin.com)

Sells his fine art photography and the collected works of others at the art and antiques gallery, *Madrigallery* (madrigallery.com)

Makes something like music—also with accomplice Robert Glassford—for the band *WereWuss* (iTunes, et al.)

Also wrote two horrific novels, *The Loving Dead* and *Hungry Woman* (available at Amazon.com and select bookstores)

To The Reader,

If you reached these final pages then I hope that means you liked the book. When I started writing books it wasn't just because I felt an LGBTQ duty to stand up and be counted, but also because I was prospecting for something—probably creativity and cash, but not just. On a deeper dig I discovered that what I really want is immortality. Maybe not in vampiric or cryogenic ways, or to be forever jailed by pearly gates, but in the manner of filmmakers and musicians, painters and poets...I need to leave something behind.

For this reason—the hope of littering eternity with evidence of my existence—I've chosen to print my books first, rather than selling them in disappearable digital formats. Two hundred years from now I want someone in space clothes to pluck me from their Ikea bookshelf, to thumb through my testimony.

In that scenario, you are the first. You're the first person(s) to know certain things about me—someone who sits alone at a bedroom computer all day, writing sickhearted stories about people who have no friends. Please do your part and keep my book on your shelf, then thumb through it again one day. And if you're feeling generous, write a review, something that tells the world we were here, you and me*.

Thank you for reading my book,
C T Madrigal

*Probably should have said *you and I*, but I didn't like the sound of it, and by now you've probably noticed I sometimes say the wrong thing.

also by the author:

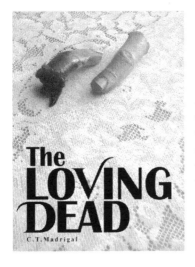

The Loving Dead
2019, PRISSPRESS

A dark, droning, half-bruised, supernatural mystery between a credulous young woman and a dislike-minded man that considers the unthinkable things two people would do to undo loneliness.

Hungry Woman
2019, PRISSPRESS

A curious couple with a devious lifestyle make a single decision that has many macabre chapters of unforeseen consequences. It's a beautifully beastly eighteen-year study in loyalty, tensility, and personal demons.

—More at CTMadrigal.com—

Made in the USA
Monee, IL
01 September 2021